ISBN 978-1-333-84114-0
PIBN 10548507

English
Français
Deutsche
Italiano
Español
Português

www.forgottenbooks.com

Mythology Photography **Fiction**
Fishing Christianity **Art** Cooking
Essays Buddhism Freemasonry
Medicine **Biology** Music **Ancient
Egypt** Evolution Carpentry Physics
Dance Geology **Mathematics** Fitness
Shakespeare **Folklore** Yoga Marketing
Confidence Immortality Biographies
Poetry **Psychology** Witchcraft
Electronics Chemistry History **Law**
Accounting **Philosophy** Anthropology
Alchemy Drama Quantum Mechanics
Atheism Sexual Health **Ancient History**
Entrepreneurship Languages Sport
Paleontology Needlework Islam
Metaphysics Investment Archaeology
Parenting Statistics Criminology
Motivational

A SECOND LOOK AT AMERICA
is one of the
Makers of History Series

Other titles in the Series include:

A SECOND LOOK AT AMERICA

by

GENERAL EMILIO ÁGUINALDO

with

VICENTE ALBANO PACIS

ROBERT SPELLER & SONS, PUBLISHERS, INC.
New York 36, New York

© 1957 Robert Speller & Sons, Publishers, Inc.
33 West 42nd Street
New York 36, New York

Library of Congress Catalog Card No. 57-11884
Vol. #VI of *Makers of History Series*

First Edition

Printed in the United States of America; Set in 11 on 13 Times-Roman by
Arrow Composition Inc.; Printed and bound by H. Wolff, New York.

FOREWORD

THIS BOOK is at once history and news. It is history because the man who fought a three-year war against the United States makes known for the first time his views on Philippine-American relations from 1898 to the present time. It is also news because, with originality and logic, he interprets present-day American world leadership in terms of its beginnings in the Philippines.

Strangely, although General Aguinaldo bitterly fought the implantation of American sovereignty over the Philippines, he presents in this book perhaps the first comprehensive and judicious account of the Philippine-American War and the subsequent Philippine-American association of half a century. He sees facts and events neither through Filipino nor American eyes exclusively but with that cineramic clarity and intimacy which can come only with first-hand knowledge, mellowed fairness and matured judgment.

Indicative of its interesting integration of the past and the present, the book rewards its readers with new and intimate glimpses of such American greats as Admiral George Dewey, William Howard Taft, General Leonard Wood and General Douglas MacArthur, as well as such Filipino heroes and leaders as Dr. Jose Rizal, Andres Bonifacio, Generals Gregorio del Pilar and Antonio Luna and Presidents Manuel L. Quezon, Sergio Osmena and Ramon Magsaysay.

Americans, Filipinos and the other peoples of the Free World, including the so-called neutralists, as well as the Communist-enslaved races, will discover in this book not only enlightenment and entertainment but also a vital, heartening message: America, having been the Nemesis of European Imperialism, cannot escape a similar role with respect to Soviet Imperialism.

General Emilio Aguinaldo

In the world's headlines at the turn of the century for successively leading two revolutions against Spain and a war against the United States, General Emilio Aguinaldo takes a new look at America and discovers that her role of world leadership today not only had its birth in Commodore George Dewey's great naval victory in Manila but also derived its shape and concept from the Philippine-American War.

During the intervening three months between Dewey's victory and the arrival of American troops in the Philippines, General Aguinaldo routed the Spaniards all over his country and, at the age of only 29, established the first constitutional republic in all Asia with himself as

6

Foreword

President. Subsequent misunderstandings with Admiral Dewey and
other Americans, starting with the staging of the sham battle the
Spaniards insisted upon before finally surrendering their last fingerhold in the Philippines, the Walled City in Manila, resulted in
Aguinaldo's leading a war against the American forces. The conflict
lasted for three years and cost the United States $600,000,000 in
gold and 10,000 in casualties. The resistance he led collapsed when
Colonel Frederick Funston of the Kansas Volunteers captured him
in a dramatic adventure over typhoon-churned seas and guerilla-
infested jungles.

Throughout America's rule of half a century over the Philippines,
General Aguinaldo lived in peaceful retirement during which he was
perhaps the keenest and most interested observer of developments in
Washington and Manila. Now 88 years old, he continues to live an
active life. One of the world's most colorful and unique fighters for
freedom, he voices for the first time his thoughts and opinions on
America. He does this in the essential context of history and of the
contemporary world situation in which America finds herself leading
the Free World in its many-faceted fight against Communist
Imperialism.

Vicente Albano Pacis

Adviser to Philippine Presidents, Vicente Albano Pacis, whose
more steady employment is teaching Political Science in the University of the East in Manila, inevitably got interested in General
Aguinaldo and his crusade for Philippine freedom and in America's
work in the Philippines and its relation to American world leadership.

Pacis learned his politics under two of the outstanding American
teachers of the mid-twenties—Professors John W. Garner of Illinois
and Frederic Ogg of Wisconsin. Having taken Journalism as his
major in college and making Sigma Delta Chi, however, he devoted his
first twenty professional years to working for the *Associated Press* in
Washington, D. C. and editing dailies and magazines in Manila.

He has worked for President Sergio Osmena, was the first Press
Secretary of the late President Elpidio Quirino, and was a trouble-
shooter for the late President Ramon Magsaysay. Happily combining
a long editorial experience and government service with both a
scholarly and practical knowledge of politics, Pacis is regarded as
one of the Philippines' keenest political analysts. He is a frequent
contributor to magazines where his articles on international politics,
American-Philippine relations, Philippine constitutional development
and politics often serve as a springboard to learned and popular
discussions.

CONTENTS

LIST OF ILLUSTRATIONS

A SECOND LOOK AT AMERICA

CHAPTER I

WHY I TALK AT LAST

IN THEIR DARK DISTRUST of the United States, Nehru of India, Sukarno of Indonesia, de Gaulle of France, and Bevan of England stand today on the same crossroad of history where I found myself 59 years ago. But I was in a worse predicament than they. Then, it was unmarked; today, it has clear and conspicuous signs.

As far as I can see today, America is only trying to extend to other countries various forms of assistance—military, financial, technical or moral. And this for a very understandable reason. Her aim is to shore up their sagging economy and morale so that they may be able to resist Communist blandishment and aggression.

Fifty-nine years ago, however, America had no clear-cut international policy. To us Filipinos, she made studiedly vague verbal offers of friendship and aid and then fairly drowned them with the boom of cannons and the rattle of Gatling guns. I was 29 and, as the President of the First Philippine Republic and Generalissimo of its forces, I was desperately fighting to keep America from occupying my Motherland. We had just liberated her from the tyranny of benighted Spain which had enslaved us for over three centuries. But due to America's intervention, our triumph was suddenly becoming our defeat. The situation was one to confuse even the most experienced statesman.

Yet I feel that there is a definite similarity between what happened in the Philippines at the turn of the century and what is happening today in Asia, Africa, the Middle East and Europe. Our own distrust of America, which nerved us into fighting an unequal and disastrous war, is echoing today in many parts of the free and neutralist worlds. It is screechy as from a worn and cracked phonograph record, it is true, but it is modulated by Communist acoustics. The chasm of misunderstanding which is today the greatest obstacle to American leadership of the free world in the search for peace and security seems vaguely familiar to me. It appears to be a couterpart of the breach which, at the turn of the century, I saw, in helpless horror, crack open, widen and deepen until it belched the fires of destruction and hate.

The great lag between good American intentions and Filipino comprehension spanned several decades. It may be that a similar length of precious time will have to lapse before America's role is understood by confused nationalists on the one hand and the great masses of people newly liberated from Western imperialism on the other. Meanwhile, this delay may spell the difference between freedom and slavery for most of humanity.

But may not the story of the Philippines under the United States serve as a bridge over the lag between America and the rest of the free world? And may I not recount that story as one who not only witnessed it from beginning to end but also played a vital and perhaps decisive role, at least in its early and critical stages?

Riding on the wings of total recall, these thoughts come to me as I am approaching 89 years and my twilight of life is on hand. I am fortunately still strong and in full possession of my faculties. In fact, I am driven every day from my home in Cavite province to the headquarters of the Association of the Veterans of the Revolution in Manila to attend to its business as its president. Until late in 1955 I also occupied the position and performed the duties of acting chairman of the Board of Pensions for Veterans of the Philippine Revolution, a government office which administers the niggardly pensions and benefits to the survivors of our war.

When I tell my visitors that several times a day I climb up and down three flights of steep stairs with a total of 64 steps to my library and bedroom up in the tower of my residence in Kawit, Cavite, they become incredulous. Their typical comment is, "At your age, General? Why, it's incredible!" They know that I was born in this house, which has since seen many expansions and remodelings, on March 22, 1869.

I realize nevertheless that at my advanced age I may be called by my Maker soon. The average Filipino longevity is less than 55 years, so that I have long outlived the average life expectation of my countrymen. All but a few of my contemporaries have gone before me. Even younger men like the late President Manuel L. Quezon, Maj. Gen. Leonard Wood, Justice Frank Murphy and all the other former American governors-general, except W. Cameron Forbes and Francis Burton Harrison, have crossed to the Great Beyond. I feel, therefore, that I should no longer put off the impulse to tell my story.

I must confess that I also have a personal motive. Before I go to meet my Maker I should naturally like to leave the record, especially my part of it, truthfully corrected.

Over the span of half a century, I have been pictured as almost every kind of bad man both to Americans and Filipinos. During the so-called Insurrection, which I prefer to call the Philippine-American War, I was written up in the American press, then unfortunately deep in its yellow era, as a cutthroat, a bandit leader, a pirate and other frightful characters. American leaders, including senators and congressmen, called me every conceivable name. Even in my own country, among some of my own countrymen, I have at one time or another enjoyed the reputation of being an assassin, traitor and other forms of infamy.

But I have kept my own peace. Above all, upon swearing allegiance to the Government of the United States, I construed it to be my obligation no longer to quarrel with America. Furthermore, most of my critics were writers, editors or government officials, while I had become only a private citizen. They enjoyed official prestige or had effective means of disseminating their opinions to the masses. I had neither official position nor a press of my own. But in addition to my disinclination to argue and quarrel, being a man of few words, I had no command of the new idiom of controversy—the English language.

Many people have wondered why I have never learned English. "You have been a school teacher, General," I have often been asked, "Why haven't you learned English during all these years?"

Not only have I been a school teacher but, when the Americans opened the first schools in the Philippines, I was still young enough to do some serious studying. I was not more than 30 years old.

I never found enough desire to learn English mainly because I believed both Commodore Dewey when he assured me that he would withdraw his forces after the Spaniards had been driven away and William Howard Taft when he announced that the Philippines would be for the Filipinos. I thought the Americans would leave us alone soon after the Spanish-American War and, since then, for over half a century, I expected them momentarily to pull up stakes and depart. I told myself that if this was to happen, there was no need for me or for other Filipinos to learn English. Most of our educated people knew Spanish, and our masses spoke their own native languages. With our eight principal native tongues and some seventy secondary dialects, we already had too many idioms. I then thought, and I know it is the case today, that the addition of a new language would complicate our linguistic problem.

I have known, observed and reflected on America's conduct in the Philippines perhaps more intimately and critically than most. I fought fierce battles with the Americans. I led them on a long and tortuous chase until General Funston captured me through an ungentlemanly and unsportsmanslike ruse. Swearing allegiance to America after my capture, I sincerely cooperated with the Americans to the extent of actively supporting the late Governor General Wood in his long and bitter controversy with President Manuel L. Quezon. With deep sadness I saw the Pacific War and the occupation of my homeland by the Japanese. And with a throbbing heart, I witnessed America proclaim my country a free and sovereign nation, restoring to us our Republic!

I cannot but conceive the great event of July 4, 1946, when President Truman proclaimed the establishment of the Philippine Republic, as the belated fulfillment of the promise made to me by Commodore George Dewey.

The perspective of over half a century has given the world, including myself, a clearer view of Philippine-American history. In addition, my own experiences and observations and continuous reflection over the years may have given me not only an advantage in appraising America's work in the Philippines but also in understanding present American intentions in other parts of the world. By talking at last, I may also have my first and last opportunity to give my side of the controversial episodes in Philippine-American history in which I have had personal participation.

So, after my self-imposed and rarely-broken silence of over half a century, I have decided to tell my story. I address myself primarily to the peoples of the United States and the Philippines. But I also hope that the Spaniards, our former masters, and the Latin Americans, once our companions in misery under Spanish tyranny, will also find my account of some interest.

CHAPTER II

BEFORE I MET THE AMERICANS

WHEN, AT THE HEIGHT of his knock-down-and-drag-out-fight with Governor General Leonard Wood in the 1920's, I succeeded in diverting the wrath of Senate President Manuel L. Quezon upon myself, he paid me this sneering compliment: "Aguinaldo was fooled by the Americans!"

Spelled out, what he meant was that, since Admiral George Dewey in Manila and U.S. Consul General E. Spencer Pratt in Singapore had supposedly double-crossed me, when the Americans first came to the Philippines, I should have learned my lesson. Instead, I was siding with Wood and the American Administration—to be fooled again.

Quezon was not quite right. Dewey and Pratt might have sold me down the river but they did not quite fool me. That is why there was a Philippine-American War.

Even that war could have been avoided if President William McKinley had understood the unfolding situation sooner. As it was, the war President oversimplified matters. Through a White House dream, he merely converted into Divine Revelation the imperialistic vision of a few articulate American leaders, the noisy rantings of the yellow and jingoistic press and the shouted exaltations of the West and Middle West over the spectacular if easy victory of Dewey against the Spanish fleet in Manila Bay.

In reality the entire situation in which the Philippines and America were involved together by Fate had the following dimensions: First, there existed a strong revolutionary movement in the Philippines antedating the Spanish-American War by several years. Second, the coming of America to the Philippines was a mere extension of her Cuban adventure which culminated in the Spanish-American War. And, third, American public opinion, at best uninformed on the Philippines, was

18

deliberately misled by a nascent imperialism conceived by a few leaders like Theodore Roosevelt, Henry Cabot Lodge and Whitelaw Reid.

My involvement with the Americans, which led so tragically to a three-year bitter war between their country and mine, began in the nearby British colony of Hongkong on the coast of China sometime in March 1898. The American officials there and, later on, in Singapore and Manila, courted me with honeyed phrases and Old-World courtesies. Three years later, I was their helpless prisoner, having been captured through a clever but certainly unsporting ruse for which Colonel Frederick Funston of the Kansas Volunteers won an immediate promotion to brigadier-general.

But, perhaps I should start my story with the Spanish rule in the Philippines and our war to obtain independence. For these, in turn, led to my interlude with the American consular service and armed forces.

Under a Spanish commission, the Portuguese navigator, Ferdinand Magellan, landed on Homonhon island on the Pacific side of my country on March 16, 1521, and the history books in all Western countries henceforth recorded this date as the discovery of the Philippines. Magellan was shortly killed in a fight with the warriors of the island of Mactan near Cebu led by their chief, Lapulapu. The remnants of his party retreated to their ships in confusion and disorder which Don Quixote would certainly have pronounced disgraceful, being unworthy of Spanish valor. Be this as it may, other Spaniards in due time followed in Magellan's wake in greater force and, in the middle of the sixteenth century, had completed the military and religious conquest of the islands. The Spaniards called them *Filipinas* and their inhabitants *Filipinos,* in honor of their king, Felipe II.*

From the conquest to the end of the nineteenth century, the Spaniards held my country in a soul-wounding stranglehold.

* Incidentally, while English-speaking lexicographers, historians and cartographers Anglicized *Filipinas* into Philippines, they left *Filipinos* in its Spanish form.

During those three and a half centuries of tyranny, there broke out sporadic regional revolts which the Spaniards were invariably able to suppress. It was not until the early 1890's, after one of our countrymen, Dr. Jose Rizal, had published two patriotic novels in succession that the Filipinos' resistance against the Iberians became generalized and crystallized. Depicting in awesome scenes the Spanish terror and Filipino degradation, the books caused as profound a stirring among our people as Harriet Beecher Stowe's *Uncle Tom's Cabin* did among the Americans, white and black.

Panic-stricken, the Spanish authorities reacted stupidly. They noisily attacked and outlawed the books. Senators and deputies in Madrid denounced them in speeches in the Cortes, and bishops and friars in Manila condemned them as anti-government, anti-Spanish and anti-Catholic. It was the sort of fuss over a book which Dr. Alfred Kinsey would love to create. It sharpened all the more the curiosity and will of the people to read them. The result was that the copies which could be smuggled into the Philippines from Germany, where they had been printed in Spanish, were passed from hand to hand until their pages were frayed and dog-eared. Their content spread by word of mouth to the rest of the populace. To all it became a common nagging and agitating knowledge. The undertow of anger against Spain soon rose to a terrible tidal wave. It was about this time that, prematurely, we began our revolution against the Spaniards.

Now they were truly desperate. When Rizal had arrived before the outbreak of hostilities, the Spanish authorities had arrested him, then had exiled him to Dapitan, a secluded spot in Mindanao. Instead of being cowed by this arbitrary action, the people had become more angered. It was then that we began to organize for resistance. Before we could mature our plans, however, our plot was exposed. We had no other recourse but to go into action, half improvising our movements.

Evidently to impress upon us their determination to stop at nothing to supress our revolt, the Spaniards brought back Rizal to Manila, court-martialled him, then publicly shot him on the Luneta, Manila's main park. But they only achieved the opposite result. By killing Rizal, who would in reality rather have reform than revolution, the Spaniards also killed our last hope of ever convincing them to improve their administration of the Philippines. By martyrizing him, they also gave us a national hero. If, in life, Rizal was our inspiration, in death, he became our great unifying symbol around whom we rallied to the defense of our homeland.

Credit for organizing the original revolutionary group, the *Katipunan,* primarily belongs to Andres Bonifacio, a warehouse employee whose patriotism had been fired by reading the novels of Rizal, *Lives of the Presidents of the United States,* and a history of the French Revolution, among others. He managed to enlist thousands of our countrymen secretly under the very sensitive noses of the Spaniards. Not only did he have an undeniable genius for organization but also great courage and patriotism. To be caught in the underground work in which he engaged meant certain death.

When in 1896 the Spaniards got wind of the society through the confession to a priest of a young sister of one of our members, the revolution had to begin prematurely. The alternative for any member, certainly for any officer who was caught, was to be shot like many other Filipino patriots before them. In truth the Spaniards soon instituted a Reign of Terror comparable to that of the French Revolution. Members and suspected members of the *Katipunan* upon whom they could lay hands were marched with regularity to the garrotes or before the firing squads. The execution of Rizal some four months after the outbreak of the Revolution was among the most revolting highlights of the Terror.

I was one of the first in my province of Cavite to join the *Katipunan.* As the 25-year old *capitan municipal,* town mayor, of Kawit, I organized and became the head of the local chapter. Patriots from the other towns joined us in increasing number until the strength of our group rivalled that of other groups including those in Manila itself. Quite naturally, I was recognized by the majority of *Katipuneros* in our province as the local leader. When our leaders in Manila gave the signal to fight the long-planned revolution, we in Cavite were ready with a compact though untrained and ill-equipped organization of about 20,000 men.

At the start of the hostility we were more ready spiritually than technologically. Long suffering, we had the will to fight. But we had very few guns and our men lacked training and experience. Our organization being secret, we could not put them through the usual military preparations of drills and maneuvers. Most of them were unshod and, for weapons, had only daggers and bolos. At the beginning they did not even have uniforms. On the other hand, our enemies were well-trained and well-equipped. Many of them were highly-experienced regulars, and their arms included the best available from Europe's arsenals.

The first battles were disastrous to our side. In San Juan del Monte, San Mateo and Morong, all in Rizal Province next to Manila, and in the suburbs of Manila itself, our forces which Bonifacio personally led were badly defeated by the Spaniards in a series of battles. Fortunately, we fared better in my province, Cavite. In strategic towns such as Noveleta, Binakayan and others, we scored heart-warming if costly victories against the enemy. Our successes soon convinced the Spaniards that the main strength of our revolution was in Cavite, and the Governor General, assembling and personally leading the strongest force he could muster, began a determined campaign against us. But we repulsed him decisively. In the battle of Binakayan which I personally directed and which came to be known in history as the bloodiest battle of the Revolution against Spain, we drove away General Blanco in defeat. But we also lost hundreds of men, including one of our bravest general officers, Candido Tirona.

The contrast between Bonifacio's defeats and my victories inevitably led to a general demand among our men for a drastic reorganization of our political and military leadership. Although acknowledging Bonifacio as an organizing wonder, having brought the *Katipunan* together, they now believed him possessed of little aptitude for government and warfare. The upshot of the new trend of thought was the holding of the so-called Tejeros convention.

The Tejeros convention was held at a time when I could not leave the field, being hard-pressed by the Spanish forces. Bonifacio and the other leaders were, however, present. After considerable discussion, the delegates decided to dissolve the *Katipunan,* which was mainly a secret society patterned after Freemasonry in organization and secret rituals, and to organize a Revolutionary Government. Proceeding with the election of new officers, they chose me as President and generalissimo. In a way the convention's decision immediately brought a double tragedy.

When a committee of the convention came to my field headquarters to notify me of my unexpected election and summon me to take the oath of office, I was far from being ready to comply. I had no previous inkling of the convention's decision to elevate me to the highest offices and I felt myself unprepared for their responsibilities. Furthermore, the notification came to me at a moment when the slightest relaxation of our defenses could turn the mounting Spanish pressure to a great victory. But my own brother, Crispulo, who was also a general officer, upon hearing my refusal to leave my forces, came forward and said, "Sir, I shall take your place temporarily while you comply with the summons of the country." With his offer, I had no choice. I left my forces and went with the notification committee to appear before the convention and take my oath. That was the last time I saw my brother alive. For the Spaniards shortly overran our position and killed him along with many others who preferred death to defeat.

An even greater tragedy was yet to come. It was probably natural that Bonifacio should have been keenly disappointed and resentful over the election's result. As the *Katipunan's* founder, he perhaps had the right to believe that he should have been maintained at the head of the Revolution regardless of the fortunes or misfortunes of our cause. I could well understand the grief of his mind and the agony of his soul when, to stave off the complete collapse of our war for freedom, the convention ousted him as our leader.

But he went too far in nursing his private grievance. Defying the decision of the Convention, which he had presided, he refused to recognize the Revolutionary Government and its duly-elected officers. His action was all the more glaring, since he was himself a high official of the new Government, having been elected its Secretary of the Interior. More than refusing to give his allegiance, he proceeded to organize his own separate government and his own separate army. He and his followers held another election and, claiming to be the true government, began to act not only independently of but even with a certain measure of hostility against the Revolutionary Government. Since a division in our ranks would have been fatal to our cause, Bonifacio and his followers were arrested as counter-revolutionists. A Court Martial condemned the top leaders including Bonifacio to death.

I should explain that, during all this trouble, the Spaniards prosecuted the war against us with great aggressiveness, no doubt trying to take the fullest advantage of the split in our ranks. The trial of Bonifacio and his co-accused had been started in Naic, Cavite, where we had established our Government, but had to be continued in Maragundong when Naic fell. The enemy followed us to the latter place, striking soon after the decision of the Court Martial had been rendered. With the Spaniards on our heels, I acted fast. I issued an order commuting Bonifacio's sentence from death to "indefinite exile to a separate island." I decided on this course because I did not want to spill Filipino blood uselessly. The Spaniards, now receiving their first reinforcements from Spain, were already spilling it in torrents. Furthermore, I recognized, as did my colleagues, the invaluable service of Bonifacio in organizing the *Katipunan*. I was in hopes that this service would in time be more generally acknowledged and that, in the context of his patriotic deeds, his error for which the Court Martial condemned him to die would also be forgiven.

But now forces beyond my control came into play. All my ranking subordinates, led by Generals Mariano Noriel and Pio del Pilar, were against my commutation of Bonifacio's death sentence and they pressed me to withdraw it. I resisted them at first. I was chagrined that they should thus disagree with my decision. But they pointed out to me that Bonifacio's act of defiance was a most serious offense even in peace time, that in war time it was doubly condemnable. On top of their legalistic argument, they added a practical consideration. They maintained that as long as Bonifacio lived, there would be Filipinos who would rally around him and with him defy the Revolutionary Government openly or secretly. And if Bonifacio should manage to escape from exile, he would be able to do us great harm. The possibilities they mentioned ranged from my assassination by his agents to joining forces with the Spaniards. Such charges had already been aired in Bonifacio's trial, and the intent to assassinate me had been proved by direct testimony. I had to yield; I withdrew my commutation order.

On the same day, the Spaniards marched against Maragundong. The officer in command of our local forces, upon learning of the imminent Spanish attack, made his own fateful decision. Major General Noriel, who had been himself the president of the Court Martial, handed a subordinate officer, Major Macapagal, a sealed order. Verbally he told him to gather a few soldiers, then take Bonifacio and the other prisoners to a secluded mountainside and there open his order and carry out its content immediately. It turned out to be an order to shoot the prisoners until dead.

Due to the confusion brought about by the successful Spanish attack on Maragundong, the fate of Bonifacio and his companions did not become known to us until later. Investigation established the fact that General Noriel had made his decision mainly on two grounds. He had construed my withdrawl of my commutation order as confirmation of the Court Martial's decision. On this matter, he was certainly hasty. It had been my intention to delay my own final decision on Bonifacio until my subordinates had cooled off. During and immediately after the trial, they had been openly hostile to him, not only because of their deep resentment of his defiance of our authority but perhaps also out of loyalty to me. Noriel offered another reason for his decision. The Spaniards were about to attack and he feared the possibility of their liberating Bonifacio and his men or taking them as captives.

In the confusion and chaos of warfare, it was quite difficult to condemn a fellow officer who had used his best judgment when decision on his part was truly urgent and inescapable. We had also just organized the Revolutionary Government, the first in the history of our country. We had not had material time to promulgate rules and regulations to govern our forces and our civilians, much less had we developed a body of precedents and practices to go by. The tragedy of Bonifacio occurred at a time of swift and disorderly transition to which he had himself contributed by his intransigence.

While I deeply deplored Bonifacio's loss, I could not show weakness. The times and circumstances demanded of me firmness and sternness however heavy was my heart. His death having left me the undisputed leader of the Revolution, together with its tremendous responsibilities and sacrifices, I could not afford to cure the disunity Bonifacio had created with another disunity which might have resulted from differences over his punishment.

Scholars who have studied the documents and other evidences pertaining to Bonifacio's trial and death have found the procedure which led to his death quite logical and legal under the circumstances. Dean Maximo M. Kalaw, an authority on Philippine politics, has stated the following: "The revolutionists could not afford to be divided. One of two courses had to be taken: either the continuation of the *Katipunan* Government under Bonifacio or the maintenance of the new Revolutionary Government under Aguinaldo which had the support of the majority the Revolutionary Government was forced to eliminate him." The elder Kalaw, Teodoro M., a noted scholar and former Director of the National Library, has also declared: ". . . the facts, judged *a posteriori*, sustained Aguinaldo's point of view.

Unity had to be maintained   All opposition had to be put down with an iron hand." These opinions are supported by equally authoritative historical writers including earlier researchers and commentators like T. H. Pardo de Tavera and Clemente Jose Zulueta.

For some time after the Bonifacio episode, the war see-sawed. As we fought more battles we gained more experience and captured more arms and ammunition from the Spaniards. As we won new skirmishes, more of our oppressed brothers rallied around us. But the Spanish Government had no intention of losing the richest of its remaining colonies without fighting to the last ditch.

It soon showed signs of acting decisively. Having failed to defeat us, Governor Blanco was replaced by the aggressive and energetic Polavieja. Equally unable to put down our Revolution, Polavieja was in turn replaced by Captain General Fernando Primo de Rivera. The successive changes of commanders was accompanied by an increasing flow of reinforcements from Spain. The Spanish fleet in the Orient, soon to be completely destroyed by Commodore George Dewey, was being enlarged by the addition of warships. These arrived escorting transports filled to the poop with army regulars. Soon, such reinforcement numbered no less than 26,000, and they were fully equipped with the most modern European arms. With the Philippine garrison and Filipino recruits and mercenaries, the latter largely made up of Macabebes from Pampanga, the Spanish armed forces in the Philippines were finally built up to a formidable war machine.

From this new position of strength, the Spaniards presently launched a counterattack. The enemy pressure was tremendous. To save our forces and at the same time decimate the Spanish forces as much as we could, we gave way gradually. In a few months, we had retreated to the mountains of San Miguel, Bulacan, northeast of Manila. There, in a fairly impregnable cave called Biaknabato, we established our headquarters. We soon also reorganized our forces and started our own counterattack. At this point, somewhat to our surprise, General de Rivera sued for peace. As peace envoy, he sent to me a respectable Manila gentleman by the name of Pedro Paterno.

Paterno performed his mission well. He told us that the Spanish forces were not only greatly stronger than at the start of the Revolution but reinforcements were continuing to arrive. On the other hand, he pointed out, we had no means of building up our strength. Manpower, we had. But we could never hope to arm our men adequately. This, he did not have to tell us; oftentimes, we had only one rifle for every ten men in the line of battle.

Paterno then touched upon our hope of receiving foreign aid. He reminded us that the *Katipunan* had hoped to receive Japanese assistance which never came. Neither had the Revolutionary Government a better prospect. His appraisal of our enemy's strength and ours, actual and potential, did not so much impress us. We had ourselves constantly assessed the situation. The consideration he offered on behalf of de Rivera which most influenced us to agree to peace, however, was the Spanish promise to introduce liberal reforms in the administration of our country.

In the resulting treaty, known as the Pact of Biaknabato, the Spaniards agreed to pay us 800,000 pesos and to institute some of the important reforms which had been previously urged by us as well as by Rizal and other earlier leaders. These included the restoration of Filipino representation in the Spanish Cortes, freedom of speech and press, and the expulsion of the friars. In return, we bound ourselves to abandon the Revolution and, as a guarantee of this, we agreed to surrender thousands of our guns, almost all having been captured from the Spaniards themselves, and I and 19 of my ranking officers consented to go on exile abroad.

Providentially, we elected to go to Hongkong, the nearby British colony on the China coast. As soon as the Spaniards paid us the first installment of 400,000 pesos, we set sail across the China Sea. The year 1897 was just ending when we reached the green and salubrious island in which I was soon to have my first contact with Americans.

CHAPTER III

DEWEY, PRATT AND I

THE PEACE proved to be only a breathing spell. The Spaniards failed to comply with their part of the bargain. They neither inaugurated the promised improvements in their administration of our country nor gave our people their promised rights. They neither expelled the friars nor paid the balance of the peace money. So it was that we decided to use what money we had on hand for the purchase of arms with which to resume our revolution at the next opportune time. I deposited the 400,000 pesos in a Hongkong bank and there kept it intact for this purpose, using only the interest it earned for the frugal maintenance of our exiled group. The next opportune time soon came in the person of Commodore Dewey.

It was perhaps fortunate that we domiciled ourselves in Hongkong. Being a British colony, the island had direct communication with England, and England was, as now, extremely sensitive to the disturbances in international relations. The British there were as well informed of developments in Cuba as were the Spaniards in Manila—perhaps even better. We had not been long there before our small group of exiles began to hear guarded mentions of a possible outbreak of war between Spain and the United States. By mid-February, with the blowing up of the *Maine* in Havana Harbor, the rumor became an open and persistent prediction; by early March, I was convinced that such a war was just around the corner.

As the hour of decision seemed on hand, my small staff and other Filipino political exiles in the British colony began to discuss freely what course of action we should take if and when the expected war broke out. We carefully explored the possibilities.

One of the plans most favored by our group called for the immediate purchase of arms with the money we had in the bank. Thus equipped, we would return to the Islands to resume our

revolution, timing our action to coincide with the outbreak of the
expected Spanish-American war. It was believed that if Spain
were involved in a struggle with the United States, the Spaniards
would have their hands full. They would defend Cuba to the
utmost and, if necessary, leave their forces in the Philippines to
fend for themselves. Even if they should attempt to send reinforcements to the Philippines, the American Navy would most
likely sink them. This was a significant consideration for it
had been the arrival of regulars from Spain which had enabled
the Spaniards to even up scores with us and back their subsequent
peace overtures with the threat of a mounting striking power.

But there was no unanimity of opinion. A small group was for
exploring the possibility of an alliance with the then rising
Oriental power, Japan. However, assistance from this direction
had been sought by the *Katipunan* in vain. Surprisingly, when
the alternative of alliance with America herself was brought up,
almost all of us felt such an eventuality impossible. Believing
that the Spanish-American conflict would be confined to the
Atlantic area, such an alliance, we speculated, would be a paper
one only. America would not be able to give us direct assistance.

Our small Filipino community was electrified to learn one day
in March that a flotilla of the American navy had arrived in
Hongkong from Nagasaki and that it was apparently on its way
to Manila. Greater still was the excitement of my small group of
officers when in the name of the fleet's commander, Commodore
George Dewey, the captain of the *Petrel,* one of the American
men-of-war, sought me for a conference. This led to a series of
secret conversations starting in March and running into April,
the last one taking place on April 6.

The *Petrel* commander, whose name was, I think, Captain
Wood, quite openly urged me to return to the Philippines to
reassemble my army and, with American advice and arms to be
supplied by Dewey, liberate my country from the Spaniards.
Swearing me to absolute secrecy, he confided that the American
fleet would soon proceed to the Philippines to attack the Spanish
fleet there. I told him banteringly that this was an open secret.

But, seriously, I asked him what the United States' move

would be after the Spaniards had been defeated and expelled from the Philippines.

"The United States, my general," he stated, "is a great and rich nation and neither needs nor desires colonies."

It was at this juncture that I suggested, "So that we may have the fullest understanding, it will perhaps be in order to put whatever we may agree upon in writing."

He replied that he agreed with me in principle but that he would have to refer my suggestion to the Commodore who alone could authorize him to do so.

My contact with the Americans was suddenly cut off early in April by what now appears a trivial matter but which at the time looked enough of a threat to make me decide to flee from Hongkong immediately under an assumed name. A countryman of ours who had served in our Cabinet at Biaknabato, Mr. Isabelo Artacho, arrived in Hongkong intent on getting his hands into our war chest. He came to demand for his services no less than 200,000 pesos, a sum equivalent to one-half of the money the Spaniards had given us. He threatened to go to court to enforce his claim if we did not settle with him amicably.

His claim was of course preposterous. He had not served our government but about two months and, at any rate, in our precarious financial condition, no one had received any salary. It was our suspicion that, with his flimsiest of alleged right, he had been sent to Hongkong by no less than the Spanish Captain General to deprive us of our sinew of war or at least tie it up in litigation so that we might be left helpless. Seeing in the threat the dying but long arm of Spain, my chief adviser, Felipe Agoncillo, urged me to leave Hongkong at once with most of the money. It was their thought that, at the least, my disappearance would avoid a scandal; that, at the most, it would save our war funds.

We decided on flight. So that my disappearance might be complete, I was accompanied by only two aides and the three of us traveled under assumed names. I, Colonel Gregorio del Pilar and Lieutenant J. Leyba, the first my aide and the second my secretary, took passage for Saigon, on the steamship *Taisang* on

April 7, 1898. After a week in this port, we boarded the *S. S. Eridan* and reached Singapore on April 21 without knowing that on the day before the Spanish-American War had begun.*

We had hardly settled down in the house of a countryman whom we had previously sworn to keep our presence a secret when, at 4 o'clock in the afternoon of our arrival a Mr. Howard W. Bray called to inquire if General Emilio Aguinaldo had arrived. An Englishman, Bray had resided as a planter and businessman in the Philippines for fifteen years and presented himself as a friend of mine. Our host played his assigned role well. Not only did he deny that I was his guest but he also requested Bray to inform him if and when I should really turn up in Singapore. Bray agreed to oblige. "But if you should see him first, please tell him that the American Consul General here has an important message for him," he bargained. "Keep this information confidential and tell it to no one else but to General Aguinaldo himself."

Mention of the American Consul General and his message made me wonder if my friend on the *Petrel* had sent out tracers for me. The fact, as I was to learn later, was that, in the crisis in which their nation found itself, all the U.S. consular and diplomatic officials in Southeast Asia were vying with each other in serving their country in general and Dewey in particular. Not only were the U. S. consuls in Singapore, Hongkong and Manila doing their utmost to assist the Commodore with information and counsel but even the U.S. Minister to Siam, Mr. John Barrett, later came all the way to Manila to render political advice to the hero of Manila Bay.

Bray returned once more that evening to inquire for me with more insistence and urgency. He came back the following morning again. Each time, my host disclaimed knowledge of my whereabouts. But when in the afternoon he called for the fourth time, I suspected that something very important had developed and I decided to talk to him.

* By an Act of the Congress dated April 25, war was declared to have existed since April 21. However, the U.S. Resolution of intervention dated April 19 was popularly interpreted as a war declaration.

"Sir," he told me after I had revealed my identity, "the American Consul General here, the Hon. E. Spencer Pratt, presents his respects and requests the pleasure of a conference with you." When I asked what the purpose of the conference was, he replied that he did not know. "But the Consul," he added, "is prepared to meet you secretly this very evening."

Wishing no longer to be kept in the dark, I consented to see Pratt. We met that night in "The Mansion," a public house on River Valley Road in a suburb of Singapore, and our conference lasted from 9 o'clock to midnight. The out-of-the-way place, the late hour and, indeed, our strange business gave our meeting a definitely cloak-and-dagger atmosphere. Bray and Leyba served as our interpreters.

It was evident from the start that Pratt had something big up his sleeves. He started by inquiring closely about our revolution against Spain and how the Peace of Biaknabato had worked out, especially how the attitude of the Filipinos to the Spaniards might have changed. I replied that as long as the Spaniards did not improve their administration of the country, the Filipinos, regardless of appearances, will always hate them in their hearts.

"That's the crux of the situation, general," he declared with a note of triumph. "As long as the Spaniards have failed to fulfill their bargain under the Treaty of Biaknabato, you have the right to resume the revolution."

I admitted that we felt exactly the same way about it. His next words had the impact of an explosion.

"As of the other day, April 19th," he said, "Spain and America have been at war. Now is the time for you to strike. Ally yourselves with America and you will surely defeat the Spaniards!"

I was dumbfounded. Before I could compose myself, he continued, "America will help you if you will help America."

"What," I asked at last, "can we expect to gain from helping America?"

"America," he replied readily, "will give you much greater liberty and much more material benefits than the Spaniards ever promised you."

As in Hongkong, I submitted the desirability of having any understanding we might reach in writing. Also like the *Petrel* commander, the consul informed me that he would convey my wishes to Dewey. But he added: "You need not have any worry about America. The American Congress and President have just made a solemn declaration disclaiming any desire to possess Cuba and promising to leave the country to the Cubans after having driven away the Spaniards and pacified the country. As in Cuba, so in the Philippines. Even more so, if possible; Cuba is at our door while the Philippines is 10,000 miles away!"

I was elated. I told him that if Dewey made official his invitation and confirmed his assurances, I would go back to the Philippines and fight side by side with the Americans

He sent Bray for me at noon the next day. At the Raffles Hotel where he resided, he told me that Dewey had sent him a reply. My summary of this interview, as I jotted it down later that day, follows:

"Pratt said Dewey replied that the United States would at least recognize the independence of the Philippines under the protection of the U. S. Navy. The consul added that there was no necessity for entering into a formal written agreement because the word of the Commodore and the U.S. Consul were in fact equivalent to the most solemn pledge, that their verbal promises and assurances would be honored to the letter and were not to be classed with Spanish promises or Spanish ideas of a man's word of honor. The Consul concluded by declaring, 'The Government of the United States is a very honest, just and powerful government' "

As I was myself anxious to return to the Philippines, in view of the fast-unfolding developments, I gave my word to Pratt to help the Americans. "If I can secure arms," I said, "I promise you that my people will rise as one man against the Spaniards."

I had my last conference with Pratt on April 25. He told me that he had received instructions from Dewey to have me proceed to Mirs Bay on the China coast, where the American warships had moved to, having had to leave Hongkong by order of the British Government, and there join his expedition to Manila.

This cave, popularly known as Biak-na-Bato and located in the mountains of San Miguel, Bulacan, became Gen. Aguinaldo's head-quarters during the last stages of the Filipino revolution against Spain. It was here that the Spaniards and Aguinaldo signed a pact ending the conflict. One of its terms was the exile of Aguinaldo and his staff officers to Hongkong which, as fate would have it, facilitated the contact between Aguinaldo and the Americans.

This dog named "Maine," after the U.S. warship whose sinking off Cuba ignited the Spanish-American War, was the mascot of Dewey's expeditionary fleet that sunk the Spanish navy in Manila Bay. Beloved by Dewey's men, it shared their labors and their victory. Cavite's inhabitants watch it admiringly.

This is a battle scene during the early part of the Insurrection or Philippine-American War. American troops are driving Filipino troops from their breastworks and advancing from trench to trench, climaxing the operation with a final victorious charge.

As it appeared that I would not be able to stop at Hongkong, I asked Pratt to help hasten the shipment of arms to us. Before leaving Hongkong for Saigon, I had started negotiations for the purchase of guns. To my request he gladly agreed. He then asked me to appoint him my representative in the United States in order to work for America's recognition of my Government once it was established. I assured him that I would gladly propose him to my associates at the proper time. In fact, although I considered it premature to tell him, I had in mind to reward him handsomely. Believing in his assurances, I thought of offering him a position in our customs department and of awarding him certain commercial privileges once our government would be organized and recognized. I also intended to pay the American Government, through him, our share of whatever might be the cost of liberating our country from Spanish rule.

With my two companions I left Singapore on the *Malacca* in the night of April 25. Pratt assured me that the commodore's launch would be at Hongkong Bay to take us to Mirs Bay to join Dewey. But when we made the British port at 2 o'clock in the morning of May 1, the launch was nowhere to be found. Instead, the American consul in Hongkong, Mr. Rounseville Wildman, met us to explain that, upon orders from Washington, Dewey had rushed to Manila but that he asked the consul to tell me that he would immediately send back a warship to take me to the Philippines.

Although I was very much disappointed that my return to my native land was put off, I had a good reason to consider the few days I was allowed in Hongkong not unnecessary. For one thing, I could look into our purchase of arms, a deal in which, upon my request, Wildman now enthusiastically took a leading part. For another, I had the opportunity to discuss general matters with the consul as well as with the rest of my staff in Hongkong. However, my contact with Wildman may be said to have cost me 67,000 pesos.

Wildman, like Pratt, premised his prediction of future Philippine-American relations on the American declaration on Cuba of April 19 presently to be known as the Teller Amendment.

Among other things, he advised me to establish a dictatorial government as soon as I reached the Philippines. He explained that it was the best government for carrying out a war. "After the war," he added, "you will do well to take the American Government as your model."

The arms purchase was also being consummated, thanks to Wildman's energy and valuable contacts. We placed orders for 2,000 rifles and 200,000 rounds of ammunition and for a launch which we intended as the beginning of a transport service which we would need in moving from island to island. I left 50,000 pesos with Wildman for the payment and shipment of these items to Manila.

The revenue cutter *McCulloch* arrived from Manila on May 7, anchoring at Kowloon across the bay from Hongkong. As I and 17* of my staff were to sail on it in a few days, I arranged to have 67,000 pesos more placed to the credit of Wildman for the purchase of another shipment of arms, an arrangement to which he agreed with alacrity. He and U.S. Minister to Siam John Barrett escorted us to the *McCulloch* in the night of May 16 and sent us off with many wishes of good luck and promises of friendship and cooperation. In due time, the first arms shipment arrived on an American warship. But the second purchase which Wildman was to pay with the 67,000 pesos never came. Perhaps the subsequent turn of events in which I became the No. 1 Enemy of the United States made him feel justified in completely forgetting the deal.

It was 10 o'clock at night when we boarded the *McCulloch*. Although, being only a revenue cutter, this ship had detached itself from the American flotilla before the Battle of Manila Bay, in which on May 1 Dewey had completely destroyed the Spanish fleet, the only American death had taken place among its crew. Its chief engineer, a man rolling in fat, had suffered a stroke from a heart condition and the excessive heat just as his vessel, bringing up the rear of the flotilla steaming into the Bay, came abreast of Corregidor. Our trip across the China Sea was uneventful outwardly; but for our small group going back home to

* Two had gone with Dewey.

renew battle with our old enemies under the strange auspices of the American navy, it was inwardly tumultuous. We spent most of our waking hours in deep reflection but each knew that virtually the same thoughts coursed through our minds.

We were returning to our native land from which we had been exiled by our enemy. We had the support of a powerful nation. But would we find our people as ready to support us as before? Certainly, the Spaniards had tried to make capital of our willingness to stop the revolution, accept money and go abroad. But our return with arms and American support should disabuse the minds of all those who had been so faithless as to doubt our determination to liquidate Spanish rule. And what about our beloved families and relatives left behind? It was about six months since we had seen them last. Had the Spaniards honored their promises to guarantee their safety? If the Spaniards should get an inkling of our return, would they not take them as hostages? Worse still, would not the enemy, once more panic-stricken, torture and perhaps kill them?

It was past noon on May 19 when the *McCulloch* dropped anchor in Manila Bay. Almost immediately, the Admiral's launch carrying his adjutant and private secretary came alongside to convey me to Dewey who was waiting on his flagship. Accompanied by Colonel del Pilar and Lieutenant Leyba, I boarded the launch and in no time I was being piped over the *Olympia* and being greeted cordially by the Admiral himself. I was given the honors due a general officer.

In his full uniform Dewey was an impressive figure. Tall and husky, though on the paunchy side, he had an honest and benevolent face made dignified by a high forehead, wavy grey hair and a thick, white moustache. Ushering us to his private quarters, he was effusive with hospitality and cordiality. He might well be, with his Manila Bay victory and immediate promotion to Rear Admiral—and the prospect of getting the Filipinos as allies.

My notes on this interview read as follows:

"After exchanging the usual amenities, I asked Admiral Dewey if it was true that he had sent the cablegrams to the Consul General in Singapore, Mr. Pratt, which the latter told me he had received, regarding myself. The Admiral replied in the affirmative, adding that the United States had come to the Philippines to free the Filipinos from the yoke of Spain. He said furthermore that America was exceedingly well off as regards territory, revenue, and resources and needed no colonies. He assured me finally that there was no reason for me to entertain any doubts whatever about the recognition of the Independence of the Philippines by the United States.

"Then, Admiral Dewey asked me if I could induce the Filipinos to rise against the Spaniards and make a short, sharp and decisive campaign.

"In reply, I said that events would speak for themselves. However, I explained, until I would receive the first arms which Consul Wildman was to send me, I would not be able to go into action. The Admiral thereupon offered to dispatch a steamer to take the arms. Indicating his anxiety for action, he also placed immediately at my disposal all the guns seized on board the Spanish warships as well as 62 Mausers and a good many rounds of ammunition which the *Petrel* had brought from Corregidor."

My record of the next conference with Dewey reads:

"I candidly informed the Admiral that when I was about to leave Hongkong the Filipinos residing in that colony had held a meeting in which they had fully discussed the possibility that after the Spaniards were defeated, the American Government might not recognize our independence and another war would follow. In that event, the Americans would surely defeat us for they would find us worn out and short of ammunition owing to our struggle against the Spaniards. I then asked the Admiral if my countrymen's misgivings had any basis. I hastened to beg him to excuse me for bringing up the matter, but I had to do so in the interest of frankness as befits allies.

"The Admiral said he was glad to have this evidence of our earnestness and frankness. In reply, he thought that Filipinos and Americans should act toward one another as friends and allies, and therefore it was proper that all doubts be expressed frankly so that explanations may be made, distrust removed and difficulties avoided. He then stated that, as he had already indicated, the United States would unquestionably recognize the Independence of the people of the Philippines, guaranteed as it was by the word of honor of Americans which, he said, was more positive, more irrevocable, than a written agreement which might not be regarded as binding when there is an intention or desire to repudiate it, as was the case with the pact we had made with the Spaniards in Biaknabato."

In this interview, the Admiral suggested that I have a Philippine Flag made which, he said, he would recognize and protect in the presence of the other nations represented in the various naval squadrons in Manila Bay. He advised me, however, that I should not hoist the flag until we had destroyed the power of Spain in the islands in order that it would, when unfurled, catch the eyes of the world at the moment of victory.

By invitation of the Admiral, I made my headquarters and home in the former headquarters of the Spanish Naval Commandant of the Cavite Arsenal. It was here where American officials came to see me or from which I sallied forth to see them. Upon their insistent urgings, we started our drive against the Spaniards almost immediately.

In the archives of the government in Washington and in almost all the history books on the Philippine-American War, it is of record that both Dewey, Pratt and Wildman completely denied having made every promise that they had made to me.

CHAPTER IV

DEWEY "EXERCISES DISCRETION MOST FULLY"

ADMIRAL DEWEY in Manila and the American consuls in Singapore and Hongkong cooperating with him were confronted by a situation, not a theory—by the facts and the perils of the hour. Ten thousand miles away from home, they had to make the best arrangements and bargains they could to insure American victory. More than any other American, Dewey had to face the brutal realities.

It may be admitted, as claimed, that neither an American Admiral nor a U. S. consular official nor a combination of them can make political commitments that are binding upon the American Government. Even so, the least Washington could have done under the circumstances should have been to ascertain if American honor might have been better upheld not by a new war but by magnanimity in victory.

One consolation is that the United States, eventually if belatedly, granted the demands of our people for freedom. Equally satisfying is the fact that America has won no war since then without applying the hard lesson it learned in the Philippines: in every victory after Manila, whether in China, Germany or Japan, it has invariably been magnanimous. My country was the sacrifice at the altar of a new gospel of international relations which America finally adopted as a firm policy.

Once ordered to go into battle against the Spaniards, Commodore Dewey naturally put into operation a plan of action which he had long been maturing in his mind. As early as in the fall of 1897, when he first aspired to the command of the American Asiatic Squadron, he had declared that, since the assignment would be about halfway around the world away, victory in battle would depend on freedom of action.

"In command of an efficient force in the Far East," he had

said, "with a free hand to act in consequence of being so far away from Washington, I could strike promptly and successfully at the Spanish forces in the Philippines."

After the Battle of Manila Bay, the distance between the Commodore and Washington became even farther. Having himself cut the cables connecting Manila with the rest of the world, dispatches from and to him had to be sent to or received from Hongkong, some two days away from his blockade line.

Buttressing the pre-conceived intention of Dewey to act freely were communications soon burning the cables from the Secretary of the Navy, the Hon. John D. Long. All this in spite of the fact that the Secretary had previously resented Dewey. The Commodore had obtained his new command through manipulations perpetrated practically behind the Secretary's back by the ebullient Assistant Secretary of the Navy, the up-and-coming Theodore Roosevelt. Much to the Commodore's disappointment, Long had denied him the pleasure of hoisting the Rear Admiral's pennant atop his flagship, the *Olympia,* a privilege enjoyed by his predecessor of equal rank. Now, however, the Secretary seemed fully to share the awesome reverence of the American people for their new hero. On May 26 Mr. Long cabled Dewey authority to "exercise discretion most fully in all matters and be governed according to circumstances which you know and we cannot know. You have our confidence entirely."

The Secretary, it is true, somewhat watered down his authorization for the exercise of the fullest discretion and his expression of utter confidence by adding a somewhat contradictory advice. "It is desirable," his cable continued, "as far as possible and consistent with your safety, not to have political alliances with insurgents or any faction in islands that would incur liability their cause in the future." Even this alien phrase in an intended *carte blanche* was, however, almost no inconvenience at all. Safety, the Secretary said, was to be the ultimate yardstick of the Admiral's discretion. And the Admiral had every reason to look to his safety which was being menaced from many directions.

There was, first of all, the peril posed by the Spaniards themselves. In Cavite alone, they had the equivalent of an infantry division; and, all over the Philippines, an estimated 50,000 men including recently-arrived regulars. There was also a considerable number of Filipino soldiers in their employ like the mercenary Macabebes. That they could recruit or inveigle more Filipinos to join their ranks was also a definite reality.

From the direction of the Suez Canal loomed an additional Spanish menace. A naval squadron consisting of armored cruisers and destroyers under Admiral Manuel de la Camara had rushed out of Spain for the Far East. Its mission was to support Admiral Patricio Montojo's flotilla and help relieve the beleaguered Spaniards in the islands. The arrival of Dewey in Manila far sooner than expected, thanks to Teddy Roosevelt's perspicacity, and the complete annihilation of Montojo's fleet by Dewey with the greatest of ease, altered the Spanish Admiralty's plans. The relief squadron was ordered to relieve itself and no one else; it was told to double back to the safety of the Mediterranean. The outbreak of the war between Spain and the United States, two nations located vis-a-vis the Atlantic, made the safety of Spain itself a more urgent consideration than the safety of the Philippines. But it was very much later that this favorable tidings reached the victorious Admiral in Manila.

Another peril beset Dewey. Enraged by the failure of the Spanish authorities to carry out their promises in the Treaty of Biaknabato, the Filipinos had been stirred up anew. They had secretly prepared for another showdown and waited only for our signal to rise once more as one man against our immemorial enemy. Such a potent human force had to be led properly if the safety of the Admiral and his flotilla was to be assured. The desperate anger of our people could as easily be directed against the Spaniards, who were in occupation of our country, as against the Americans if they tried to succeed the Spaniards in the role of masters.

A third danger, perhaps the greatest potentially, was intervention by other nations in an attempt to obtain a share of a possible Philippine loot. With the exception of Great Britain and France, the nations of Europe regarded the United States as an upstart in the colonial game and sympathized with Spain though some of them were not averse to succeeding her. Several deliberately refused to declare neutrality. One such nation was Germany, and its public press was unanimous in vehement condemnation of America. At least one Oriental country also had more than a passing interest in the Philippines.

There was a widespread suspicion, which records since revealed have shown to be well-founded, that Japan and Germany were alertly watching for opportunities, like vultures on the prowl, to at least snatch a morsel of the Philippines if and when the picking became good. It was indeed a time for picking the last obtainable colonies in the Orient. Germany had just leased Shantung Peninsula, Britain had signed up for Wei-hai-wei, and Russia had followed suit in Manchuria. True, Japan was still to acquire the status of a world power, but subsequent documents have revealed that it was also observing developments eagle-eyed and drooling.

The Germans were however the more aggressive. They sent a full squadron to Manila, one greater in tonnage than and superior in firepower to Dewey's flotilla and commanded by an officer who outranked Dewey even with his new title of Rear Admiral gratefully given him by a nation glutted with victory. Vice-Admiral Von Diederichs, the German commander, had three cruisers, two destroyers and a naval transport loaded with 1,400 men equipped for landing and land operations. His total manpower alone was almost twice that of Dewey's full complement of only 1,743 men.*

The German Admiral committed so many violations of the laws of blockade with arrogance and impunity that Dewey was driven to threaten, with tacit backing of the commander of the English flotilla which was also on the scene, that if Germany wanted war he would give it to Von Diederichs there and then. Highly suspicious to Dewey must have been the visits of the German commander to the Spanish Captain-General in Manila, who returned his calls. German officers, among them Prince

---

* Dewey's flotilla was composed of the lighter warships *Olympia, Baltimore, Raleigh, Boston, Concord* and *Petrel,* and the revenue cutter *McCulloch.*

Lowenstein, freely fraternized with the Spanish troops. The Germans even took soundings off the mouth of the Pasig River, occupied lighthouses and quarantine stations, landed their men for drill at Mariveles harbor and other places, and the Admiral himself occupied a former Spanish official's quarters.

The conduct of the German fleet convinced a large majority of the American press and people that Germany had dark designs upon the Philippines. Indeed secret German documents discovered after World War I reveal that the Kaiser had issued instructions to the German forces to pick up such parcels of real estate in the Pacific area as they could manage to get away with. Apparently about to change ownership, the Philippines was a made-to-order objective.

Guided by competent studies of these documents, former Philippine Governor-General W. Cameron Forbes, in his monumental work, *The Philippine Islands,* discusses in detail the German interest in our country and proves that it was definitely predatory. As early as May 11, 1897, Prince Henry of Prussia, commanding the Asiatic Squadron, cabled Von Bulow, the minister of state for foreign affairs and later German chancellor, that a German merchant in Manila had advised him that our rebellion against Spain had a good chance to succeed and that "the natives would gladly place themselves under the protection of a European power, preferably Germany." This information was presently amplified by the German consul in Manila who reported that we planned to estabilsh a kingdom and that we would probably offer the throne to a German prince.

Von Bulow forthwith submitted this information to his sword-rattling megalomaniac Kaiser with the comment, "The control of the sea in the end may rest on the question of who rules the Philippines." In a marginal note, the emperor expressed agreement and added that the Philippines, wholly or in part, must not pass to another power "without Germany receiving an equivalent compensation." The German appetite was further whetted by the U.S. Ambassador to Berlin who publicly voiced the then prevalent American opinion that his own Government would not occupy the Philippines. He added gratuitously that it was desirable that the German colonial system be extended there.

Typical of the American anger over the German feints in Manila was the editorial of the *Atlanta Constitution*. "Americans resent any kind of arrogance," it said, "but when it is displayed by a despot whose lunatic reign has excited the contempt and indignation of all who enjoy human liberty, the feeling goes deeper." It added that a war with Germany might not be a bad idea, saying, "Who knows but the imperial war god of Germany may cause to be fired the shot that will be the signal of a conflict, the result of which may be indirectly to redeem all Europe from the fraudulent government of kings and emperors."

When the German Squadron at last went slinking away from Manila Bay after Spain and the United States had signed an Armistice, it saved the Kaiser's face by grabbing the spilled crumbs of the disappearing Spanish empire, the Marianas and the Caroline islands.

With Germany and Japan known to be interested in a Philippine colony, it was typical American foresight for Dewey to score the decisive advantage of alliance with the Filipinos. And, modesty aside, I was the key to such an alliance.

Dewey had at least two good reasons to seek my cooperation even before he had fired a shot: to head off Japan and Germany and to have us clear the Philippines of Spaniards while he had no land troops of his own. Aside from the possible danger to the American position of a Japanese or a German Alliance with the Filipinos, there was the other peril that if Spanish land power were not weakened but on the other hand were allowed to build up, the subsequent operation by the American forces would have been difficult and costly. Furthermore, there was always present the possibility that Germany might pact alliance with Spain against the United States for a price—the Philippines or at least a parcel of it.

The expressions of the fullest confidence in Dewey and the instructions to use complete discretion must be considered together with the brutal realities in the light of America's lack of Philippine policy up to mid-October 1898, a period of six months after the Battle of Manila Bay. And, during these fateful six months, while President McKinley put his ears against the ground listening for some decipherable rumblings of public opinion, American officials from Secretaries Day and Long, through Admiral Dewey and General Anderson, down to Consuls Pratt and Wildman, necessarily suffered from a Teller-Amendment mentality.

Through the Congress and the President, the American people had declared on April 19, 1898, that, in intervening in Cuba, the United States "disclaims any disposition or intention to exercise sovereignty, jurisdiction, or control over said island except for the pacification thereof, and asserts its determination when that is accomplished to leave the government and control of the island to its people." Here was the concrete and specific statement of purpose behind the Cuban intervention and the war with Spain.

Since America came to the Philippines as an incident of the Spanish-American War, it was logical and inevitable, in the absence of contrary statements or indications of a different policy, to suppose that her purpose in the Philippines was exactly the same as her purpose in Cuba. This was the assumption on which American officials in the Orient proceeded in their respective missions, it was the assumption America wished the world to accept, and it was the assumption on which we ourselves in the Philippines based our understanding of American statements and deeds.

One can therefore imagine with what supreme confidence the victor of Manila Bay exercised the "fullest discretion" all, of course, for the sake of Old Glory. And why not? Widest discretion in the field has since been justified as "operational necessity" by no less than the U.S. Joint Chiefs of Staff.

When General Eisenhower, during the last phases of the invasion of Germany, decided to depart from the plan concerted and approved by the Combined Chiefs of Staff at Malta— plans which had received the final approval of President Roosevelt and Prime Minister Churchill—and communicated his decision to Marshal Stalin before either the Combined Chiefs of Staff or Churchill and Roosevelt themselves learned about it, Churchill protested vigorously. Not only did he charge that Eisenhower's move was a "short-circuiting of the highest authorities, both military and constitutional," but he pointed out that Eisenhower's decision to bypass Berlin for Leipzig and Dresden and leave it to the Russians was both a military and political error of the gravest character.

"The Russian armies," he predicted in a protest to President Roosevelt, "will no doubt overrun all Austria and enter Vienna. If they also take Berlin, will not the impression that they have been the overwhelming contributor to our common victory be unduly imprinted in their minds and may this not lead them into a mood which will raise grave and formidable difficulties in the future?"

As Churchill had feared, the Russians not only took Berlin but also fanned out deep into the vacuum in western Germany created by Eisenhower's diversions. This reduced Berlin to a beleaguered city in a red German sea. When later the vanquished nation was divided into occupation zones, the western Allies found their position most precarious. From their own sectors of Berlin, they had to administer their zones as well as feed and supply their Berlin population through roads, railroads and other means of transportation and communication in Russian-held territory. As if holding the plunger to a dynamite charge, the Russians were able to create crises at will. One such crisis resulted when they blockaded Berlin. To defeat the blockade, the Allies resorted to the expensive and dangerous if heart-warming Berlin airlift.

General MacArthur's case in Korea also involved a question of discretion in the reverse manner. Instead of exercising the fullest discretion and bombing the privileged sanctuaries of the enemy in Manchuria as an operational necessity, he vigorously protested the restrictions imposed upon him by Washington. The result was his discharge by President Truman as Supreme Commander of the United Nations Forces in Korea and the Allied Forces in the Pacific.

The case of Dewey is more similar to Eisenhower's than to

MacArthur's. He had solicited and obtained our armed assistance as an obvious "operational necessity." But it is a pity that instead of standing up courageously for what he had already done, like Eisenhower, he chose to follow what appeared to be the line of least resistance and repudiated our reiterated understanding. I think that his decision eventually proved to be the more disastrous alternative.

It is beyond all doubt that Dewey had been most anxious to obtain our military cooperation. Documents since discovered reveal that Pratt had cabled to him his opinion that "Aguinaldo is the man for the occasion." To the consul's information that I was willing to return to Hongkong to "arrange with Commodore for general cooperation insurgents Manila," Dewey had cabled the urgent reply, "Tell Aguinaldo come soon as possible."

Naturally the reasons for the Admiral's great anxiety were not then fully clear to me. A complete knowledge of the true state of affairs at the time, pieced together from official and private documents, however, makes possible a more judicious and comprehensive appraisal of the situation, together with the true motives behind Dewey's words and acts and those of the consular officials eagerly cooperating with him. In the light of this more ample and documented knowledge, together with over half a century of mulling over the entire incident of 1898-1901 —embittered as I had the right to be by the turn of events and my defeat and capture in war—I continue to hold that, prior to August 1898, the commitments, promises, assistance and other acts of American officials indicative of willingness to help us obtain our freedom and set up an independent government were given in full good faith.

CHAPTER V

AMERICAN GOOD FAITH

IN A NEW BIOGRAPHY of Admiral Dewey written with the assistance of his only son, George Goodwin Dewey, by Laurin Hall Healy and Luis Kutner, this interesting sentence appears:

> Dewey was especially careful never to put anything in writing, a step which permitted Aguinaldo later to allege that he had received from the Admiral numerous promises of sovereignty.

What interests me most is the first part: "Dewey was especially careful never to put anything in writing . . . ." Although I wish to be charitable and say that this statement is more naive than revealing, it nevertheless invites comment. Should the Admiral have been especially careful not to have a record in black and white of his promises and assurances? Or should he have exercised the greatest care not to promise or assure anything that he did not mean or had to deny later?

If a man is in urgent need of the support and cooperation of another, yet meticulously avoids making any commitments in writing, he would seem to be acting in bad faith. Putting the terms of an understanding or agreement on paper is generally accepted as the logical and natural procedure among men who intend to carry out their part of a bargain to the best of their ability. Dewey's consistent and inflexible refusal to write anything down in the course of our negotiations, in the manner in which his latest biographers present the matter, would seem to be nearer bad faith than good.

In the light of the difficult situation I have previously described in which the Admiral found himself, it was possible that if he were disposed to act in good faith he was still compelled by circumstances to proceed in bad faith. Men in desperate situations tend to invoke the end in justification of the means. This is natural as well as legal. The instinct of self-preservation is nature's highest law; and the laws of men, in their supreme tests, often fall upon it for support. In self-defense a man may kill another, and both the courts and society itself understand and forgive his crime. National survival is also the supreme national law, and in its name men have fought wars. Admiral Dewey not only had his own life and the lives of his 1,743 officers and men to preserve; over and above the fate of individual Americans, he had in his exclusive custody and protection in Manila the security, fortune and sacred honor of America.

Personally, nevertheless, I know and believe that Dewey and the men who assisted him dealt with me in full good faith, at least during the first months of my contact with them. I make this statement most deliberately. I base it on their spoken words, their written statements once officially secret but since revealed, their acts and their concern over my country and myself in the fluid historic context prior to the fall of Manila in August and perhaps to as late as October 1898. In the latter month, President McKinley at last undertook to fuse together and articulate into official policy the sentiments of Captain Alfred T. Mahan of the Navy; Senator Henry Cabot Lodge and Theodore Roosevelt; the intensifying pressure of power politics; the editorial opinions of the *New York Tribune*; and the victory hysteria of the provincial West and Midwest.

The American field commanders in Manila were like the members of an orchestra, determinedly perceptive and sensitive to every grimace and gesture of their conductor. Unfortunately, while the orchestra pit was in the Philippines, the podium was in Washington. Since during the first few months the signals were not only often hesitant but also delayed in transmission, each performer was inevitably and frequently on his own. An unfortunate dissonance was the result.

As to the promises made to me by Dewey, Pratt, Wildman and others, I have only my own words against their denials.

My aide, Col. Gregorio H. del Pilar, and my secretary, Lt. J. Leyba, who might now be my witnesses, long ago joined their Maker. But I do assert what is only most logical and natural: that I agreed to their request for military cooperation only because they accepted my own conditions. These conditions were substantially the same as those set down in the Teller Amendment: The American and Filipino forces would cooperate in fighting the Spaniards and liberating the Philippines of their rule; the Americans would advise in the establishment of a new Philippine government, extending it protection if necessary; and, this done, they would leave my people and country entirely free and independent.

The maximum qualification to this assertion that I admit is the natural difficulty and imperfection of communication in two different languages, English and Spanish, through itinerant interpreters. Although he had lived long in the Philippines, Howard W. Bray spoke a halting Spanish and, being a Briton, conversed in British English. Lt. Leyba was his exact opposite; while he spoke excellent Spanish, he had before met English mainly in books and not so many of them.

But no matter. The sentence I have quoted from the new Dewey book can at least serve the purpose of illustrating how language, even in the hands of native experts in its use—and even when written rather than merely spoken—is imperfect as a means of communicating thought. Where two or more languages are used orally by non-experts, the deficiency naturally aggravates, and profound misunderstanding and conflicts can arise.

It is possible more than probable that in their transmission through our interpreters, the Americans' ideas and mine not only suffered curtailments but also acquired elaborations. The first might have been due to the linguistic limitations of the interpreters as well as of ourselves, but the second could have been the result of good if mistaken intentions of over-enthusiastic subalterns.

But if all this is controversial, the documents which had previously been confidential but since declassified and the acts of the Americans, which speak louder than words, should be conclusive. There are many facts which, to use Secretary Long's choice phrase, Washington could not know at the time but which, on the basis of documents since made accessible, can now be learned, evaluated, and pieced together. They can, I believe, speak conclusively for Dewey, Pratt, Wildman and me.

Among these papers are manifestoes and press reports contemporaneous with my interviews with the American officials. These were surely read not only by them but also by other American officials at home, for the American consuls are now known to have sent copies or clippings of them to the State Department.

While I was still on my way back from Singapore to Hong-kong, the Filipinos in the latter city, led by my associates, issued a Manifesto to the Filipino people, copies of which were brought to the Philippines by two of my men who accompanied Dewey to Manila. "Divine Providence is about to place independence within our reach," it declared. "The Americans, not from mercenary motives have considered it opportune to extend their protecting mantle over our beloved country. . . . The Americans will attack by sea and prevent any reinforcements coming from Spain. . . . We insurgents must attack by land. . . . Where you see the American flag flying, assemble in number; they are our redeemers!"

On May 24, just a few days after my return to the Philippines on the *McCulloch* and nearly a month after the battle of Manila Bay, I myself issued a Manifesto, in which I said the following: "Filipinos, the great nation, North America, cradle of liberty, and friendly on that account to the liberty of our people has come to manifest a protection . . considering us with sufficient civilization to govern by ourselves this our unhappy land."

Accompanying our words with action, we established a dictatorial government on June 18, and a revolutionary government on June 23. On August 6, I issued an appeal to foreign governments to recognize the independence of the Philippines.

All these events happened before the reference month of October when President McKinley finally came out with his decision to keep the Philippines.

Two most interesting documents, the existence of which I was not aware until years later, were a news story and an editorial in the Singapore *Free Press* of May 4, 1898. Although I had been brought to the offices of the *Free Press* by Bray and there interviewed by the editor, Mr. W. G. St. Clair, I had, in the fast succession of earth-shaking events that followed, forgotten the visit. Clippings of the newspaper were however immediately transmitted to the State Department by Consul General Pratt, the records reveal. In his covering letter, Pratt declared, "Though the facts are in the main correctly given, the dates are not quite accurate, and a certain amount of conjecture has been indulged upon as regard my action on the matter and that of the Commodore."

The story relates the chain of historic events leading to my interviews with Pratt, from the outbreak of the revolution against Spain in 1896 to my presence in Singapore. The most pertinent portions of the story, which occupied about two columns, are perhaps the following paragraphs:

> During the conference, at which Mr. Bray acted as interpreter, General Aguinaldo explained to the American consul general, Mr. Pratt, the incidents and objects of the late rebellion and described the present disturbed state of the country. General Aguinaldo then proceeded to detail the nature of the cooperation he could give in which he, in the event of the American forces from the squadron landing and taking possession of Manila, would guarantee to maintain order and discipline among the native troops and inhabitants in the same humane way in which he had preferred to conduct the war and to prevent them from committing outrages on defenseless Spaniards beyond the inevitable in a fair and honorable warfare. He further declared his ability to establish a proper and responsible government on liberal principles, and would be willing to accept the same terms for the country as the United States intends giving to Cuba.
>
> The Consul General of the United States, coinciding with the

general views expressed during the discussion, placed himself at once in telegraphic communication with Admiral Dewey at Hongkong.

The long narration concludes with this statement:

> The substance of the whole incident in its relations to the recent course of affairs in the Philippines, has been fully telegraphed by the editor both to New York and London.

The editorial is entitled "Aguinaldo's Policy" and attempts to describe the government to be established in the Philippines by ourselves. It opens with this significant sentence: "General Aguinaldo's policy embraces the independence of the Philippines, whose internal affairs would be controlled under European and American advisers." It continues, "American protection would be desirable temporarily on the same lines as that which might be instituted hereafter in Cuba . . . entire freedom of the press would be established. . . . There would be general religious toleration, and steps would be taken for the abolition and expulsion of the tyrannical religious fraternities.   . . Spanish officials would be removed to a place of safety until opportunity offered to return them to Spain. .   "

By word of mouth and by print our intentions and plans were, I think, made sufficiently clear. It can almost be said that there was no possible chance that the Americans could have misunderstood them. In fact they did understand them. And while they did not agree to them in writing, their request for and use of our valuable cooperation, together with our sacrifices of life and property, their active support and encouragement of our military operations and their cognizance of our political activities, created a definite American obligation.

Reporting on our various interviews, Pratt himself told the State Department on April 13, 1898: "The General further stated that he hoped the United States would assume protection of the Philippines for at least long enough to allow the inhabitants to establish a government of their own, the organization of which he would desire American advice and assistance."

Although he concluded his dispatch with the statement,

"These questions, I have told him, I have no authority to discuss," Pratt as late as June 10, 1898 said in a letter addressed to me:

> Allow me to tender you my most sincere congratulations on the brilliant success of your recent military achievements. . . . All is coming to pass as I had hoped and predicted, and it is now being shown that I was right in arranging for your cooperation with Admiral Dewey and equally right in asking that you are given the support and entrusted with the confidence of the American Government.

This is exactly in line with another letter written to me by Consul General Wildman in Hongkong, since embodied in the *Congressional Record,* like Pratt's and many other documents on Philippine-American relations. "Do not forget," it reiterated, "that the United States undertook this war for the sole purpose of relieving the Cubans from the cruelties under which they were suffering and not for the love of conquest or the hope of gain. They are actuated by precisely the same feelings for the Filipinos."

The Teller-mentality asserted itself at every opportunity.

Although Dewey wrote me no letters, for reasons which his latest biographers have naively given warrant, he sent dispatches to the Secretary of the Navy, prepared a memorandum for the Peace Commission in Paris, testified before congressional committees, and finally wrote his autobiography. His references to me and the Filipinos in this great mass of documents reveal definite stages of thought and attitude which were sensitive and responsive to and paralleling those of President McKinley.

On June 27, he concluded a cable to Secretary Long with what appears to be intended as an indirect justification of his dealings with me in this wise:

> In my opinion these people are superior in intelligence and more capable of self-government than the natives of Cuba.

As Dewey told a congressional committee later, he instructed me on the day of my arrival from Hongkong, "Go ashore and start your army." From that date until the arrival of substantial

American troops in July, Dewey saw me almost daily, watched and encouraged my military and political activities, describing them frequently to Washington in a series of progress reports.

Here are samples of the Admiral's earlier dispatches to Secretary Long:

> May 24—Steamer has just arrived from Amoy with 3,000 Mauser rifles and great ammunition for Aguinaldo, whose force is increasing constantly.

As the blockading power, Dewey had to approve the entry and landing of all war materials we were able to bring in from abroad. This shipment, in fact, came on one of his ships.

> May 30—Aguinaldo visited *Olympia* yesterday. Expect to make general attack May 31. Doubt ability to succeed.
>
> June 6—Insurgents have been engaged actively within the province of Cavite during the last week. They have had several small victories, taking prisoners about 1,800 men, 50 officers. They are Spanish troops, not natives.
>
> June 12—Insurgents continue hostilities and have practically surrounded Manila. They have taken 2,500 Spanish prisoners, whom they treat most humanely. They do not intend to attack city proper until the arrival of U.S. troops as I have advised.

Dewey was able to give the assurance that we would not attack Manila alone, only because I had agreed to his insistent plea that we wait for the American troops.

> June 19—I have given Aguinaldo to understand that I consider insurgents as friends, being opposed to a common enemy.

After the U.S. Troops had built up to a few thousands, however, Dewey began to alter his attitude. He told the congressional committee in 1902, "I had not much to do with him (Aguinaldo) after the army came."

But Gen. T. M. Anderson had somehow already caught, if only briefly, the Admiral's earlier spirit. For some time after his arrival in Manila at the head of three transports carrying the first batch of troops, he showed the same symptoms of Teller-Amendment infection which originally afflicted his countrymen.

On my part, as Anderson himself states in his record of our first conversation, I continued to be obsessed by the desire to know if America would live up to the promises of its officials.

Dewey and Anderson called on me on July 1, the day following the troops' arrival. "He (Aguinaldo) asked me point-blank," Anderson said of this visit, "if the United States had recognized or would recognize his government." The general failed to record his reply but I can say that, though he was evasive, he was not unsympathetic. Both in his correspondence and conversations with me, he treated me as an ally.

Under date of July 4, he sent me an official letter in which he stated the following:

> I have the honor to inform you that the United States of America, whose land forces I have the honor to command . . . has entire sympathy and most friendly sentiments for the native people of the Philippine Islands. . . . I desire to have the most amicable relations with you and to have you and your people cooperate with us in the military operations against the Spanish forces.

In another document, Anderson commented on my return call upon him as follows:

> I told him that in 120 years we have established no colonies. He then made the remarkable statement: "I have studied extensively the Constitution of the United States and I find in it no authority for colonies and I have no fear."

But this spirit of understanding was not to last long. Our faith in the Americans was first rudely jolted in mid-August when they allowed themselves to be inveigled by the Spaniards into excluding us from participating in the taking and occupation of Manila. In the United States itself, developments were taking place which would soon completely disillusion us. On October 10-21, President McKinley toured the West and Midwest and spoke before audiences which were naturally exultant and jubilant over the spectacular feat of American arms in Manila.

The crowds, as Mr. Andrew Carnegie observed, "of course

cheered when he spoke of the flag and of Dewey's victory."
Walter Millis adds, "As those waves of patriotic applause broke
upon him, the President began to see a new light." Following
the Western swing, "Uncle" Joe Cannon, soon to become
Speaker, immediately noticed the President's transformation.
"He returned to Washington," he commented, "convinced that
there was no way out of it, and he would have to take over all
of the Philippines." Added another future speaker, Champ
Clark: "The jingo bacillus is indefatigable in its work."

The plain truth is that Commodore Dewey fought and won
the Battle of Manila Bay as a very distant repercussion of the
genuine American concern over Cuba. The battle having been
won, America was slow in making up her mind as to what to do
next in the Philippines. The decision to retain the entire archipelago, as President A. Whitney Griswold of Yale points out,
was reached slowly and was the integrated end-result of many
pressures and considerations. The most important of these were
the envisioned prospects of American profits in the markets of
Asia, "British persuasion, German rivalry, the machinations of
Lodge and Roosevelt, the doctrines of Mahan, and the growing
imperialist sentiments of the voters."

Gradually the McKinley Administration succumbed to what
Viscount Bryce called "the sudden imperialistic impulse of
1898-1900" and President Griswold describes as "this *fin de
siecle* mood." But once it had succumbed, it succumbed completely. During this brief fateful period, the United States established a protectorate over Cuba, annexed Hawaii, secured title
to American Samoa, and acquired Guam, Wake, Puerto Rico
and the Philippines.

Following is the approximate "chart" of America's rising
imperialistic fever:

August 1897—Captain Alfred T. Mahan, leading advocate of
big navy and American expansion, is appointed to the Board of
Naval Strategy.

September—Theodore Roosevelt, assistant secretary of the
Navy, is urging both President McKinley and Secretary of the

Navy Long to launch a naval attack on the Philippines the instant war with Spain breaks out.

October—Roosevelt orders Commodore George Dewey to sail for Nagasaki, Japan, to assume command of the American Asiatic squadron.

February 25, 1898—Roosevelt cables Dewey to proceed to Hongkong, take on a full load of fuel and, in the event of war with Spain, "your duty will be to see that the Spanish squadron does not leave the Asiatic coast, and then offensive operations on the Philippine Islands." (This order was issued when Secretary of the Navy Long took the afternoon off and Senator Henry Cabot Lodge dropped in on Roosevelt.)

May 1—Battle of Manila Bay, Dewey destroys Spanish fleet.

May on—Memorials from business groups and chambers of commerce, urging retention of the Philippines as the key to the markets of eastern Asia, pour into the Department of State and the White House.

May on—The publications of churches of all denominations maintaining missions in the Far East strongly urge Philippine annexation.

May 3—Ambassador Hay reports from London to Secretary Day that on excellent authority the Germans intend to seize the Philippines. He urges prompt action to forestall them.

May 4—Lodge tells Henry White, "We must on no account let the Islands go.   "

May 24—Lodge to Roosevelt: "In confidence but in absolute certainty" the administration is now fully committed "to the large policy that we both desire."

June 12—Roosevelt to Lodge: "You must get Manila and Hawaii; you must prevent any talk of peace until we get Puerto Rico and the Philippines. . . ."

June 15—Lodge to Roosevelt: "The whole policy of annexation is growing rapidly under the irresistible pressure of events."

June 20—Lodge and Mahan talk to Secretary of State Day for two hours. Lodge reports the conversation to Roosevelt: "He (Day) said at the end that he thought we could not escape our destiny there. The feeling of the country is overwhelming against giving the Philippines back to Spain."

July 18—Lodge to Roosevelt: "McKinley is worrying over

the Philippines—he wants to hold them evidently, but is a little timid about it."

July 28—Ambassador Hay in London to the State Department: "British Government prefer (to have us) retain Philippine Islands.   "

Late July—Cabinet meeting of several days results in draft protocol drawn up by Secretary Day proposing to return all of the Philippine Islands to Spain except "sufficient grounds for a naval station." This was debated with the cabinet equally divided.

August 12—The United States signs protocol with Spain, Article 3 providing that American forces "will occupy and hold the city, bay and harbor of Manila pending the conclusion of a treaty of peace which shall determine the control, disposition and government of the Philippines."

August 13—Spaniards surrender Manila to American forces on condition Filipino forces are excluded.

September—American Peace Commission named: Whitelaw Reid, Senator Davis of Minnesota, and Senator Frye of Maine, expansionists; State Secretary Day, middle ground; and Senator Gray, anti-annexationist.

September 16—McKinley instructs Peace Commissioners: "   . The United States cannot accept less than the cession in full right and sovereignty of the island of Luzon."

October 1-November 28—Commission meets in Paris. During this period, according to Griswold, "the dispatches from the expansionists peace commissioners, particularly Whitelaw Reid's, added to the various other influences already noted, finally swayed McKinley to demand the cession of the entire archipelago."

October 10-21—McKinley tours Midwest and West and observes victory hysteria among the people, interpreting it as support for expansion and imperialism.

October 26—McKinley instructs Secretary Hay to give final instructions to his Commissioners to the effect that "the cession must be of the whole archipelago   "

November 28—Treaty signed with provision for the cession of the entire Philippine archipelago to the United States upon payment of $20,000,000 to Spain.

January-February 6, 1899—Treaty debated by Senate behind closed doors.

February 4—Philippine-American war breaks out.

February 6—Treaty ratified with only one vote to spare.

If President McKinley succumbed to the persuasion of Great Britain, the pressure and machinations of the expansionists and the apparent snowballing of the more articulate public and press opinion in favor of Philippine annexation, what was expected of Admiral Dewey? Was it not his great victory that had given point and urgency to every expansionist emotion and reason? Had Dewey then and there courageously come out to declare that he and his emissaries had made me—and through me, the 8,000,000 Filipinos—understand that we would be treated like the Cubans and given back our country and independence—had he done this most honorable thing, what might have been the consequences?

To America, it might have meant the prevention of the Philippine-American War and all its harmful effects on American honor and prestige. To Dewey, however, it might have resulted in his transformation from a beloved hero to a despised heel. Yet had he stood for the truth and won over the American people, he might have become a hero many times over—resolute in war, magnanimous in victory, and honorable in peace.

But even heroes are human. And field commanders, like Caesar's wife, must not only be faithful to the commander-in-chief but must not appear as if they were unfaithful to him. Remember MacArthur. So now, as the President zigged, the Admiral zigged; as the former zagged, so zagged the latter. Fortunately, as his latest biographers point out, he had been "especially careful not to put anything in writing." Certain that no proof to the contrary could be produced, he denied having promised me independence. He denied having received me on the *Olympia* with military honors. He called my claims "a tissue of falsehoods." At least, he could not deny that he had requested and we had given him military aid.

To the Schurman Commission, the Admiral made a blanket and emphatic denial of all his political commitments to me. The key paragraph in his letter said:

I never, directly or indirectly, promised the Filipinos independence. I never received Aguinaldo with military honors, or recognized or saluted the so-called Filipino flag. I never considered him as an ally, although I did make use of him and the natives to assist me in the operations against the Spaniards.

This denial is obviously beyond logical and sane credibility. We had fought a revolution against Spain and had set up a provisional Government. Finally facing superior forces, we had reluctantly accepted the Pact of Biaknabato, given up the struggle and dissolved our Government. We had saved the cash indemnity the Spaniards had paid us and, at the opportune time, had begun to purchase with it arms and ships for a new revolution.

Then Admiral Dewey came along.

He wanted my assistance and that of my forces badly, urgently. He had me contacted in Hongkong, had me sent back from Singapore. He transported me to the Philippines, gave me arms and instructed me to start land operations against the Spaniards, since he himself had no land forces. He asked me and thousands of other Filipinos to embark upon an adventure in which we would risk our lives and drag our homeland to a new blood bath.

Is it believable that I could agree to undertake his vast request without assurances that our second war against the Spaniards would be more fruitful than the first? Is it credible that, obsessed by the determination to secure the freedom and independence òf my motherland, I should plunge headlong to do the Admiral's bidding without getting his promise that, before exposing ourselves to a second jeopardy, this objective would be realized?

There are conclusive proofs that we had asked for a promise of eventual independence from Pratt, Wildman, Dewey and others. That we had asked is a fact never at any time denied. Well then, if our request had been denied flatly or even only taken under advisement indefinitely, ignored or maneuvered out of our conversations, it is inconceivable that we should have been on terms of friendship and cooperation with the Americans at all, at least after we had returned to the Philippines.

The Admiral would have the Schurman Commission and, through it, the American Government and people think that asking a people to fight a war is as simple as asking a passer-by to help fix a flat tire. "I did make use of him and the natives to assist me in the operations against the Spaniards." Indeed! It was as simple as that—as simple as hitching a donkey to a wagon or a carabao to a cart! This is oversimplification to the point of absolute absurdity. To believe the Admiral is at once to believe us naive, simple-minded, stupid and idiotic.

It is also interesting to note that even where the Admiral had recorded his opinions and reactions in writing, he subsequently reversed himself, also in writing. To the Secretary of the Navy, he cabled on June 23, 1898 a voluntary categorical opinion that the Filipinos were far more ready than the Cubans for self-government. Yet, on October 24, when our formerly amicable relationship was fast deteriorating, he concluded a cable to the Secretary, "The natives appear unable to govern." In justice to the Admiral it should be added that in a still later Memorandum to the U.S. Peace Commissioners in Paris, he went full circle and reiterated his generous first estimate of Filipino political capacity.

I stick to my statement that Dewey, Pratt, Wildman and others dealt with me in good faith prior to the fall of Manila and perhaps up to the moment President McKinley finally made up his mind to keep the Philippines. General Anderson's candid opinion on his fellow Americans is of interest at this juncture. This is what he told the American Government:

> Whether Admiral Dewey or Consuls Pratt, Wildman and Williams did or did not give Aguinaldo assurances that the Filipino government would be recognized, the Filipinos certainly thought so, probably inferring this from their acts rather than from their statements. . . . Admiral Dewey gave them arms and ammunitions as I did subsequently. They were permitted to gather up a lot of arms which the Spaniards had thrown into the bay; and, with 4,000 rifles taken from Spanish prisoners and 2,000 purchased in Hongkong, they proceeded to arm three brigades and also to arm a small steamer they had captured.

One of the most respected American historians of the early Philippine-American period was John Foreman. Sometime late in 1898, before the Paris Peace Commission, he declared: "Aguinaldo and his inexperienced followers were so completely carried away by the humanitarian avowals of the greatest republic the world had seen that they willingly consented to cooperate with the Americans on mere verbal promises, instead of a written agreement which could be held binding on the U.S. Government."

Foreman was even nearer the truth than Anderson. By the nature of things we were indeed inexperienced. We had been an oppressed subject people who had risen in arms against our oppressors for having been pushed beyond the limit of endurance. That is why we welcomed the Americans so readily and looked upon them for advice and even for protection. Definitely, we did not regard the United States as Spain's successor in the ancient game of imperialism. And we cooperated with her with abiding good faith.

In what Walter Millis calls the "splendid improvisation" stage of American statesmanship, there could naturally be no consistency whether in policy or in principle. McKinley himself furnished the explanation for the changing American attitude to the Philippines. "The march of events," he declared, "rules and overrules human action."

I like to think that on January 7, 1899, almost a full month before the Philippine-American War broke out, Admiral Dewey, who was still in Manila, suffered a pang of conscience and sent the following cable to Secretary Long:

Affairs are very disturbed in Philippine Islands. Natives excited and frightened and being united by false reports spread by Spaniards who should be returned to Spain as soon as possible. Strongly urge that the President send here as soon as possible small civilian commission to adjust differences. This should be composed of men skilled in diplomacy and statesmanship.

The Schurman Commission, which was primarily intended as a conciliation body, was the result. But it did not reach the Philippines until March 4, fully a month after the outbreak of hostilities. I feel that had it arrived before February 4, the war could have been avoided.

It is only fair to President McKinley to recollect that about a year after he had taken the Philippines he seemed to have become conscience-stricken and somewhat relented. Apparently doubting that the series of events which had led to the taking of the islands and to the Philippine-American War had had earthly logic or legality, he suddenly announced a heavenly explanation for his Philippine decision. Appropriately enough, he made the revelation to a delegation of the General Missionary Committee of the Methodist Episcopal Church which called on him at the White House. Following was the President's interesting story:

> Hold a moment longer! Not quite yet, gentlemen! Before you go I would like to say just a word about the Philippine business. . . . The truth is I didn't want the Philippines, and when they came to us as a gift from the gods, I did not know what to do with them. . . . I sought counsel from all sides—Democrats as well as Republicans—but got little help. I thought first we would take only Manila; then Luzon; then other islands, perhaps, also. I walked the floor of the White House night after night until midnight; and I am not ashamed to tell you, gentlemen, that I went down on my knees and prayed Almighty God for light and guidance more than one night.
>
> And one night late it came to me this way—I don't know how it was, but it came: (1) That we could not give them back to Spain—that would be cowardly and dishonorable; (2) that we could not turn them over to France or Germany—our commercial rivals in the Orient—that would be bad business and discreditable; (3) that we could not leave them to themselves—they were unfit for self-government—and they would soon have anarchy and misrule over there worse than Spain's was; and (4) that there was nothing left for us to do but to take them all, and to educate the Filipinos, and uplift and civilize and Christianize them, and by God's grace do the very best we could by them, as our fellow men for whom Christ also died. And then I went to bed and went to sleep and slept soundly.

The President's handling of the Philippines henceforth until his death from an assassin's bullet evinced a spirit of contrition which enabled him to lay the basis of a sound, enlightened and far-visioned peace-time Philippine policy.

Years later, no less than Theodore Roosevelt, now an ex-President, declared, "If we act so that the natives understand us to have made a definite promise, then we should live up to that promise."

And yet, in retrospect, I cannot help but be glad that the expansionists won over McKinley completely. For the alternative to annexing the Philippines entirely might have been partition. The Philippines might have been another Poland with Japan annexing the Batanes group in the north, the United States keeping Luzon, Germany grabbing the Visayan Islands, and perhaps Great Britain taking over Mindanao which is proximate to its territory of Borneo. Had the Philippines been dismembered in this or a similar manner, we should have lost all chances of becoming a free and independent nation. In the teeming East where populations are reckoned in hundreds of millions, Luzon alone, not to mention the Visayas or Mindanao alone, would have been too negligible an entity to ever aspire for a separate and independent international personality.

Reviewing the swift march of events, Walter Millis declares: "It was all, of course, with the best of intention and in the loftiest of motives, but General Emilio Aguinaldo, one regrets to report, had been neatly double-crossed."

I would not so greatly simplify it. I believe that Dewey and the others acted in good faith. But we were all caught by the accident of history, and since we could not extricate ourselves together, we tried to wiggle free separately. Repudiating their promises to me became their easiest way out. It was the hardest for me. But I thank God that He has vouchsafed me a long life for I have thus come to see and understand the historic accident as perhaps neither McKinley nor Dewey ever saw and understood it—I have learned its ultimate meaning for my country and for America.

American mortar battery at Caloocan, Rizal, near Manila.

American battery ready for action near Caloocan, Rizal.

This photograph, showing American volunteers in action during the battle of San Roque near Manila, is said to have become famous as a part of the celebrated Brady collection of war pictures.

These American soldiers are firing from a captured Filipino breastwork during the battle of San Roque near Manila. The Americans found the breastwork quite substantial and, had they been defended with adequate fire-power, would have been hard to capture.

CHAPTER VI

WE FIGHT FOR AMERICA

AS A MILITARY STATESMAN, Dewey was born half a century too soon. He discovered and applied successfully a sound basis of American international military leadership. His discovery was the use of native soldiers, with American leadership, in the liberation of their own countries from imperialism. It is a formula which is only now, two world wars later, being rediscovered and advocated notably by General James A. Van Fleet, as a means of fighting communism. But the hero of Manila Bay later disowned and repudiated it completely. When he saw its great potency he feared he had unknowingly been another Frankenstein who had created a new monstrosity. So believing, he invited its destructive force upon himself and his country.

General Van Fleet, drawing from his experiences in Greece and Korea and writing after a tour of free world defenses across no man's land from the Iron and Bamboo Curtains, in effect urged the revival of Dewey's system. "Indo-China is tottering," he declared, "in spite of the $400,000,000 in American aid.

I can tell Paris (and even Washington) that this war never will be won with French troops—or American. Had only half of our money been spent in building an Indo-Chinese army under native command, it would have brought the free world many tough native divisions as effective as our Koreans, which would be more than enough to clear the peninsula." His prediction came true in Geneva where the Communists virtually dictated the humiliating Indo-China settlement.

Concluding, Van Fleet advocated the extension by America all over the free world of the use of native soldiers. "Preparedness packages of about . . . ten-division size," he stated, "should also suffice to keep Communists out of Thailand, Malaya, Indonesia .   the Philippines . . Pakistan . .

Iran . . . Turkey. . . . We cannot furnish the world with American ground armies. If we try, it will drain us of manpower and throw us into bankruptcy without ever firing a shot, which is what the Soviets want."

What Van Fleet strongly advocates today as the most practical method of fighting Communist imperialism globally Dewey practiced successfully in the Philippines over half a century ago against European imperialism.

When the Spanish-American War exploded during a lull in our revolution against Spain, three avenues of action were wide open to us. We could have followed a policy of strict neutrality until the war had been over, then made friends with and wangled the best bargain we could from the victor. But this would have been too passive a way of shaping our future. We might, on the other hand, have pacted alliance with the Spaniards. Although they were our bitter enemies, we were then technically at peace with them and we were their subjects. Nearly 400 years of association had forged strong ties between the Filipino and Spanish peoples. Our official language was Spanish, our religion was the religion of Spain, and our culture in general was basically Spanish. It wouldn't have been too hard to discover convincing bases for a new Filipino-Spanish cooperation. And Spain might have rewarded our show of loyalty when she sorely needed it with liberal political reforms.

The third alternative open to us was alliance with America. The circumstances favored this course. We had grown extremely doubtful of Spanish goodwill and honor. It also happened that at the moment of decision on our part, I and some of my ranking officers were led by fate across the path of the American spearhead in the Orient. This and American alertness put me into early contact with Commodore Dewey who then brought me back to the Philippines. We therefore irrevocably threw our lot with America.

Dewey was a naval victor without land troops. He was in command of a squadron of four protected cruisers, including his flagship, the *Olympia*, two gunboats, and a revenue cutter, the *McCulloch*. Under him were 1,743 officers and men, all navy personnel. As a belligerent, he was denied the use of neutral ports. His Manila Bay victory would have been empty if the Spaniards could have completely denied him landing and perhaps mounted guns to keep him away at a respectful distance.

Back in the United States, troops were indeed being frantically readied for the Philippines. Even so, Dewey must have known that it would take some time to enlist, train, equip and ship them. As a matter of fact fully two months had passed after the battle of Manila Bay before the first trickle of American troops reached the Philippines. Free to make preparations on land during the intervening period, the Spaniards might have been able to offer such a strong resistance to subsequent American landings that there might have been bloody carnage on the beaches.

Invasion by water was then as for some time later, regarded as a suicidal military operation. Up to World War II, when air power made the reach of an invading force almost limitless, no less than Gen. Douglas MacArthur—and perhaps also Lt. Col. Dwight D. Eisenhower, then on his staff in Manila—stood foursquare behind the proposition that a land-based force was at least ten times stronger than a sea-borne invasion of equivalent proportions. On this conviction, which he fortified by citing such military epics of frustration as the British failure to land on the Dardanelles in World War I, General MacArthur built the Philippine national defense plan as military adviser to the Philippine Commonwealth.

While Dewey waited impatiently in Manila Bay for American troops and had only a precarious fingerhold on Philippine territory consisting of a restricted perimeter around the Cavite navy yard, we reassembled our armies and resumed our war against the Spaniards.

We had the upperhand from the very beginning due partly to the unenviable situation of the Spaniards. They had just lost their Asiatic fleet, the remnants and ruins of which littered the Bay for all to see. Afloat in its place was the victorious fleet of Dewey, now blockading the Bay. The walled city of Intramuros, the center of Spanish authority, was well within the range of its guns. Although a Spanish relief fleet had started on its way to the Orient, the Spaniards in the Philippines could not be certain of its arrival. They were cut off from home, the almost total losers in a great naval battle, blockaded by the United States Navy, and menaced within by a new Filipino revolution. Their morale had hurtled down to the low level of despondency.

On the other hand, our morale was the highest possible. Never before did we have such an abundance of arms, such universal support from our people and the active backing of a powerful nation. We purchased arms from abroad which the American blockading authorities either transported themselves or gladly permitted to enter. We received additional arms from the Americans. We could have all captured Spanish arms, whether by the Americans or ourselves. The people rallied perfervidly around us as they had never done before. In our previous revolutions, many of our wealthy and educated citizens had shown no sympathy for our cause, preferring to play safe by not antagonizing the Spaniards. Now, believing perhaps that the Spaniards could not escape defeat, they joined our ranks with apparent sincerity and patriotism. There was unity among ourselves the equal of which had never been witnessed before.

The main and common reason for both the morale collapse among the Spaniards and the morale upsurge in our ranks was of course the Americans. They were Spain's enemy but our allies. In the complete conviction that their mission in the Philippines was the same as in Cuba, we welcomed them as liberators and friends. And, certainly, their words and acts during their first months in the islands fully confirmed our belief and gave no indication of any contrary purpose.

Almost immediately we went into action. In two months, more or less, we had the Spaniards completely on the run. In another month we had captured about 10,000 of them, and those who had escaped had taken refuge behind the walls of Manila and in a few fortified outposts elsewhere. Most important of the outposts was Baler, the birthplace of President Quezon, then within a Spanish military reservation. The military force there was however so small that we gave it little importance.

Naturally, we accompanied our military success with political action.

Scarcely a month after the Battle of Manila Bay, we proclaimed the independence of the Philippines and unfurled the first Filipino flag, the result of Admiral Dewey's suggestion, at a formal ceremony in my hometown, then known as Cavite Viejo, now Kawit, Cavite. We followed this with the promulgation of a provisional Constitution which declared our purpose "to struggle for the liberation of the Philippines until all nations, including Spain, shall have expressly recognized it, and to prepare the country for the establishment of a Republic."

I next announced the establishment of a dictatorial government, accompanying my announcement with the following declaration: "As the great North American nation has evinced interest in our welfare and has extended her hand to help us obtain our liberty, I again assume control of our forces in their endeavor to attain the supreme object we all have in view, establishing a dictatorship and issuing decrees on my own responsibility, with the advice and approval of illustrious fellow-countrymen, until such time as all the Islands are under our sway, when a properly constituted popular assembly can be formed to elect a President with a Cabinet into whose hands I shall surrender the supreme authority."

By July 25, we had constituted our Cabinet and on September 15, we assembled the first Congress in the town of Malolos, Bulacan. The latter forthwith approved a Constitution in accordance with which we proclaimed the first Philippine Republic. I was then elected its first President.

The Republic we established was the first crystallization of democracy in all the East, just as Rizal's literary activities had been the vanguard of nationalism in all that part of the world then enslaved by European imperialism. Pioneers though we were, competent observers have since agreed that our efforts were comparable to those of the American Fathers.

Our Constitution embodied almost all of the basic democratic postulates. It made the categorical declaration, "Sovereignty resides exclusively in the people." It followed the trinitarian theory and the separation of powers. "The government of the Republic," it stated, "is popular, representative, alternative and responsible, and is exercised by three distinct powers which are denominated legislative, executive and judicial. Two or more of these powers shall never be vested in one individual alone."

The Constitution's Bill of Rights included all the basic rights of citizen. Under the title, "The Filipinos and Their Individual Rights," it listed in thirty-two articles such rights as due process of law, freedom of speech and press, freedom of domicile, property right, and all the usual rights a person accused of crime may invoke to insure himself a full opportunity to prove his innocence.

The members of the Congress were elected by popular vote and they, in turn, selected the President of the Republic by an absolute majority. We introduced a parliamentary feature by giving members of the cabinet the right to enter the session hall of the Congress and, upon their request, participate in debates over measures affecting their departments. We also provided for the impeachment of the President and other high officials by the Congress "for crimes committed against the security of the State."

All in all, the basic principles upon which we founded the Republic were democratic. It is nevertheless true that, due to the state of war soon forced upon us by the American forces, it was not possible to carry them out fully in their letter and spirit. Even in today's great democracies, however, a state of war invariably gives rise to departures from normal, peace-time democratic processes.

American Minister to Siam John Barrett, who became one of Dewey's advisers, writing at about that time for the American *Review of Reviews* commented on our activities as follows:

"After Aguinaldo's arrival at Cavite, he organized with wonderful rapidity a provisional government, and in short time had an army which was capturing Spanish outposts with the frequency of trained regulars. . . . Before Aguinaldo had been in Cavite a month, he not only had more soldiers than he could arm, but also contributions of large sums of money and unlimited amounts of rice and other raw food supplies brought in by the people for the support of the army. . . . He had over twenty regiments of comparatively well-dressed soldiers carrying modern rifles and ammunition. . . . The people in all the different towns took great pride in this army."

Discussing the political aspects of our activities, Barrett further said:

"By the middle of October, Aguinaldo had assembled a congress at Malolos of 100 men. . . . These men whose sessions I repeatedly attended, conducted themselves with great decorum and showed a knowledge of debate and parliamentary law. . . . The executive portion of the government was made up of a ministry of bright men who seemed to understand their respective positions."

A dispatch to the *Chicago Record,* signed by John T. McCutcheon, concluded as follows:

"Our respect for the insurgent prowess had grown a great deal, for by June 30 they had taken almost every province in Luzon with the exception of isolated garrisons and were hammering away at the doors of Manila."

When we organized the Republic, Spanish authority had completely disappeared in the Philippines. Almost all the sad remnants of Spanish officialdom and citizenry were already huddled tightly together within the Walled City surrounded by our forces on land and blockaded by Admiral Dewey's fleet in the Bay. We had cut off their water and food supplies. It was only a matter of time before they would surrender or starve. We had them completely at our mercy.

It may be asked why we did not move directly into Intramuros and thus complete our victory. There was a special reason. From the very moment we gained the upper hand over the Spaniards to a few weeks before the actual surrender of Manila, Admiral Dewey kept begging me not to take the city.

"American troops have already left San Francisco," he used to tell me. "They will be here in a matter of weeks. I beg you to wait for them and let them take part in the final battle. Let them share your final victory."

When the first troopships arrived, he rushed to me to explain that there were still others on the way and requested me to wait for them also.

"Our troops are coming gradually," he said. "They are being gathered in various parts of our country, then sent over many miles of railroad to San Francisco. There, they wait for ships sometimes for many weeks more."

Since I had given my word of honor to the Admiral to cooperate with him in every reasonable way, I acceded to his request. I assured him I would wait for all the American troops so that, shoulder to shoulder, we would march to Intramuros, rout the Spaniards and complete my country's liberation. Thus we would be brothers-in-arm to the final victory.*

Even as we were on the eve of final victory over the Spaniards, however, indications of trouble between the Americans and ourselves began to crop up. The first batch of American troops arrived on June 30 under the command of Brigadier General Thomas M. Anderson. At intervals thereafter other transports arrived with additional troops. By the time Major General Wesley Merritt, overall army commander, landed he had a command of about 6,000 men.

The accelerating troop build-up began to trouble me. Since the Spaniards had been virtually defeated by us and Manila itself was ready to surrender momentarily, I began to wonder whom the Americans expected to fight. Only the very remote possibility that Spain could somehow bring in reinforcements would they have any enemy with whom to do battle.

The first American troops landed on the area around the Cavite naval yard which constituted the precarious land toe-hold of Admiral Dewey. As additional troops came, they began

* This fact has been generally ignored. On the magnificent monument to Commodore Dewey's victory in Manila Bay rising majestically in the center of San Francisco's beautiful Union Square, this inscription appears: "On the night of April 30, 1898 Commodore Dewey's squadron entered Manila Bay and undaunted by the danger of submerged explosives reached Manila at dawn May 1, 1898, attacked and destroyed the Spanish fleet of ten warships, reduced the port and *held the city in subjection* until the arrival of troops from America." (Italics supplied)

to need a more extensive beachhead. But we held practically all the rest of the rim of Manila Bay. The Admiral therefore came to me and requested me to withdraw part of my forces to give way to the Americans. As we were still working together harmoniously, I readily acceded to his request. I ordered the beaches of Tambo, Baclaran, Paranaque and Pasay evacuated. Part of this area is today traversed by Dewey Boulevard, Manila's beautiful and broad bayfront driveway named in honor of the Hero of Manila Bay.

The troops affected by my withdrawal order were under the command of General Mariano Noriel. His headquarters was housed in Fort Antonio Abad located on the Pasay sector of the beach in one of our most forward positions. An interesting incident occurred during the turn-over which proved Noriel's military efficiency as well as his uncanny intuition.

When I gave him the order to withdraw and move his head-quarters somewhere in Makati, he was reluctant but he nevertheless obeyed. When however he saw the Americans replacing the Filipino flags with American flags along his erstwhile trenches, he turned to me almost in tears.

"Look, general," he urged me, pointing to the drama of the flags, "look what they are doing! If we don't look out, they will be replacing our flags with their own all over the country!"

I must have smiled at him tolerantly when I told him, "You are being tragic. They're our allies, always remember that!"

Naturally Noriel had also to turn over Fort Antonio Abad to the Americans. During the process, a sudden skirmish around the Fort attracted our attention. After Noriel and his men had withdrawn but before the Americans could take full possession of the Fort, the Spaniards suddenly moved in and ejected the Americans. In their disorderly retreat, the latter left two field pieces which the Spaniards also quickly siezed.

Upon realizing what was happening, Noriel unhesitatingly led back his troops to the Fort and recaptured it from the Spaniards together with the American guns. They then held the place until the Americans moved back in. Outside of the walls of Intramuros, the Fort was the only permanent military structure in the entire bay area. It would have meant much to the morale of the Spaniards to have retaken it permanently.

Noriel felt entitled to have the last word. "Our allies don't seem to realize they're at war," he said. "I only hope that if we ever have to fight them, they will be that slow and careless." I am sure he had many occasions later to change his opinion.

The seed of suspicion in our minds began to sprout and grow when the Americans agreed to the strange terms of the Spaniards for surrendering Manila. The latter demanded that we be excluded from the attack, the surrender and the city itself. We had invested the city for some time and we had desisted from attacking and capturing it only on the plea of Admiral Dewey not to take action until the American troops would arrive in order to share the credit and victory. We followed his wishes in the spirit of sincere comradeship. Now the Americans alone took the city, which we had softened to a pulp, after the briefest exchange of shots. And the Americans excluded us from its gates, threatening to fire upon us if we should disobey. In a telegram dated August 13, the day when Manlia fell, Anderson sent me this veritable ultimatum: "Do not let your troops enter Manila without permission of the American commander. On this side of Pasig River you will be under fire."

This was a heavy blow we found hard to bear. It stunned as well as puzzled us.

We had done all the land fighting. Admiral Dewey himself subsequently testified before the U.S. Congress to this effect. "I was waiting for troops to arrive and I thought that the closer the Filipinos invested the city the easier it would be when our troops arrived to march in," he declared. "The Filipinos were our friends, assisting us; they were doing our work . . . . saving our troops . . . . Up to the time the army came, Aguinaldo did everything I requested. He was most obedient; whatever I told him to do he did. I saw him almost daily."

How much we had saved the American troops was obvious to all. So completely devoid of fighting spirit had the Spaniards been reduced by us that, although the arriving Americans landed on the beaches along the Bay within the range of Spanish guns atop Manila's walls and the outer breastworks, they fired not a shot. The Americans found no Spaniards to fight except in the Walled City, and these had already been so starved and demoralized that they were no longer able to offer more than token resistance

In this tragic predicament to which we had reduced them, the Spaniards in fact soon thought of surrendering. General Basilio Augustin Davila, the Spanish commander, as early as July 24, sent a cable to Madrid reporting the untenable situation of his exhausted forces and the sufferings of the Spanish soldiers and civilians alike and suggesting surrender. For his suggestion, he was summarily dismissed, and in his place was appointed General Fermin Jaudenes. But the change of commander did not, of course, improve the Spanish situation; if at all, it made it worse.

Jaudenes himself presently explored the possibility of surrendering. Approaching the Americans through the Belgian consul, M. Andre, he proposed to give up on two conditions. First, to save Spanish honor, there should be some sort of a battle during which the Americans would demand surrender by international signal flashed from the mast of the *Olympia*. In reply, the Spaniards would raise the white flag. Second, that to insure the safety of the Spaniards, the Filipino forces would be kept out of Manila. These terms the Americans accepted. So, strictly following this script, the Spaniards surrendered Manila and the Americans took and occupied it.

In fact, however, the sham battle was doubly unnecessary. On that day, August 13 in Manila, August 12 in Washington, Spain and America signed in the latter place the cease-fire agreement which ended the hostilities. Article II of the protocol of agreement stated: "The United States will occupy and hold the city, bay and harbor of Manila pending the conclusion of a treaty of peace which shall determine the control, disposition and government of the Philippines." Admiral Dewey himself said later that if the cable had not been cut (at his own order), the news of the cease-fire would have been received in time to prevent the battle. The Americans could have then moved into the city led by a brass band.

But Spain's honor had to be saved, there had to be a battle. In the process, the Americans lost four men killed and three officers and 32 men wounded. Being the beneficiaries, the Spaniards paid a little more; they lost 49 killed and 300 wounded.

The obvious truth is that the Americans could have pushed the Spaniards into unconditional surrender. They had been ready to surrender for some time. We ourselves could have forced their surrender long before August 13. It was only the insistent plea of Admiral Dewey that kept us from delivering the *coup de grace*.

All in all, indeed, we had done virtually all the land fighting and paid all the price. In the battle of Manila Bay the American squadron lost only one man and it was from heart attack. In the course of investing the city along with our forces, they had suffered 30 men killed and seven officers and seven men wounded. In the sham battle for the surrender of Manila they lost four men in addition to 35 wounded. Against their losses were our own losses of thousands in killed and wounded. Our reward was our exclusion and snubbing in the hour of final triumph. It was an insult and a betrayal hard to take.

The Spaniards gave as their reason for insisting on our exclusion the fear that neither the Americans nor ourselves would be able to restrain our men from taking inhuman revenge such as looting their goods, killing their men, and abusing their women. But this was, of course, mere fear and fantasy. In our control as prisoners were about 10,000 Spaniards, including women, whom we were treating in accordance with the laws of war and humanity. In his dispatches to the Secretary of the Navy, Dewey himself repeatedly testified to this effect. One of his wires concluded: "Have advised (Aguinaldo) frequently to conduct war humanly which he has invariably done."

It was indeed the honorable American Consul General in Hongkong, Rounseville Wildman, who insistently but vainly counselled me to treat Spanish prisoners inhumanely. In a letter he wrote in reply to my inquiry as to what we could do with our Spanish prisoners, since we had a very hard time feeding so many of them, he sent this interesting advice:

> In case your prisoners can pay their steamship fare to Hongkong and H.E. the Admiral has no objection to their leaving, I see no objection to your relieving yourself of them on their oath not to take up arms again. If you find any of them break oath and you capture them with arms in their hands *give them the full penalty.*
>
> However, do not let any of your prominent prisoners leave or escape. Keep them as hostages. You may need them to redeem some of your Generals. *Never mind about feeding them three meals a day. Rice and water will be a good diet. They have been living too high for the last few years.*

I realize that sensational newspaper stories had started to create the impression among Americans that we were indeed savages who treated their war prisoners only a little short of boiling them for dinner like the proverbial African cannibals. And until now I know that this impression, confirmed time and time again by similar press stories during the subsequent Philippine-American War, still lingers in the minds of many Americans.

In war, the basest human passions being dominant, a certain amount of atrocity is inevitable. Even the Americans treated many of our men in a manner that in 1941-45 would have constituted war crimes. They gave them the water-cure and killed them after capture. They reconcentrated the population and killed the able-bodied men. I cannot deny that some of my men might have committed comparable offenses against the Spaniards and later against the Americans also. But the fact is that in general we meticulously followed civilized practices. Our Christianity, if not our inherent humanity, dictated this course. In addition we were eagerly and earnestly inviting the nations of the world to recognize our independence and sovereignty. We knew that one of the most important proofs of our worthiness to recognition would be our ability to uphold civilization even in so impossible a context as war.

We were the victims of the yellow journalism of the day. War atrocities are so much better reading than stories proving meticulous observance of the laws of war. If the atrocity is so insignificant that it is not worth the cable toll it can be magnified and embroidered upon to satisfy the editor. And it is my experience from having been many times at the wrong end that, once a slander or libel gains currency, no correction or denial can ever fully catch up with it.

Apparently falling for justification upon the propaganda which the American press had perpetrated, Admiral Dewey, when he wrote his autobiography in 1913 some 15 years after the fall of Manila, stated that the Spaniards had wished to surrender the city earlier but that he had refused to accept their proposition. "I had no force with which to occupy the city," he reasoned out, "and I would not for a moment turn it over to the undisciplined insurgents who I feared might wreak their vengeance upon the Spaniards in a carnival of loot."

I fear that this is merely hindthought to justify a *fait accompli* of which he was the principal author and which became one of the leading causes of the Philippine-American War. Indeed, in the light of the facts and of his previous contrary statements, there is no other way of justifying it.

I have never yet heard nor read any truly satisfactory explanation of the Spanish-American agreement to exclude us from the capitulation of Manila. I cannot myself explain it with authority. Yet even now, over half a century later, I still wonder if the Spaniards, in getting the Americans to agree—although the latter could have demanded and gotten unconditional surrender—did not deliberately plant a time bomb against the Americans. Knowing our fierce racial pride and our obsessive aspiration to be recognized as equals, the Spaniards could almost have foretold that the American agreement to shunt us would so cruelly wound our sensibilities that, if unappeased, we would fight even the Americans.

It is a pity that Admiral Dewey, having been the first American military leader to apply what General Van Fleet only recently urged upon America—the use of native soldiers to fight off aggressive imperialism—he and the army commanders completely discredited the system by lightly scorning the friendship, the pride, the honor and the patriotism of the natives which alone could make it successful.

CHAPTER VII

WE DID NOT WANT TO FIGHT THE U.S.

IF THE SPANIARDS did plant a time-bomb against the Americans by getting them deliberately to hurt our pride, they succeeded in their purpose by the merest chance. We did not want to fight another war. Neither apparently did President McKinley wish to wage a war against us. But the good will among the officers and men on both sides was drying so fast like grass in mid-summer that it took only a spark to start a prairie fire. And General Elwell S. Otis, rather than cooperate in stamping it out, allowed it to take its destructive course until it became a conflagration.

I must admit that we had thought of the possibility of our having to fight a war with America. I should be a military commander lacking in the most elementary qualities if I had not thought of the various possible shapes of event, including the most unlikely. For the situation, from the beginning, was fluid. The merest untoward incident could and did veer the course of history.

Even before I left Hongkong for Manila, our group of political refugees and exiles had discussed the possibility, then next to impossible in our calculations, of having to fight America after disposing of Spain. In one of our first interviews, as I have previously mentioned, I reported to Admiral Dewey the fear expressed by my countrymen that we might have to defend ourselves against the Americans after we had been exhausted by our war against the Spaniards. The Admiral allayed our fear by considering my frankness as an additional proof of friendliness on our part. After that interview I reported to my colleagues that we could forget all thoughts of having to fight the Americans. My calculation proved too sanguine.

In any event, we had no ready reason to fight the United

States. We had, on the contrary, overpowering motives why we wished to cultivate American friendship.

The attainment of our paramount objective demanded friendship with and not hostility to the United States. In its simplest form, we envisioned our country as an American protectorate until such time as we could safely become a free and independent republic. We made this clear from the time I had my first interviews with Pratt, Wildman and Dewey. Even after we had organized a Government of our own under a Constitution of our own making, our pronouncements were consistently for a nation temporarily under the sheltering wings of the United States. It would have been the most illogical conduct on our part to wish to attain this purpose by plotting war against America.

I must admit that there was some ambiguity and perhaps even inconsistency in our position. We bracketed together sovereignty with protection. We also clamored for the recognition of our Government by other nations of the world. This confusion was largely due to our unfamiliarity with the niceties of international affairs. But we indicated ourselves in all ways to be ready and eager to negotiate with America. Such a negotiation could have clarified and improved matters and avoided bloodshed.

Our position was nevertheless most reasonable and it has since been completely vindicated. After the Philippine-American War, Washington formulated and followed a policy which was generally identical with the program which we ourselves had offered. Having established sovereignty over the Philippines by treaty, purchase and conquest, the United States extended to us gradually-increasing self-government. This program logically resulted in the proclamation and restoration of the Philippine Republic in 1946. Had war been avoided—and it could have been prevented by a greater measure of goodwill on the part of American military authorities approximating our own—the period of American rule in the Philippines would have been far shorter and America's moral stature today would be far more massive.

Our greatest effort towards preventing the Philippine-American War was probably the sending to Washington and Paris of one of our ablest men at the time, Don Felipe Agoncillo, on a mission of peace. After we had somewhat recovered from the emotional crisis caused by our exclusion from the Walled City, we were inclined to interpret the incident as a mere indiscretion on the part of the American field commanders without sanction whatsoever from their Government. Almost immediately after the fall of Manila I instructed Agoncillo, then in Hongkong, to proceed to the United States to seek a basis of understanding with Washington. His mission as I defined it was to acquaint President McKinley with the history of our independence movement, prevent the return of our country to Spain, should this be contemplated, and inform the President of our desire to run our own affairs with American advice and military protection.

Our envoy sailed with General Francis V. Greene on a U.S. Army transport. This hospitable arrangement ingratiated the U. S. Army with us anew and gave promise of an open-minded and frank discussion of the future of the Philippines in the American capital. Having arrived there on September 28, Agoncillo immediately sought an audience with the President of the United States.

It is now possible to know the real facts of the Agoncillo mission, including the interesting behind-the-curtain interludes. This is due mainly to a fine if altogether brief study of the documents of early Philippine-American history, including some of the approximately 400,000 different papers captured from us by the American Army, made recently by Professor Honesto A. Villanueva of the Department of History of the University of the Philippines. These source materials are unfortunately still in the possession of the Government in Washington, the Library of Congress and other American libraries.

The interesting records of Agoncillo's memorials to and interview with President McKinley are found in memoranda written for the Secretary of State by Alvey Augustus Adee, Second Assistant Secretary of State for 36 years and often referred to by historians as "the anchor of the State Department." It was also he who interpreted Agoncillo's Spanish into English and McKinley's English into Spanish.

McKinley received Agoncillo in the White House on October 1. Through Adee, the President asked the envoy for the purpose of his visit. The latter replied that he desired, on behalf of the Filipino people and myself, to present to the American President and, through him, to the American people, the facts of the political situation in the Philippines, together with their historical background, so that they might be given due consideration in the final determination of the terms of peace between the United States and Spain.

Given permission by the President to convey his message, Agoncillo proceeded to recite the long history of Spanish oppression and the consequent revolution of 1896. He explained the events leading to the Treaty of Biaknabato, its terms and the perfidy of the Spaniards which justified the Filipinos in resuming the revolution. He concluded by reporting to the President my various interviews with Admiral Dewey and Consuls Pratt and Wildman.

"At the outbreak of hostilities between the United States and Spain," he declared, "General Aguinaldo was invited by Admiral Dewey to proceed to the Philippines and renew the revolution. Aguinaldo returned and faithfully fulfilled his part of the agreement, operating with his forces against the Spaniards and referring all matters to the superior judgment of Admiral Dewey, his sole desire being to cooperate with him in establishing the independence of the Filipinos."

The President then inquired if he had further matters to communicate to him. At this point in our struggle for liberty, we still did not suspect any American intention to occupy our country more or less permanently. In the mind of Agoncillo, therefore, the fear was paramount that the United States might give back the Philippines to Spain. This fear was bred by the lack of a written and official American commitment similiar to the Teller Amendment in the case of Cuba, and our belief that even without such commitment the United States would not embark upon a career of imperialism. For if it were to do so, especially beyond the Western Hemisphere, it would violate its own basic political principles.

Agoncillo, therefore, informed President McKinley that the Filipinos would like to be represented in the Paris Commission which was negotiating the Treaty of Peace. When he sensed that this request was impossible of fulfillment, he broached the lesser alternative of wishing to be heard at least by the U.S. Commissioners. President McKinley suggested that, in view of the difficulty of language and of the necessity of precise knowledge as to the desires of Agoncillo, perhaps it would be better if the Filipino envoy were to write down his proposed statement before the Paris Commission. Agoncillo readily accepted the President's suggestion and on this indecisive note the interview ended.

On October 4 the envoy submitted for the President a statement of the Filipino position with respect to the Treaty. It contained ten principal points. Starting with a recital of the part of the Filipino forces in destroying Spanish power and sovereignty in the Philippines, all in accordance with previous agreements of cooperation with Admiral Dewey, the statement asserted that the only existing legitimate government in the Philippines was that organized by the Filipinos and that the Filipinos should, therefore, have a decisive voice in the disposition of their country in the forthcoming Treaty of Paris.

Gaining the impression that President McKinley was sympathetic to the Filipino position, Agoncillo went to Paris. There, unfortunately, he was refused a hearing by the Peace Commissioners. As a last resort, under date of December 12, 1898, he issued a formal protest, which he sent to the press and the foreign legations in Paris, against "any resolutions agreed upon at the peace conference in Paris as long as the judicial, political, and independent personality of the Filipino people is entirely unrecognized." The Treaty having been drafted without any heed to either the situation in the Philippines or the importunities of Agoncillo, the disappointed Filipino diplomat decided to return to Washington and work against its ratification in the American Senate, arriving there on December 24.

By this time Agoncillo and the Filipinos knew all too well the terms of the Treaty. With respect to the Philippines, it provided for the cession of the entire archipelago by Spain to the United States. To lighten the blow to the Spaniards and as a concession to the Spanish Peace Commissioners who feared that outright cession without any consideration whatsoever might force their Government to repudiate them and their work, the United States agreed to pay Spain the amount of $20,000,000. In the text of the Treaty the final decision of the United States to occupy our country, replacing Spain as the sovereign power, was finally revealed in its nakedness.

This American decision hit us with the devastating effect of an atomic blast. It was at once disillusioning, disappointing and tragic. Yet we went on working for a peaceful understanding between the Philippines and America. Agoncillo himself continued to counsel us to exhaust all the means of diplomacy before resorting to arms. In turn we urged him to exert his utmost efforts to prevent the ratification of the Treaty and to get America to negotiate with us around a table for the purpose of establishing American protection over our Government and country.

But the fight in the Senate over the Treaty became a political war with the Democratic leader, William Jennings Bryan, following a strategy that was at once nearsighted, selfish, and unstatesmanlike.

Up to almost the time of actual voting on the Treaty, the administration lacked the two-thirds vote required to ratify it. Largely aroused by the activities of the Anti-Imperialist League, which included such puissant figures as former President Benjamin Harrison and Carl Schurz, American public opinion began to crystallize against the idea that the United States was embarking on a career of imperialism. The popular opposition, while not necessarily against the ratification of the Treaty, supported the demand for some assurances that America would not colonize the Philippines but that, like the Cubans, the Filipinos would be left alone after they had established a more or less stable government of their own.

But Senator Lodge of the Republican side and Mr. Bryan, the defeated Democratic candidate for President in 1896, turned the tide in favor of the Treaty. The first disposed cleverly with the arguments of fellow senators against the Treaty, and the second, frantically working behind the scene, convinced additional senators to insure the necessary two-thirds vote by arguing that ratification would give the Democratic Party, with him as candidate, of course, a winning issue in the 1900 presidential election.

Against all the attempts in the Senate to get the American Government to declare that the Philippines would never be colonized or annexed to the United States as a condition for ratifying the Treaty, Senator Lodge argued that ratification alone did not in the least imply a policy of colonization or annexation. Any previous declaration of policy, he maintained, was therefore an expression of distrust in the sense of justice and honor of the United States.

"I believe," he said, "we can be trusted as a people to deal honestly and justly with the Islands and their inhabitants thus given to our care . . . To the American people and their Government, I am ready to intrust my life, my liberty, my honor and, what is far dearer to me than anything personal to myself, the life and liberty of my children and my children's children. If I am ready thus to entrust my children to the government which the American public create and sustain, am I to shrink from intrusting to the same people the fate and fortune of the Philippine Islands?"

The Lodge argument was more emotional than logical. But it placed many Senators on the defensive; the thought that a vote against the Treaty was a vote of non-confidence in the American Government mesmerized them. Once this proposition was accepted, it became tantamount to treason to oppose the Treaty.

Mr. Bryan, instead of upholding the honor and prestige of America, was concerned only with the fate of his Democratic Party in 1900. He was certain that if the Treaty were ratified, we Filipinos would go to war against America. He therefore wanted the Treaty ratified so that America would be involved in another war which he could blame on the Republican administration. "Paying 20 millions for a revolution," he told the Democratic senators, "would be enough to defeat any party." It was however his party that subsequently suffered defeat—on the issue of free silver.

The Philippine-American War started on February 4, 1899. The vote on the Treaty was taken the following Monday, February 6. Yet in spite of Senator Lodge, Mr. Bryan and the war which he had predicted, the Treaty was approved with only one vote to spare. It seems possible that had the American people and Government known more widely our exact position in the Philippines, the Treaty would have been defeated. The defeat of the Treaty might have subsequently led to a sort of peaceful negotiations with us, resulting in more or less complete understanding.

On January 30 Agoncillo submitted to the Senate of the United States, through its secretary, his last Memorial. The gist of this document is that, notwithstanding Admiral Dewey's Manila Bay victory, it had been the Filipinos under my leadership who had finally defeated the Spaniards and destroyed Spanish sovereignty over the islands. It added that we had established a Republican Government which in effect had replaced the Spanish Government, that our Government had the support of our people, had restored peace and order and was in control of the country. It concluded that, with or without the consideration of $20,000,000 Spain was neither legally nor physically able to deliver possession of the Philippines to the United States. In its confused mood, thanks largely to the efforts of Senator Lodge, the Senate ignored the Memorial.

This was Agoncillo's last act in America. On February 4 he went to Canada to file a message to us. His departure happened to coincide with the outbreak of hostilities in Manila, giving rise to the suspicion in some quarters that we had given him the signal to flee. The truth is that we had instructed him to send his confidental and urgent messages in code, and he had been prohibited to do so in the United States. He had simply gone to Montreal to comply with his instructions. Because on the following day, Sunday, the hostilities in Manila had become known in America, he did not return to Washington but proceeded to Paris.

The course of history might have been different if Washington had dealt with Agoncillo less gingerly and warily. If he had been given a fair hearing, the Senate might have passed at least one of the many resolutions offered in which it was attempted to declare that it was not America's policy to colonize or annex the Philippines. Not only was there heroic efforts in the Senate to bind America to such a concrete policy but important leaders like General Joseph (Fighting Joe) Wheeler, Andrew Carnegie and others also earnestly urged President McKinley to appease the Filipinos by giving them just one assurance that they would sooner or later be free and independent. This in the belief, which was completely justified, that it was all we needed to renew our shaken confidence in the American Government and people.

The President not only was deaf to such entreaties but, having resolved in his mind to take over the Philippines and to have full freedom to decide its fate in due time, he also treated the mission of Agoncillo more as a nuisance than an assistance to a wise decision. There is evidence, however, that McKinley had earlier shown some interest in our proposition that the Philippines become a protectorate of the United States. For among the documents in Washington is a memorandum signed by David J. Hill, Assistant Secretary of State, on the subject "Protectorate." He had evidently been assigned by higher authorities to make a study of the advisability of extending a protectorate status to the Philippines. Meanwhile, however, the Administration set its course in the direction of occupation. Mr. Hill also virtually vetoed the idea himself with his conclusion that "where no responsible or effective government is in operation with which it (the protecting power) may form relations, protectorate is impossible." There is no evidence that President McKinley gave the matter a second thought.

When Agoncillo first went to Paris in the hope of being heard by the American Commissioners, McKinley instructed the Acting Secretary of State, Mr. John Hay, to notify Secretary of State

W. R. Day, the head of the U.S. delegation, that "the President does not propose to commend them (Agoncillo and his secretary, Sixto Lopez) to you." This was, of course, tantamount to a directive not to bother with the Filipinos.

McKinley himself received Agoncillo in the White House with complete reservations. Before opening the interview, he instructed Adee to explain clearly and repeatedly to Agoncillo that the President was receiving him unofficially and informally and that, in doing so, did not recognize either his position as an official envoy of the government or association which had sent him. Adee himself preluded each contact with Agoncillo with similar reservations and explanations.

At a time when the American nation was once more confronted by an urgent situation and not an abstract theory, American officials were being sanctimoniously technical rather than eminently practical. Under international law, the act of the chief executive of a nation or his representatives of officially receiving a foreign diplomatic envoy implies recognition of the envoy's government. Unreasoning fear of this implication straitjacketed Washington officials and prevented them from rendering justice to my people and serving America with honor and patriotism.

And yet when the crisis in the Philippines was fast coming to a head, President McKinley attempted to make use of Agoncillo in a manner which seems to me unwarranted.

On January 7, as I have already mentioned, a message had been received in the Department of the Navy from Admiral Dewey in Manila in which he had reported with evident concern the dangerous deterioration of Philippine-American relations and had suggested that a group of civilian diplomats be rushed to the islands to try and patch up matters. On January 10, three days later, the White House and the Department of State, now thoroughly alarmed, tried to utilize Agoncillo for their own purposes.

Working through General Greene, who had befriended the envoy while they were traveling together from Hongkong to Washington, the highest officials of the American Government tried to induce Agoncillo to send me a cable, solely however as his own message, warning and advising me against violence as such a course would work against our own cause. The final draft of the cable which President McKinley, rejecting one prepared in the Department of State, had himself apparently drawn up, and which Greene, obeying higher orders, presented to Agoncillo as his own and without revealing to Agoncillo the part, anxiety and interest in it of the President and other high officials, read as follows:

> Nothing would be so unfortunate for the Filipinos as a conflict with the United States. Hasty or inconsiderate action now would only delay the realization of our hope for generations. You should know that nothing can be done for us until the sovereignty of the United States is recognized. I am firmly convinced that the United States has no motive but our good and want to be our friends and not our enemies.

Naturally, Agoncillo refused to send me the cable. Purely as his own, in accordance with the secret desire of McKinley, and in the false knowledge that the only American official interested was Greene and only in an unofficial and personal capacity, Agoncillo believed that such a message would be tantamount to a betrayal of the mission we had entrusted to him and therefore regarded by us a treasonous act. With tears streaming down his face, he told Greene that he would do anything in his power to prevent bloodshed in the Philippines. But he pointed out that he was powerless to prevent it unless the United States would grant "absolute independence to the Filipinos under American protection."

Here I must disagree with Professor Villanueva who believes that "if Agoncillo had sent this telegram to Aguinaldo, it is probable that Filipino-American relations would have taken another course. . . . The outbreak of February 4, 1899, leading to destruction of life and property would have been avoided." It should have been McKinley or the War Department that ordered their commanders in Manila to avoid a fight. On our part, even without the proposed Agoncillo cable, we were resolved to avoid war. All the pertinent documents show plainly that we were

neither willing nor prepared to fight; that the war was started by
the Americans; that, once it had started, we tried to stop it; and
that the American commanders turned us down with arrogance.

But let General Otis, in his official report as land commander
in Manila, describe the actual outbreak:

> An insurgent approaching the picket of a Nebraska regiment
> refused to halt or answer when challenged. The result was that our
> picket discharged his piece, killing the Filipino, when the insur-
> gent troops near Santa Mesa (hearing the firing) opened fire on
> our troops there stationed . . . During the night it was confined
> to an exchange of fire between opposing lines for a distance of
> two miles. . . . *It is not believed that the chief insurgents wished
> to open hostilities at that time . (The fighting) was one strictly
> defensive on the part of the insurgents and one of vigorous attack
> by our forces.*

As Otis truly reported, we were not ready for a new war. The
historian, Charles B. Elliot, a strong McKinley supporter, also
recorded that we were "unprepared for attack or defense." "The
unexpected battle," he wrote years later, "came when they were
off guard, most of the higher officers being absent in Malolos."
That we were only defending ourselves, and weakly, was the
unadulterated truth. During the initial American advance of
February 5, we lost 3,000 in killed and wounded while the
American casualty was negligible.

I can't here resist the temptation to reproduce the graphic
version of the American private, W. W. Grayson, who had fired
the first shot, of how the shooting started:

> I yelled "Halt!"   . The man moved. I challenged him with
> another "Halt." Then he immediately shouted, "Halto" to me.
> Well, I thought the best thing to do was to shoot him. He dropped.
> Then two Filipinos sprang out of the gateway about fifteen feet
> from us. I called "Halt" and Miller fired and dropped one. I saw
> that another was left. Well, I think I got my second Filipino that
> time. We retreated to where our six other fellows were and I said,
> "Line up, fellows, the niggers are in here all through these yards."
> We then retreated to the pipe line and got behind the water work-

main and stayed there all night. It was some minutes after our second shots before Filipinos began firing.

The morning after the night shooting, I sent a ranking member of my staff under a flag of truce to General Otis to convey the message that the firing on our side the night before had been against my orders and that I wished to stop further hostilities. To prevent future outbreaks, I also proposed the establishment of a neutral zone between the American and Filipino forces, wide enough so that accidental contact would be impossible. To my proposals, Otis replied roughly, "The fighting, having begun, must go on to the grim end!"

This attitude was soon adopted by President McKinley himself. Justifiably fearing, however, that the American people would not accept so tough and rough an explanation as that of General Otis, he embellished it with some untruths. "The first blow was struck by the inhabitants," the President repeatedly claimed in public speeches soon after the outbreak of hostilities. "They assailed our sovereignty, and there will be no useless parley, no pause, until the insurrection is suppressed and American authority acknowledged and established."

Armegeddon was loose—against our desires and in spite of our earnest and sincere efforts to befriend America.

CHAPTER VIII

THE ONLY HONORABLE COURSE

IT WAS TRULY the Spanish time-bomb that exploded in the night of February 4, 1899.

The Spanish Government and what remained of the Spanish military and citizenry had taken refuge behind the walls of Intramuros, a massive fort completely enclosing the heart of Manila. To support their guns atop the walls, they had mounted additional batteries in blockhouses which they had constructed along a perimeter some three to five kilometers outside the walls. To invest this remaining Spanish island, we dug trenches and constructed breastworks around it, north, east and south, just beyond the range of the Spanish guns. Dewey blockaded the harbor.

Except Intramuros, two or three outlying unimportant forts, including those of Baler and Zamboanga, the towns of Iloilo and Bacolod, and the Moro areas of Mindanao, our forces controlled the whole country. They also besieged Baler and Zamboanga forts. But the Spaniards held Iloilo while a group of misguided counter-revolutionists seized Bacolod. The U.S. Navy held the Port of Cavite and its arsenal.

Our almost complete control of the country was recognized by the American authorities, including Admiral Dewey and General Anderson, as well as by the foreign consulates in Manila. American authorities invariably requested us for passes whenever they sent any of their men beyond Manila to the provinces. Whenever other foreign nationals wished to travel for legitimate reasons, they likewise sought our permission through the intercession of their respective consular or diplomatic officials. Our ships, the *Filipinas, Bulusan* and several others, which constituted our transport system linking our forces deployed in the various islands, flew our flag. Upon sailing in and out of Manila

Bay, they received and returned the salute of the units of the American squadron which happened to be nearby.

When the American troops began to arrive, they naturally disembarked at the Port of Cavite where Dewey could protect them. Then, section by section, Dewey and later their own commanders requested us to yield our southern sectors along the Bay. As more troops arrived, they began to land nearer Manila, expanding their beachhead even to areas within the range of the Spanish guns which, however, remained silent. As we yielded segments of our lines, our displaced forces pulled back southward and eastward to form a new line.

When Manila fell, the Americans also replaced the Spaniards in their defense positions in the line of blockhouses and behind and atop the city walls. Our main forces remained in their prepared positions, except where we further yielded territory to the Americans on their demand that the terms of the Spanish-American protocol of August 12, as to the control of the harbor and the City of Manila, should be carried out to the letter. After all these shifts in position, our line finally ran from the Paranaque beach almost joining the American line in the south, through Makati, Pandacan, Sampaloc and San Francisco del Monte in the east and up to the Caloocan beach in the north. Within this semi-circle were almost enclosed both Manila and the American land forces. It was now the Americans instead of the Spaniards who in effect faced us across no man's land. This set-up was made-to-order for the incident of the night of February 4 which started the three and a half years of Philippine-American war.

It is tempting to speculate what might have happened if the Filipino and American forces had cooperated in the taking and occupation of Manila. With the common enemy finally liquidated, perhaps the trenches and earthworks would have been abandoned and obliterated. The comradeship in arms would have fortified Philippine-American friendship. Peaceful negotiations with us might have followed as a matter of course, and an agreeable common *modus vivendi* might have been easily found. But this was not to be.

To us the war with America was no less than a great tragedy.

From my first contact with the Americans in Hongkong and Singapore, I had envisioned my Motherland, long chained in slavery by benighted European imperialism, at last free and happy. To that dream we had dedicated every ounce of our efforts and our energies. We had at long last defeated the Spaniards on our own soil. This victory had been made possible to a great extent by the arms, the advice, and the buoying promises of independence given to us by Admiral Dewey and other American officials. Now the Americans were our enemies in war. Dashed were all our hopes of an independent nation under American protection.

We had no great expectations of being able to drive away the Americans from our shores by force. Our two wars with the Spaniards had cost us a great deal of life and money. Many of our most valuable and capable men had paid the supreme sacrifice on the battlefield. Our residual army was, for the most part, a motley crowd of crude recruits and volunteers. Much of the arms which we had been able to accumulate had become unserviceable, and our ammunition was almost exhausted. Without war industries, we depended on purchases abroad and captured enemy guns. With the American Navy blockading our country, the trickle of foreign arms, which it had gladly permitted to reach us while we had been fighting the Spaniards, would completely stop. The 40,000 stands of rifle and the considerable store of ammunition which we had at the height of our power had been dangerously depleted. We had used them up in the service of America. We had no artillery. And the Filipinos were weary.

On the other hand, the United States forces were fast swelling in size and strength. A powerful unit of the American navy was on hand. The U.S. troops were well-trained and modernly equipped. The replacement and build-up of men and material were continuous. At the outbreak of the war the American armed forces in the Philippines numbered about 20,000 men with at least 14,000 effectives. Washington now called for more volunteers while it readied regulars to reinforce further this already powerful contingent.

The army and navy had in effect already flung across the

Pacific a bridge of transports and warships over which an end-less flow of men and equipment now came from San Francisco to the Islands. Before long, the Eighth Army Corps under the over-all command of General Otis was assembled and ready for action. It was of course equipped with all the modern arms known, including powerful artillery and the Gatling gun, the first version of the machine gun.

There are those who claim that the American commanders, following secret orders from Washington, deliberately started the war to insure the ratification of the Treaty which ran against a hurricane of opposition in the Senate. Our efforts to maintain peace and our obvious unreadiness for war on the one hand, and the trigger-happy readiness and expanding strength of the American forces, on the other hand—together with the fear that the Treaty might be shipwrecked—would seem to give credence to his theory.

Personally I feel that starting the war—and fueling it to a holocaust once begun—was entirely the idea of the Americans in Manila. However, just as Dewey and the other American commanders and officials in the Philippines adjusted their views and actions to the gradually shaping annexationist policy of the Commander-in-Chief, so it may be said that Washington adapted itself to the situation created in Manila by the Americans. So eventually perfect was this hand-in-glove relationship that the American people never learned the undeniable facts that the American forces had started the firing and that within 24 hours I had taken steps, if vainly, to effect a cease-fire. On the contrary Washington officially accused us of having started the shooting and of having sworn to fight to the bitter end. Undoubtedly the flame of American anger fanned by our supposed action of challenging American arms and sovereignty helped to cook the goose for us as far as the Treaty was concerned. It was ratified.

But we had to fight back. We had to defend our people, our home, our Motherland. We were at bay. We had no honorable course but to resist and sell our lives dearly.

The seat of our Republic being Malolos, Bulacan, 25 miles north of Manila, our natural defensive strategy was for our main

A portion of the 22nd U.S. Infantry waiting for orders to advance during a battle near Pasig, Rizal, a few miles outside of Manila.

American firing across the rice fields at the Filipinos concealed in the

Gen. Charles King and staff at Manila.

forces to fall back northward to protect it. There we had our official personnel, including our highest dignitaries. We were resolved to prevent their capture so as to insure the continuity of the Government. In the event of defeat, we also should have them as symbol of unity and resistance.

But even before any shots were exchanged between Americans and Filipinos, our Government had suffered defections which left us shaken by its unexpected and bitter impact. Many of the rich and educated countrymen who joined us only when the defeat of Spain was certain and our alliance with the Americans unquestioned, now crossed the line and went over to the Americans.

But not wishing to cast any reflections of my own making on these ex-colleagues of mine, I shall limit my reference to their misconduct by simply quoting the following paragraph from the book on the Philippines of former Governor-General Forbes:

As President of the revolutionary republic, General Aguinaldo named as cabinet officers and councilors many of the ablest Filipinos of the day. The brilliant and irreconcilable Apolinario Mabini exercised a predominant influence in determining the policy pursued by his chief leading up to and following the rupture of friendly relations with the Americans. Dr. Trinidad H. Pardo de Tavera, later member of the Taft Commission, and Don Cayetano Arellano, who became Chief Justice of the Philippine Supreme Court, were named by General Aguinaldo in the department of foreign affairs in his first cabinet. Don Gregorio Araneta, who was Secretary of Justice in the Malolos cabinet was later appointed by General Otis Associate Justice of the Supreme Court. Afterward he became Attorney-General and finally in 1908 Commissioner and Secretary of Finance and Justice. Don Benito Legarda, an able official of General Aguinaldo's department of revenue, later became a member of the Taft Commission, from which he was elected one of the first two Resident Commissioners from the Philippine Islands at Washington. *All of these, with the exception of Mabini, withdrew from the Malolos government prior to the outbreak of hostilities with the United States. They represented the conservative, well-educated class, and following them many others in minor posts also withdrew from the Malolos government and*

ey saw *o* *e* *o insurgent organiza*
armed resistance to American sovereignty. (Italics supplied.)

It should be noted that these defections had occurred before the outbreak of hostilities on February 4, and, of course, before the ratification of the Treaty on February 6. America, therefore, had not yet acquired sovereignty over the Philippines, whether by virtue of treaty, purchase, or conquest. On the other hand, we had almost complete control of the Archipelago.

We contended then, and I feel that we were in the right, that Spain could not convey sovereignty over the Philippines to the United States because we had superseded the Spanish government with our own. Our act of resistance against American attack was not, therefore, a defiance of American sovereignty. We were in our own country upholding to the death the sound and sacred Jeffersonian principle that government should be with the consent of the governed.

But the period of discussion was over. Logic palled before the brutal facts of war. Self-defense was our only choice.

The Americans had a well-coordinated plan of aggression and they now put it into immediate execution. They launched a three-pronged attack. The columns were led respectively by Generals Lloyd Wheaton, Henry W. Lawton, and Arthur MacArthur. Wheaton's column pushed eastward along the Pasig River as far as the Laguna Lake, cutting our forces in the middle of our semi-circle around Manila. General Lawton moved north-north-east along the eastern rim of the Central Luzon Valley. General MacArthur's column followed the railroad track northward on the western side of the valley near the China Sea coast. The original American beachhead begged from us was expanding like an explosion.

After having broken our lines and pushed us northward and southward to a safe distance from Manila, Otis ordered the campaign slowed down while he waited for further reinforcements. This gave General Antonio Luna, our Director of Operations, time to prepare some defensive positions along the Rio Grande. When shortly the Americans resumed their advance, the greatest battle of the war took place there, although it resulted in our defeat.

With American reinforcement now arriving in torrents, the war became intense and relentless. MacArthur, commanding several divisions, resumed his northward push while Lawton and Wheaton, with reinforced columns, doubled back to mop up in the provinces of Bulacan, Pampanga, Rizal and Cavite. The fearless Lawton was killed in the battle of San Mateo, Rizal, December 18, 1899, after having previously made a brilliant thrust into Cavite, culminating in the battle of Zapote in which our southern forces, always inferior in equipment and training, suffered tremendous losses. By now, the American land forces had mounted to over 100,000 well-trained and well-equipped men.

Meanwhile, as we yielded ground, we moved our Government farther north behind our crumbling lines. As Malolos fell on March 1, 1899, we transferred our Government to San Isidro, Nueva Ecija. When San Isidro became an untenable government seat in June, we shifted to Cabanatuan in the same province. Soon we moved again to Tarlac, Tarlac and here we were able to hold our own ground until November 12, 1899. When we evacuated Tarlac, we inaugurated guerrilla warfare, and I moved my headquarters to the mountains of Northern Luzon.

While our Government was still located at Malolos, an American Peace Commission, headed by President Jacob Gould Schurman of Cornell University, arrived. It was sent by Washington upon the frantic urging of Admiral Dewey. Alarmed by the worsening Philippine-American tension, the Admiral had cabled to the Secretary of the Navy, earnestly asking for a civilian commission "to adjust differences." President McKinley acted on the suggestion expeditiously and within a few days created the Commission and appointed its members.

But travel being what it was then, the Commission did not reach Manila until March 4, a full month after the outbreak of hostilities. Yet, since its primary mission was to pacify the Filipinos, it immediately addressed itself to this task. "To win the Philippine Republic over to the cause of peace with the recognition of American sovereignty," Dr. Schurman later said, "was the supreme object of all our endeavors."

Almost immediately, the Commission made overtures to us. But in addition to arriving in the middle of a shooting war, its peace effort was accompanied by a marked intensification of the American armed drive. This was perhaps the idea of Dewey and Otis whom McKinley also named to the Commission. Thus, while our Government was still in Malolos when the Commission arrived in March, we had already retreated to San Isidro, Nueva Ecija in May when the Schurman conciliation efforts reached their critical stage. Had the American forces agreed to a truce and given the Schurman Commission the fullest opportunity to negotiate with us in peace, it might have accomplished its mission successfully. But the bitterness engendered by the war inevitably soured the sweetness and reasonableness which the Commission tried to generate. The Americans were determined to negotiate from strength.

The theoretical issue between the Commission and ourselves was sovereignty. It wanted us to recognize American sovereignty before negotiating a settlement. By way of tempting us, it made public an offer of autonomy in which the government, under an American Governor-General, would include qualified Filipinos in the highest levels of the legislative and judicial departments. We tried sincerely to meet the Commission more than halfway. In May, our Congress voted for the cessation of war and the acceptance of peace on the basis of the Commission's offer of autonomy. Although I disagreed, I accepted the decision of the Congress. We forthwith reorganized our cabinet so as to give preponderance to those in favor of peace, like Paterno and Buencamino. I was then empowered to create a Commission with authority to proceed to Manila and negotiate with the Schurman Commission on the terms of peace and the extent of Filipino self-government.

But there were two high officials in our Government who were inflexible in their determination to continue the war against the Americans and were, therefore, not in conformity with our move for peace. They were Apolinario Mabini, the Premier in our

Cabinet before its reorganization, and General Antonio Luna, the Undersecretary of War and over-all field commander of our forces. Mabini was a paralytic but a man of great intelligence and stubbornness. Luna was a fiery and fanatical commander who, in the words of Forbes, seemed to have soaked in some of the fierce spirit of the French Revolution during his long stay in Paris. These two vehemently and implacably refused peace. But while Mabini, the intellectual, willingly resigned from the premiership to give way to Paterno, Luna, the man of action, decided to take matters in his own hands.

In one of the first meetings of the cabinet following its reorganization and transfer to Cabanatuan, Nueva Ecija, Luna gave a sickening demonstration of his terrible temper. The scene was the convent of the town, my temporary residence, and the day, May 25. Luna started to hurl insults at our colleagues, berating their willingness to negotiate peace with the Schurman Commission. A heated argument followed. In a moment, the debate descended to personalities. Luna upbraided Buencamino for the supposed cowardice of his son in the recent battle in San Fernando, Pampanga. Embarrassed, Buencamino also accused Luna of having lost the battle of Bagbag because of his fiery temper.

In that battle, Luna had withdrawn two battalions from the front line to the rear area to discipline a subordinate general. The subordinate had apparently committed no offense worse than to be interested in the same wench on whom Luna also had his eyes. Luna's action had left a breach in our line through which MacArthur's forces had immediately poured in, forcing a general retreat on our part. The break-through had contributed to the fall of Malolos. It was truly a black blot on Luna's record, and its mention so infuriated him that he violently slapped Buencamino, knocking him down. He was about to attack the others as well when I stopped him.

Not satisfied with this undignified tantrum, Luna, several days later and without my knowledge, ordered a unit of his troops to arrest most of the members of the Cabinet on the charge of treason. Later he recommended that I punish them with exile.

Although I found the entire proceeding disturbing and distasteful, I told Luna that I would order an investigation of his charges. After he had left for the front, I released his prisoners.

One may wonder why, against the advice of Mabini and the Cabinet, I took in Luna and named him Undersecretary of War and gave him the rank of brigadier general. One may even ask why we put up with him at all. The main reason was that we were short of capable military leaders. None of our general officers had had any formal military training. Practically all of them had recruited their own soldiers from among their tenants and neighbors and the latter often obeyed no one else. While most of our officers were men of intelligence and courage, they were generally incapable of large commands.

Neither indeed did Luna go to a military school, for he was a pharmacist by training, but outside of his undeniable personal valor, he was an avid student of military theory and history. Not only was he our ablest commander but he had the foresight and ability to open and operate a military school in which to train most of our officers. We needed him to keep our forces as a coordinated unit. And we needed even his terrible temper to impose discipline on our unschooled army.

A tragic sequel to the slapping incident swiftly followed. On June 4 Luna sent word that he was coming to Cabanatuan to call on me. He fixed no date and specified no purpose, but I presumed that the latter would have relation to the recent developments in the Cabinet. As it happened, his call coincided with the day I went out to inspect our troops in the field, having received reports of demoralization. It also happened that the captain of the presidential guards, Pedro Janolino, and his brother, Sergeant Joaquin Janolino, who were at my headquarters at the time together with other guards, had also had a previous personal clash with Luna.

Captain Janolino had been in command of a company in Calumpit some months earlier. There, he had supposedly disobeyed Luna, allegedly saying that he took orders only from me. Luna had the entire company disarmed and accused Janolino of insubordination and cowardice. I learned of this incident later in connection with the subsequent investigation of Luna's violent death.

No one knew exactly the details of what happened within the convent when Luna went up there to inquire for me. But shortly after he had entered the place, gun reports were heard. Luna himself soon staggered out of the building and reeled to the center of the Plaza, bleeding from bullet and knife wounds. In another moment he was felled by a volley of shots from various members of the presidential guard.

Upon receiving report of the tragedy, I ordered my Secretary of the Interior, Severino de las Alas, to investigate the entire incident. In his report, which he submitted about a week later, Secretary de las Alas declared that the attack had been the result of "the insulting and assaulting of the sentinel and guard," and "slurs directed against the person of General Aguinaldo by General Luna." To the assassins, commensurate punishment was meted out. The loss of Luna was, of course, a very heavy blow to our armed efforts.

These tragic developments within our Government and Army were avidly propagated in the Philippines and America by the Schurman Commission and the American forces. But as usual they were twisted and exaggerated. They reported that Luna had arrested the members of our Commission which had been created to negotiate with the Schurman Commission and had shot most of them and imprisoned the rest. They added that these developments had caused the complete dissolution of our Government. They then attributed the failure of the U.S. Commission's peace efforts to the supposed absence of a Government with which to negotiate. Schurman reported as follows:

> In its patriotic effort to bring about peace, the Philippine Republic itself suffers collapse. Done to death by its own false friends, I shall never forget that its last expiring voice was for peace and reconciliation on the basis of the proclamation issued by our Commission. But what the congress, cabinet, and president of the Philippine Republic so unanimously resolved, Luna, the general commanding their army, completely frustrated. He arrested the delegates who had been so solemnly authorized by congress,

cabinet, and president to proceed to Manila, accused them of treason, and sentenced some to imprisonment and others to death.

Years later, my enemies accused me of having personally engineered the assassination of Luna. To furnish the necessary motive, they also accused Luna of having plotted to replace me as head of the Philippine Republic. The first charge is totally false; as far as I know, the second is also completely unfounded.

Because it was known that I was lukewarm to peace at that stage, Luna's frustration of our peace gesture was not cited as my motive for supposedly wishing to eliminate him. A new motive had, therefore, to be concocted; namely, that Luna had been out to eliminate me. I cannot, of course, be very certain what ambitions Luna might have secretly harbored in his own heart, but the fact is that I was never aware that he had such intentions and I do not believe that he had any. It was also pointed out for its implication that Luna's assassins were men loyal to me. This, too, is a superfluous and misleading statement. There was nothing strange in the fact that every officer and man in our armed forces, including my own guards, was loyal to me, since I was the Commander-in-Chief.

Former Governor-General Forbes records in his *Journal*, that, sometime in 1906, he had occasion to discuss with the late general's brother, Joaquin Luna, then the governor of the province of La Union, the probable truth about his brother's death. The governor, who had undertaken his own thorough investigation, assured him that "in his opinion, General Luna's death had not been planned by General Aguinaldo but by some of the other leaders."

A far more credible motive than that attributed to me could have been, indeed, revenge for Luna's arbitrary and summary handling of the members of the cabinet, especially Buencamino. This is not to mention the smouldering fires of revenge in the hearts of many subordinate officers who had tasted bitter humiliation in Luna's hands. Had there been a previous plot to murder Luna and had I had a hand in it, I would certainly have had the dastardly crime committed as far away as possible from my own premises.

The Luna incident did create such a grave crisis in both our governmental and military organizations that it was all I could do to stave off their immediate and complete collapse. Both our Cabinet and our military command had to be quickly and properly reorganized. I took tighter control of the Government and personally assumed over-all command of our armed forces. In the midst of this crisis the American forces further intensified their assaults against us. It seems that they interpreted our delay in contacting the Schurman Commission as an abandonment of our desire for peace. As if to express their displeasure, they now let loose the full force of their military might on the remnants of our northern army.

The stepped-up American offensive forced us once more to order a general retreat, moving our Government to Tarlac, the capital of Tarlac Province, at the same time. Here in spite of the increasingly fiercer American thrusts from various directions, our forces and our Government held for six months more. But not more.

By November 12, 1900, our ammunition having been critically depleted, I decided to abandon open warfare and resort to guerrilla tactics. We evacuated Tarlac, and from that point we gave up attempts to keep our Government together and concentrated on our armed efforts. I moved my headquarters to the mountain fastnesses of Northern Luzon. By now the American forces were able to prowl over most of Luzon at will. General Malaria also came to the Americans' aid. I and many of my soldiers were attacked by the disease. I had to move from place to place in this condition until finally I established myself, together with my small staff and fifty armed guards, in Palanan, Isabela.

Even my ranking field commanders did not know my hideout. We divided the country into guerrilla districts, each under a general officer. Through a system of codes and couriers, I was able to continue the direction of our scattered forces until, through a most unsoldierly ruse, Col. Frederick Funston of the

Kansas Volunteers, assisted by Macabebe mercenaries and renegade Filipino and Spanish officers, effected my capture and three of my staff on March 23, 1901.

Before giving my version of my capture—for the American version, principally that of Funston's, is not quite correct—I should like to recall one of the most heroic acts of the entire war on our side. I hasten to add that it was nothing short of heroism for any of my men to fight the unequal war against the Americans. The fight to the death of General Gregorio del Pilar, who was in command of my rear guard, was, however, a classic of courage and loyalty.

As November 1899 turned into December, it was necessary to stop or at least delay the slashing spearhead of the column under General Samuel M. B. Young in order to give me time to retreat northward to safety. By now, the American power build-up was at its maximum and, with the disappearance of our Government, the Americans were also at the highest level of their morale. Various columns pursued my group without let up, and I had narrow escapes such as that in Pozorrubio, Pangasinan on November 15, when Young so closely pressed us that he managed to capture my mother, my wife and my son Miguel, together with Secretary Buencamino.

Del Pilar had joined our revolution against Spain as a very young man. He had first come to my notice when, as a captain in our uniform, he had presented himself at my headquarters and had asked for permission to lead a commando attack on the Spanish garrison at Paombong, Bulacan. Although he had looked very young, for he was indeed still in his teens, who was I to object to youth? I was myself below thirty, and the boyish young man with cleancut features looked dashing, trustworthy and capable. I gave him permission.

I had almost forgotten the incident which I had subsequently taken as a mere show of youthful bravado when, about a week later, he came back to report that he had accomplished his mission. He had killed most of the Spaniards and captured 14 Mauser rifles which he delivered to me. Impressed by his feat, I then and there promoted him to the rank of Major, and a lifelong friendship between us began.

A short time afterwards, I took him as my aide and promoted him to the rank of Lieutenant Colonel. I had lost a brother, General Crispulo Aguinaldo, in one of the earlier clashes in Cavite against the Spaniards and I regarded Del Pilar as more or less his replacement. I believe he reciprocated my brotherly attitude with a truly fierce loyalty. From that time on he was my inseparable companion. He was at my side when we signed the 'Pact of Biaknabato and he followed me to exile when I went to Hongkong in compliance with the terms agreed upon with the Spaniards. It was he who accompanied me to Saigon and Singapore and he was on hand during my various interviews with Consul General Pratt and others. He returned with me to the Philippines on the *McCulloch* and shared the thrill and pride of receiving the honors due a General when I boarded the *Olympia* to make my first call on Admiral Dewey.

When, however, we organized the Republic, having by now observed closely and long his qualifications of leadership, I raised him to Brigadier General and appointed him Military Governor of Bulacan. But he was a born fighter and preferred to be in the midst of action. So it was that before long he once more joined us in the field. The erect figure of this young man on his white charger soon became a familiar inspiring sight wherever the action was thickest.

After the dissolution of our army into guerrilla bands, I assigned Del Pilar to command my rear guard while I myself, together with a small retinue and the precious records of the Government and the war, sought places of safety in various provinces in Northern Luzon. Toward the end of November 1899, Major Marsh's battalion of the 33rd Infantry, under Young's command, was in hot pursuit of my small group. Fleeing, we feinted northwestward, then veered northeast up the rugged southeastern end of Ilocos Sur through a mountain pass called in the local dialect "Tirad," meaning "sharp point." When Del Pilar noticed the peculiar terrain of the place, he offered to make a delaying stand there while my group would continue on in search of safety. I approved his plan.

A narrow opening that cuts a fairly high range of mountains, the pass is a natural defensive redoubt. Del Pilar figured that, for the Americans to be able to pursue us, they would have to go through this gap, and that as long as it could be defended we would be safe on the other side of the range. With him were sixty men armed only with rifles. Immediately, he set them to digging a series of trenches on the shoulders of the pass, all of them so located as to overlook the southwestern approach, the range being in a northwesterly direction. Del Pilar then left his men and accompanied me to the town of Cervantes further in the interior where we all spent the night. The following day, he and I parted for the last time. My own group continued on towards Bontoc, Mountain Province, while Del Pilar returned to the pass and his men.

It was 10 o'clock in the morning of December 2 when Major Marsh's battalion was sighted approaching the pass, nearly a thousand men against sixty! Del Pilar placed himself just behind the forward trench and ordered his men to wait until the Americans would be near enough for their Mausers to pick out. Scenting their quarry, the Americans pressed on and, after a brief while, began shooting. Del Pilar's men replied, and the battle was joined.

In Young's battalion was a company of sharpshooters. While the rest of the American unit peppered the defenders with mountain gun and rifle fire, the sharpshooters, Indian-fighting fashion, clambered up the cliff. It was not long before the forward trench, on which the entire fire of the battalion was now zeroed in, became untenable. Noting the heavy casualty, Del Pilar ordered the survivors to retreat to the second entrenchment. They fell back under a concentrated fire which cut down some of their thinning number.

Almost immediately, the American fire located the new target. His men were being killed mercilessly, but Del Pilar, himself fully exposed to danger, held on until all his soldiers were either killed or disabled. Then mounting his inseparable white horse and apparently oblivious of the barrage which continued un-abated, he began to ride slowly down the winding trail in the direction of Cervantes. He was no doubt saddened and made careless of his own fate by the apparent failure of his mission and the loss of most of his men. He could not know and never would know that the morning engagement gave us all the time we needed to increase our distance from the Americans to safety. His service was as noble and heroic as the sacrifice of Leonidas and the other heroes of Thermopylae.

The next moment was memorably described by an American war correspondent, Richard Henry Little, whose touching eye-witness dispatch was published in the *Chicago Tribune* on February 4, 1900, as follows:

> Then we who were below, saw an American squirm his way out to the top of a high flat rock and take deliberate aim at the figure on the white horse. We held our breath, not knowing whether to pray that the sharpshooter would shoot straight or miss. Then came the spiteful crack of the Krag rifle and the man on horseback rolled to the ground, and when the troops charging up the mountain side reached him, the boy general of the Filipinos was dead.

On his death, Del Pilar was only 22 years old. In his diary, which Major Marsh retrieved from an American soldier, he had written under December 2:

> The General has given me the pick of all the men that can be spared and ordered me to defend the pass. I realize what a terrible task has been given me. And yet I feel that this is the most glorious moment of my life. What I do is done for my beloved country. No sacrifice can be too great.

The American soldiers, upon knowing that they had killed no less than Del Pilar, gave vent to the usual American craze for souvenirs. They picked him clean of every removable object including his trousers, shoes, cuff links, spurs, suspenders, handkerchief.

"It suddenly occured to me," concluded Little, "that his glory was about all we had left him."

There was left, too, a void of desolation in our hearts. General del Pilar's death caused me great personal sorrow and was an irreparable loss to our cause. If Luna sinned on the side of temper and recalcitrance, del Pilar erred on the side of loyalty and duty. Both, however, loved our Motherland devotedly and only wished above all to see her free and happy.

With his life and the lives of fifty-three of his sixty brave men, the heroic del Pilar bought us respect and time. Major Marsh later ordered a stone marker placed on his grave reading:

GENERAL GREGORIO DEL PILAR
KILLED
AT THE BATTLE OF TIRAD PASS
DECEMBER 2, 1899
COMMANDING AGUINALDO'S REAR GUARD
AN OFFICER AND A GENTLEMAN

The report of his heroism inspired in the minds of even the top American commanders a sober second thought on the Filipinos. And he gave us a year and two months more of freedom before my much-fictionized capture took place in Palanan, Isabela on March 23, 1901.

CHAPTER IX

FUNSTON AND I

COMMODORE GEORGE DEWEY won the Battle of Manila Bay and a few days later was a Rear Admiral. Colonel Frederick Funston captured me in Palanan, Isabela, and within the week was a Brigadier General. The Battle of Manila Bay signalized the beginning of American action against the Spaniards in the Philippines and has been called the greatest single event of the Spanish-American War. My capture marked the end of organized Filipino resistance to America and has been described as the most dramatic and outstanding event of the Philippine-American War. In due time, Dewey and Funston returned to America, each to be received as a great hero. Cities welcomed them with bands, parades, banquets and oratory, and the ladies with ah's, oh's, swoons and kisses.

But how empty a supposed act of heroism can be—sometimes!

As the generalissimo of our war against America, I was naturally the greatest prize the Americans must capture. This was even more obviously true after our army had broken up into guerrilla bands. Our field commanders and their scattered forces defended no specific territories but struck only where and when it suited them. In such a war the short-cut to victory is the straight line to the over-all commander whose inspiration and leadership are the life of the resistance.

The anxiety and puzzlement of the Americans as to my activities and the location of my headquarters were recounted by Funston himself. "For more than a year," he said, "the exact whereabouts of the elusive chieftain of the insurgent Filipinos had been a mystery. Rumor located him in all sorts of impossible places. . . . It was realized that Aguinaldo from his hiding-place, wherever it might be, exercised through their local chiefs a sort of general control over the guerrilla bands, and as he was insistent that the Filipinos should not accept American rule, and as he was still recognized as the head and front of the insurrection, many of us had long felt that the thing could not end until he was either out of the way or a prisoner in our hands."

Concluding his own account of my capture, Funston made this significant statement: "We posted guards all about the building (our Palanan headquarters, a former schoolhouse) and searched it thoroughly, finding great quantities of the correspondence of the insurgent government, showing that Aguinaldo had all of the time been in touch with his subordinates, even with those in the far-away Visayan islands."

Contrary to the claims then made in America that our war was not supported by the generality of our people, we Filipinos were firmly united in our natural determination to protect our homeland. Unwittingly the Spaniards had welded us into a compact nation. To the natural bonds of common race, history and native land, they had added common culture, language and religion—and the even more binding power of tyranny.

Americans who came to know us by actual contact and observation soon realized our unity and learned to respect it. Typical was the reaction of General MacArthur who had led the column which took Malolos and who on March 15, 1900 replaced General Otis as Military Governor and over-all commander.

"I did not like to believe that the whole population of Luzon was opposed to us," he told a U.S. Senate committee, "but having come thus far, and having been brought much in contact with both insurgents and *amigos,* I have been reluctantly compelled to believe that the Filipino masses are loyal to Aguinaldo and the government which he leads."

On a later occasion he stated, "Aguinaldo was the incarnation of the insurrection."

The Americans wondered why, after our Government had collapsed and our army had been disbanded, we kept on fighting. They had expected us to surrender as soon as we would feel the full impact of American might. Yet, long after we had evacuated Tarlac, we kept on fighting. Behind our continued resistance were hope against hope, despair, the readiness to die for our country, and the determination to win for our people at whatever cost the decent respect of mankind.

From the outbreak of the war, I realized our difficult position and the impossibility of winning over the Americans. While the Spaniards had been slow in sending reinforcements to the Philippines, the Americans, once they had started, were fast. While the Spaniards had had more or less obsolete equipment, the Americans used modern arms (although some considered the Spaniards' Mauser rifle superior to the Americans' Krag). Where the Spaniards had been slow and leisurely fighters, the Americans were energetic, persistent and resourceful. And, believing what we had seen, the American navy could cut the Spanish navy to pieces at will. We fought the Americans with the greatest of reluctance and regret.

Once the war had started, however, we built up hopes to give the semblance of reason to our course. We hoped that, with the Democratic Party and the Anti-Imperialist League openly opposed to the taking of the Philippines, the American people would soon demand an end to the war. The war was also proving very costly. Indeed, it eventually cost the United States some $600,000,000, not to mention subsequent benefits to the War's veterans, together with about 10,000 casualties among the 126,467 men eventually sent to the Philippines.

On top of the enormous cost in money and human life, the basic political principles on which the American Government was founded were being violated and repudiated in the American action. We hoped for an American ideological reaction which, on top of the other considerations, would force America to pull out of our country. This failing, we went so far as to believe the possibility that some European powers, perhaps Germany, might champion our cause—even for a price.

Our esteemed cabinet colleague, Apolinario Mabini, voiced still another reason why we were resisting the Americans with all our might. "The Filipinos realize," he stated, "that they cannot expect any victory over the American forces. They are fighting to show the American people that they are sufficiently intelligent to know their rights . . . . to know how to sacrifice themselves for a Government which assures them their liberty and which governs them in conformity with their wishes and needs."

We neither hoped for victory over the Americans nor hated them. But we wanted to gain their respect. Dewey, Pratt and Wildman had disowned their promises. Dewey seemed to have taken our cooperation for granted and had later denied us the considerations of decency and honor as they are known among civilized men. The American armed forces, in keeping us off with their guns from participating in the taking of Manila, had thought us unfit of trust and comradeship. In killing five Filipino soldiers for every one wounded, thus exactly reversing the proportion between killed and wounded in previous wars, the Americans seemed to have denied us the protection of the laws of war on the treatment of the wounded and prisoners. President McKinley himself had refused to give our pleas serious consideration.

How could we prove that the Americans were wrong?

Our only recourse was to show them that we knew how to fight for our rights and our ideals with fierce courage and to die for our native land with unbowed pride. It was our hope that, if we ourselves should perish, we would at least earn for our children the decent respect of others, especially the Americans who now seemed set to govern us in place of the Spaniards.

One of my greatest satisfactions is that, even before our full sacrifices were known, some of the ranking American leaders in the field had already begun to show us respect and admiration. For instance, General Lawton. "Taking into account the disadvantages they have to fight against in arms, equipment and military discipline—without arms, short of ammunition, powder inferior, shells reloaded until they are defective, inferior in every particular of equipment and supplies," the General reported, "they are the bravest men I have ever seen . . . . What we want is to stop this accursed war. . . . These men are indomitable."

I for one resolved to die. After that brief moment of hesitation in San Isidro when it appeared that the Schurman Commission might be the means of obtaining what Dewey and the others had promised me, I never again faltered. I took for granted finally that I would die fighting. But it is perhaps God's way of reminding us of our human frailty to dispose of our plans as He pleases. For even as Funston's hired renegades closed in on me, and I started to sell my life dearly, I found myself in the friendly but firm hug of one of my own men and could not use my gun.

Funston's own version of my capture was immediately accepted as gospel truth. Sometime in 1911 when he published his memoirs, he devoted an entire long chapter to the exploit which had made him a hero and a general. In various condensed forms, his account has since been part of the history books. I claim no different knowledge of his plans, preparations, movements and other details, but I strongly dissent from his versions of how he secured my secret messages to some of my field commanders and how my actual capture was made by his renegades and hirelings.

Even as he has fictionized these parts, his account unashamedly admits the commission by him of forgeries, the use of disguises and abuse of hospitality. To his own admissions should be added brain-washing and torture. His whole stratagem was indeed a cross between the Greek Trojan Horse, the British Major Martin and the Russian tribunal-confessional.

Briefly, the Funston version is as follows:

One day early in February 1901, a courier from our headquarters, Cecilio Segismundo, surrendered to the American garrison at Pantabangan, Nueva Ecija, and handed over various coded messages of mine to several of my field commanders. They were signed with various *noms de guerres,* also in code and known only to the addressees. Funston and Lazaro Segovia, the latter a renegade and deserter but evidently a talented Spaniard, puzzled over the messages over black coffee all of one night. Finally breaking the code, they were able to learn in two of the letters the tell-tale fact that the courier knew the name of the town where I had established my headquarters; and in one, that I conveyed vital instructions to my cousin, General Baldomero Aguinaldo. I directed him to replace General Jose Alejandrino as commander of Central Luzon and, when he had assumed this position, to order the four zone commanders under him to send me detachments of picked troops eventually aggregating about 400 to deploy as guerrillas in the Cagayan Valley.

Funston seized upon my request for troops as the germ-idea of his stratagem. As he finally shaped it, a company of Macabebe mercenaries under Tagalog officers would pretend to be the first of the troops I had requested and would claim to have captured on the way five Americans, namely Funston and four other officers.

Such a group was finally embarked on the ship *Vicksburg* at Manila and brought around south of Luzon through the San Bernardino Strait and then up on the Pacific off Casiguran Bay where, shortly after midnight on February 14 during a heavy downpour, it anchored off shore with all its lights screened and secretly landed Funston and his men by the ship's boats. The Americans had been told by their spies that any suspicious party anywhere within one hundred miles from my hideout would be reported to me by my men within 24 hours. Casiguran Bay was eighty miles south of my headquarters.

During the eight-day sea voyage, Funston, assisted by the four other Americans, Segovia and three renegade Filipino officers, Hilario Tal Placido, Dionisio Bato, and Gregorio Cadhit, had carefully grilled their men in what to do and say, all in accordance, of course, with the story that the group was a detachment being sent to my camp.

To complete the ruse, the Macabebes were made to leave their American uniforms on the boat and to put on varieties of second-hand outfits to simulate my bedraggled guerrillas. They were also armed with Mausers and Remingtons but given a few Krags as extras to serve as supposedly captured arms from the Americans. Segovia and the three Tagalogs were similarly dressed. The American officers took good care to put on well-worn outfits.

Marching to the town of Casiguran, the Filipinos were welcomed by the town officials and people as minor heroes, while the Americans were stared and gazed at in various degrees of curiosity and emotion. The Filipinos asked for food and guides. These the town officials gladly furnished them. The provisions hastily gathered together during the party's brief stopover was however enough only for a few days. Funston and his men nevertheless preferred to make time and started for Palanan.

Before leaving Manila, Funston had had a Filipino clerk in his employ, Ramon Roque, forge the signature of General Lacuna, one of my field commanders. In one of their previous raids on the headquarters of Brigadier-General Urbano Lacuna, the Americans had seized, among other booties, Lacuna's supply of stationery bearing the letterhead "Brigada Lacuna." After Roque had practiced imitating Lacuna's signature to perfection, Funston had him write it at the bottom of each of two sheets of Lacuna's stationery. Later, on the *Vicksburg*, Funston had Segovia fill in the body of the two letters in Spanish.

One letter dated February 24, 1901 purported to be an answer to my own letter to Lacuna. It thanked me for my confirmation of his promotion to Brigadier-General recommended some time before by General Alejandrino. It added some supposed reports on the progress of the guerrilla warfare in his zone and ended with what Funston called "some airy persiflage about the things the writer was doing to the hated invaders."

The second letter, dated over a month later, stated that Lacuna had received orders from General Baldomero Aguinaldo, who had assumed command of Central Luzon, to send one of his best companies to me. It said further that he was complying with the order and was sending a company under the command of Lt. Col. Hilario Tal Placido whom I may recall as one of my former officers.

The letter went on to explain that Placido had been previously compelled to take the oath of allegiance to the United States but that, on order of Lacuna, had returned to active service under the Philippine flag. The second in command, the letter added, was a gallant Spaniard by the name of Lazaro Segovia who had shown himself so much addicted to our cause. Both letters bore the signatures of Lacuna as previously forged by Roque.

These, together with a third letter signed by Tal Placido, were now sent ahead to Palanan by couriers selected by the vice-president of Casiguran, a man loyal to us, so that we in Palanan would know in advance of the coming of the group. Tal Placido's letter, dictated by Segovia and addressed to me, was to the effect that the writer, by order of Lacuna, was on his way to Palanan with a company of troops. He had with him five American prisoners, it explained, whom his company had captured after a brief skirmish against a small detachment mapping the country into whom they ran while crossing the mountains between Pantabangan and Baler. As he could not detach men to escort the Americans back to Lacuna, he was taking them along to Palanan.

After having marched for days, climbing craggy mountains and fording numerous streams and swamps and having exhausted their food supply, the motley group was stumbling along in a weak and hungry condition when on March 22, at a point some ten miles below Palanan, they were met by a courier sent by my Chief of Staff, Colonel Simon Villa. He carried a letter instructing Tal Placido to proceed with his men to Palanan but to leave the Americans with a guard of ten men at a place known as Dinundungan on the road to Palanan. This created an emergency which Funston had not foreseen.

The party proceeded to Dinundungan which it found to be merely a place without inhabitants. Here one of our men, aided by Negrito laborers, was already building sheds for the American prisoners and their guards. Funston and Segovia spent a supperless and sleepless night figuring out how to meet the unexpected crisis. By day time they had a plan: the Americans with ten Macabebe soldiers under a corporal would remain in Dinundungan as ordered. But on the way, Segovia would rush a note back to the corporal stating that a messenger from Palanan had been met on the trail bearing another letter from Villa which revoked previous instructions and directed that the guards and their prisoners also proceed to Palanan.

The night before, Funston had coached Tal Placido to write a note to Villa reporting the party's arrival at Dinundungan and his compliance with the instructions to leave the Americans there with guards. He added that the party had been without food for several days, that they were very weak and hungry and could not possibly negotiate the eight miles to Palanan without first eating. So, would Villa send some breakfast for the entire party? The letter was rushed to Villa by a Negrito messenger, and early the next morning the requested food came. Funston and his group cooked and ate breakfast and, thus refreshed and strengthened, started on the last lap of their journey.

In about an hour, two Macabebe soldiers were sent running back to Dinundungan with Segovia's letter. This they ostentatiously handed to the Corporal of the guard. Shown the letter and not suspecting anything amiss, the man directing the construction merely somewhat resentfully remarked that Palanan should not have put him to so much trouble building shelters which were not to be used after all. Funston and his fellow Americans together with their guards then departed to catch up with the larger group.

Funston's verbatim account of what happened at the camp follows:

> The main interest now centers in the adventures of the main column, the one by which the actual capture was made. About a mile outside town it was met by a couple of insurgent officers, who escorted them the remainder of the distance. About three o'clock they approached the Palanan River, here about a hundred yards wide and quite deep, and saw the town on the other side. The only way to cross this stream was by means of a rather good-sized *banca*. Hilario and Segovia crossed with the first load, leaving instructions for the men to follow as rapidly as they could, form on the opposite bank, and then march up to Aguinaldo's house. The boat was to be sent back to await our arrival.
>
> Segovia and Hilario now had a most trying half-hour. They called on Aguinaldo at his headquarters, and found him surrounded by seven insurgent officers, all of them armed with revolvers. Outside, the fifty men of the escort, neatly uniformed and armed with Mausers, were drawn up to do the honors for the reinforcements that had made such a wonderful march to join them. Segovia and Hilario entertained those present with stories of the march from

Lacuna's headquarters, and were warmly congratulated on having made it successfully. Segovia took his position where he could look out of one of the open windows and see when the time had. arrived.

Finally, the Macabebes under Dioniso Bato and Gregorio Cadhit marched up, Segovia stepped to the head of the stairway outside the house, for they were in the second story, and signalled to Gregorio, who called out, "Now is the time Macabebes. Give it to them." The poor little "Macs" were in such a nervous state from their excitement over the strange drama that they were playing a part in that they were pretty badly rattled. They had loaded their pieces and were standing at "order arms," as were the men of the escort facing them on the other side of the little square. They fired a ragged volley, killing two men of the escort and severely wounding the leader of Aguinaldo's band, who happened to be passing between the lines when fire was opened. Aguinaldo, hearing the firing, and thinking that the men of his escort had broken lose to celebrate the arrival of the reinforcements, stepped to the window, and called out, "Stop that foolishness. Don't waste your ammunition."

Before he could turn around Hilario had grasped him about the waist and thrown him under a table, where he literally sat on him, and Hilario was a fat man. I had given the most positive orders to the effect that under no circumstances should Aguinaldo be killed, and that no lives should be taken unless it was absolutely necessary. But as Segovia dashed back into the room several of the officers started to draw their revolvers, and he opened fire on them hitting Villa three times, who was tugging to get a Mauser automatic pistol out of its holster, and also wounding Major Alhambra. Villa surrendered, as did Santiago Barcelona, treasurer of the socalled republic. Alhambra and the other officers leaped from one of the windows into the river, the house standing on the bank, and escaped by swimming. As Hilario grasped Aguinaldo, he said, "You are a prisoner of the Americans," so that the fallen "Dictator," as he now called himself, had some sort of a vague idea of what had happened to him.

In the meantime we Americans with our supposed guard had reached the river, jumped into the *banca* waiting for us, and had paddled across in frantic haste. Running up the bank toward the house, we were met by Segovia who came running out, his face aglow with exultation and his clothing spattered with the blood of the men he had wounded. He called in Spanish, "It is all right. We have him."

We hastened into the house, and I introduced myself to Aguinaldo, telling him that we were officers of the American army, that the men with us were our troops, and not his, and that he was a prisoner of war. He was given assurance that he need not fear any bad treatment. He said in a dazed sort of way, "Is this not some joke?" I assured him that it was not, though, as a matter of fact, it was a pretty bad one on him. While naturally agitated, his bearing was dignified, and in this moment of his fall there was nothing of the craven. He is a man of many excellent qualities, far and away the best Filipino I ever was brought in contact with. It was well known that he was a man of humane instincts, and had done all he could to prevent the horrible bands that now made up his forces; but under the circumstances his control over them was limited. The wounded Villa was more inclined to stand aloof, but we dressed his wounds, thereby mollifying him somewhat. Barcelona was as mild as could be.

Funston's story, as I have stated, is fictionized. He has added some dramatic details and omitted unfavorable facts. I would simply call attention to some of its discrepancies. I realize of course that everything is supposed to be fair in love and war. But just as there are laws on some aspects of love, such as breach of promise, there are also laws regulating war.

Funston had no compunction in committing forgeries. Not only did he have Lacuna's signature attached to spurious letters but he ordered the writing of other letters containing counterfeit messages.

One of the strangest hoaxes of the last World War was the use by the British intelligence of a dead body which they dressed up as a Royal Marine Major and falsely identified as William Martin. In the pockets and wallet, they stuffed papers and letters. The letters were intended to mislead the Germans into believing that the next allied invasion objective after North Africa was not Sicily but an unidentified place in the Western Mediterranean or the Peloponnesus in Greece. The body was then planted in the sea off Huelva, Spain, on the correct assumption that the Spanish authorities, upon recovering it, would make sure that the Germans would surreptitiously learn the letters' contents.

But it should be noted that the letters were not forged but genuine. They were actually written and signed by Lt. Gen. Archibald Nye, vice chief of the imperial general staff, to General Alexander, commander of the 18th Army Group in Africa, and Lord Louis Mountbatten to Admiral Sir Andrew Cunningham, commander-in-chief of the Mediterranean area. On stolen stationery, Funston addressed messages to me above the forged signatures of one of my field officers. The cynics would say the Germans would have been too smart to fall for forgeries, and it was my own hard luck that I did. I would say that what Funston did was not exactly cricket.

Funston apparently had the knack of utilizing rascals and renegades for his own purposes.

The Macabebes were of course mercenaries. They had served in the Spanish army and switched their allegiance to the Americans as a matter of course. We ourselves had no Macabebes in our forces. It is said that the original paternal ancestors of the Macabebes were western Mexican Indians brought to the Philippines as recruits by the Spaniards and later permitted to settle in the region of Macabebe, Pampanga. The original Indians naturally felt foreign among the Filipinos and looked upon the Spanish Government for assistance and protection. This feeling seems to have been transmitted from generation to generation to their descendants who continued to serve the Spaniards. After the Spanish defeat, they transferred their loyalty to the Americans almost instinctively.

Segovia, Placido, Bato and Cadhit were plain renegades. They had succumbed to American gold and all served as spies. Segovia had deserted the Spaniards to join us, then deserted us for the Americans. Placido and the two other ex-officers in our army had been repeatedly disciplined by their superior officers for various military offenses. Selling to the Americans was their idea of getting even.

Renegades and knaves as they were, only Segovia among

them had been told of the purpose of the expedition before the group boarded the *Vicksburg* at Manila. Only after they were safely on board and completely in his power did Funston dare inform the others.

"I sent for Tal Placido. Bato and Cadhit, the three ex-insurgent officers with us," Funston admitted without qualms, "and told them that we were going after their old chieftain, and that they would be expected to play their part.   If they were faithful they would be well rewarded, if not, there would be but one penalty and that would be inflicted if it was the last thing done. They seemed thunderstruck.   "

Are there not here admitted the crimes of kidnapping, coercion, intimidation and threat?

The use of disguises by supposedly uniformed soldiers and officers is highly questionable. It is, I think, a law of war that soldiers under false colors are beyond the law's pale and subject to punishment. Our fighting forces, to be sure, had discarded their uniforms to fight as guerrillas, but had they used American uniforms they would have been denounced as scoundrels who did not observe the rules of civilized warfare. Yet, Funston proudly admitted,   the only recourse was to work a stratagem, that is, to get to him (Aguinaldo) under false colors."

Funston's careless abuse of hospitality is unworthy of the tradition of American officers who are expected to be gentlemen as well. He had deceived the Casiguran officials into feeding and provisioning his group in the belief that they were friends. He begged us for food when he and his men were starving, in order that they may have the strength to reach and destroy us. Than this there never has been a stranger payment for kindness and charity. But Funston was not one to be squeamish. Referring to the Vice-President of Casiguran, who had fed, housed and provisioned him and his men, he said: "Of the numerous ones that we made fools of, he was the only one that I ever had the slightest qualms about."

Some time after the war, when I had had opportunities to compare notes with my former officers in Central Luzon, I learned that Funston had started his heroic work by subjecting our courier,

Segismundo, and his escort to various tortures including the water cure. I was told that this poor fellow and his companion had been betrayed by the President of Pantabangan whom they had taken for a man loyal to us. The result was their capture by the Americans.

At that time, the Americans subjected to various degrees of grilling and torture everyone even remotely suspected of knowing where I was ensconced. So now they worked on Segismundo and his escort. The men withstood the preliminary tortures, but an unguarded reply of Segismundo to a question about me led them to concentrate their sadistic efforts on him. In his answer, he had mentioned knowing no one else as chief except a certain "Capitan." They now pounced on him and gave him everything, finally resorting to the water cure.

At the risk of offending the sensibilities of mid-twentieth century readers, but wishing to make them understand how terrible the water cure was which the Americans practiced on many of my men, I should like to reproduce hereunder an account of how it is administered. It is that of an early American visitor to the Philippines who denounced the torture in a letter to a New York newspaper:

But the water cure! If the tortures I've mentioned are already hellish, the water cure is plain hell. The native is thrown upon the ground, and, while his legs and arms are pinned, his head is raised partially so as to make pouring in the water an easier matter. An attempt to keep the mouth closed is of no avail; a bamboo stick or a pinching of the nose will produce the same effect. And now the water is poured in, and swallow the poor wretch must or strangle. A gallon of water is much but it is followed by a second and a third. By this time the victim is certain his body is about to burst. But he is mistaken, for a fourth and even a fifth gallon are poured in. By this time the body becomes an object frightful to contemplate. While in this condition, speech is impossible, and so the water must be squeezed out of him. This is sometimes allowed to occur naturally, but it is sometimes hastened by pressure, and "sometimes we jump on them to get it out quick," said a young soldier to me with a smile—a young soldier, a mere boy hardly ten years out of his

mother's lap . . we learned that many times the cure is twice
given ere the native yields. I heard of one who took it three times
and died   These things are not lovely but they are true.

It was only after he had been revived from a second water
cure that the unfortunate Segismundo, now certain that he
would be killed if he held out further, admitted everything and
finally led his tormentors to the place where he had cached my
letters to various of my field commanders.

Funston himself almost lets the cat out of the bag in that
part of his narrative which tells how he had contacted the vice-
president of Casiguran, a man loyal to us, through one more
of his forged letters. "We sent this missive by Segismundo, he
being accompanied by Gregorio Cadhit and two armed Macabebes," he reported. "The last-named men had their instructions as to what they were to do in case of treachery." After
having both picked and washed his brains, Funston kept the
luckless Segismundo as a captive to utilize for other purposes.

But nowhere in his account does Funston indulge more in
fiction than in the part describing how I was actually captured.
He mentions that there were seven officers with me in the room
and that only Segovia and Placido had come up to us. The
Macabebes and two other Tagalog officers marched by themselves later to the small plaza before our headquarters. My
officers and I, Funston also makes of record, were each armed
with a revolver. How was it possible for the two, who had come
pretending friendliness, to go into action after their Macabebes
had started firing at my guards who were extending them hospitality, and "beat us all to the draw"? Only Segovia was using
his gun, according to Funston, yet he immobilized us all and
wounded Villa and Major Alhambra several times. He must
have been as fast with the gun as Jesse James or Shane of the
movies. But this just was not so.

What actually happened was this: When Segovia and Placido
began repeating themselves while waiting for the Macabebes,
four of my seven officers left the room, one after another, for
various reasons—to see the incoming troops, answer a call of

nature, get a drink, etc. Only Villa, Santiago Barcelona, Alhambra and myself remained. The limping Segovia himself had stepped out to the head of the stairway and staggered back to the room with his gun drawn just as the Macabebes' fire was heard. In the same instance, Placido, forgetting to draw his gun, lunged at me.

But in the same moment, with guns drawn, Barcelona, Alhambra and Villa placed themselves around me. It was Barcelona who took command of the situation. He warned Segovia not to shoot, as we would surrender peacefully. He had at the same time held me in an enfolding bear hug, then quickly said to me, "My general, you owe it to our people to live and continue your fight for freedom!"

I had myself drawn my gun and had decided to die fighting. Then, before I could raise it, Barcelona had pinioned my arms while Villa and Alhambra had placed themselves between me and Segovia, forming a protective shield. When Segovia started shooting, Villa, without faltering yet without replying so as not to draw more fire, received the shots with his body. However, when Alhambra was also hit, this officer lit off through the window. Really, with such an opportunity, Segovia was the poorest shot I have ever seen. And, when everything was over, Placido was still dazed.

But neither villainy nor treachery, brainwashing nor torture could change the fact that I was captured by the Americans. I was put on the *Vicksburg* together with Villa and Barcelona the next day and, sailing around the end of Northern Luzon, brought to Manila Bay. From here, Funston and an officer of the *Vicksburg* took me on the ship's boat to Malacanan by way of the Pasig River. General MacArthur, then the military governor, received me not, I felt, without respect and kindness.

My capture, together with the treachery and betrayal that accompanied it, left me deeply angered, then distressed, then almost completely numbed. I was at first incredulous, believing everything to be a bad dream from which I would surely awaken. Then, when my senses had surrendered to the facts and I at last realized that I was a captive, I was overwhelmed by a feeling of disgust and despair. I had failed my people and my Motherland.

And yet, I also felt relieved. I had known for some time that our resistance was doomed to failure. But having gone thus far, I felt that I must keep on until death. Now, it was over and I was alive. There was the humiliation and degradation, but there was, too, the future and the new and better things that it may bring. For somehow, with all the shabby treatment that individual Americans had given me—forced, I thought, by circumstances—I could not bring myself to believe that the United States as a nation could be as bad a master as Spain. A sixth sense somehow assured me that America would sooner or later redress the sins of her individual sons.

Strangely, I developed an undefinable admiration for Funston. He had previously been in the Cuban war and spoke Spanish quite tolerably. The fact that we had both fought against the Spaniards gave us a common background, and the Spanish language enabled us to communicate directly. I now observed him to be a diamond in the rough.

A husky, almost muscle-bound man, he was literally as hard as nails. But I felt, too, that he had a big heart. A man who adventured into war as a volunteer to help liberate the Cubans must have possessed a broad humanitarian sympathy. That he was fighting in the Philippines to enslave the Filipinos was, I thought, something he did not quite mean—nor, somehow, did America. He had fierce courage. He was resourceful to the extreme. And, at the height of his personal triumph, he was simple, matter-of-fact, and even humble.

CHAPTER X

THE REDEMPTION BEGINS

I KNOW EXACTLY how Alexander Kerensky felt in 1917. Earlier in 1901 I had gone through the identical extremity of despair and disappointment.

Kerensky had led a successful revolution against the Czar. Having become the Premier, he proceeded to establish the first popular government known to the oppressed Russians. But within the year the infant democracy was trampled to death by the heavy-heeled Bolsheviki led by Nikolai Lenin.

In 1896 we had started a revolution against Spain and in 1898 had established the first Republic not only in the Philippines but in all the East. But in 1899 the American forces crushed our army and our Government and in 1901 captured me in Palanan and made me prisoner.

Yet today I can justifiably pity Kerensky and congratulate myself.

His Russia is still prostrate and bleeding under the hobnailed boots of its Red masters, but the Philippines is once more a free and democratic Republic. What is more, while the Soviet masters have made Russia the greatest active peril the world has ever known, the Americans have made the Philippines the symbol of a new and enlightened international relationship. Whereas the Bolsheviki have many times condemned and convicted themselves as the murderers of the freedom and peace of the world, the Americans have redeemed themselves by developing a new pattern of assisting backward nations to learn self-government and achieve self-determination and independence. While America has thus insured the doom of the old and oppressive European imperialism, the Communist have spawned a far more terrible imperialism—conquest of the world through propaganda, sabotage, hate and revolution.

This is the American gatling gun, the precursor of the machinegun. This rapid-fire gun was typical of the immense technological advantage the American Forces enjoyed. While they had mountain guns, mortars and other modern artillery, the Filipinos had a Mauser or Remington rifle for every ten men, reloaded their cartridges over and over again, and could count with only a few cannons.

In this interesting group may be seen Col. Kessler, Maj. Fitshugh and Lt. Knowlton of the American Army and V. Tokizama, Japanese military attache in the Philippines.

Gen. Pantaleon Garcia, one of the ranking general officers in the army of Gen. Aguinaldo which fought the Americans.

I shall now proceed to tell how America redeemed itself in my country far and above the sins it had committed.

American redemption was, in effect, the end-result of many confluent forces—our war against America, a great American act of contrition led by President McKinley, the diplomacy and humanity of William Howard Taft, and American and Filipino public opinion. The redemption has enhanced America's moral stature and added a new buttress to democracy as the best form of government and way of life.

In the last years of the nineteenth century, Uncle Sam became infected with the highly contagious fever of imperialism. He had rushed into Cuba, like a good Samaritan, to stamp out the rampaging epidemic that, under General Valeriano Weyler, the Butcher, had gotten out of control. Unfortunately, the virus somehow invaded his bloodstream.

While within him the disease was incubating, he also came to the Philippines. Having taken our country, he was undecided and uncertain as to what to do with it. If at all, he was inclined to treat our homeland in the same manner that he was handling Cuba. But in a matter of months, the disease's prodromal stage began; the fever presently raged, rising to dangerous temperatures. The patient was delirious. The impassioned oratories of Senators Lodge, Albert Beveridge and Cushman K. Davis were his feverish ravings.

But by 1900 the virulence was over. The antibodies in his system, reinforced by the wonder drug of sobered-up public opinion, had at last prevailed. Yet, the ordeal was not all in vain: from the experience he emerged with a clearer vision of world affairs.

I do believe that we Filipinos contributed a great deal to the return of America to normality, sobriety and morality. We forced Washington to raise, equip and transport over 100,000 men and spend some $600,000,000. We inflicted casualities of about 10,000. We convinced America, without leaving room for any doubt, that we Filipinos were determined to win our liberty at any and all cost. We made the Americans realize that our love of freedom was akin to their own—that it was over and above our lives, our fortunes and our sacred honor. We proved that as a nation we possessed unconquerable dignity.

Had we acted in the contrary, had we been cowardly and craven, we should have deserved slavery. But Jose Rizal had taught us well. "There are no tyrants," our great patriot had said, "where there are no slaves." No one can ever accuse us of having given the least reason to America to tyrannize us. All this must have been a great sobering American experience.

In their own good time the Americans also discovered that the Filipino people, even in sober second thought, completely approved the attitude we had taken and defended to the last.

The richer and better educated Filipinos who had deserted our Government in Malolos and crossed the lines to join the Americans, together with the leaders of the Bacolod counter-revolutionists, organized the Federal Party in 1900, a year before my capture. This was the only political group the Americans allowed until 1906. From its ranks they naturally drew the first Filipinos appointed to high positions in the military government and later in the civil establishment. The most talented among them became advisers to the military governors and justices of the Supreme Court. In 1901, three of them became the first Filipinos appointed to the Philippine Commission, which exercised both the executive and legislative functions. The Federal Party completely monopolized patronage.

In 1907, by authority of the Cooper Act of 1902, the first national election in the Philippines was held. The purpose was to choose the first members of the Philippine Assembly, the new lower house of the Legislature. The Federal Party was at the height of its power and enjoyed full and active American support. This was understandable. Since its organization it had advocated Filipino cooperation with the Americans and annexation of the Philippines to the United States. To oppose it, a new party, the Nacionalista, was organized. Led by Sergio Osmeña, it advocated immediate Philippine Independence.

The pre-election campaign was conducted freely on a high level. In the press and in public meetings in every town and village, the annexation and independence issues were debated.

When the votes were counted, the Federal Party elected only 16 assemblymen while the Nacionalista Party won 58 seats. Overwhelmingly repudiated, the Federal Party disintegrated. From that time on, immediate independence was the only winning political slogan. In peace as in war our people completely vindicated us.

These developments were, of course, duly noted in America. American public opinion, never at any time overwhelmingly in favor of taking the Philippines, began to sober up. After all, the cheers and shouts inspired by Dewey's Manila Bay victory were only the manifestations of a passing national intoxication. Regarding the emotional outburst with disgust from the beginning, the Anti-Imperialist League and the Democratic Party fought American expansionist ambitions with hard and clear logic. The League commanded respectful attention for it included many respected figures like former Presidents Harrison and Cleveland, Andrew Carnegie, Jane Addams, Carl Schurz and Moorefield Story. Its determined work of information directed from its headquarters in Boston was systematic and effective.

The Democratic Party, following Bryan's preconceived strategy and inspired by the classics of constitutional and humanitarian orations with which Republican Senators Hoar and Bacon caused the Senate to tremble with guilt, made Philippine independence the "paramount issue" in the 1900 presidential election. Even indeed at the zenith of the imperialistic fever, temporarily abetted by Mr. Bryan's wall-eyed political scheme, the Senate ratified the Treaty of Peace with only one vote to spare. And the Bacon-McEnery Resolution, which was intended to define a transient American policy in the Philippines in a similar manner that the Teller Amendment guided U.S. policy in Cuba, was defeated only by the Vice-President's vote cast to break the tie.

By early 1900, President McKinley was inaugurating a completely new Philippine policy. Utilizing his war powers he sent the Taft Commission to the Philippines and armed it with a Letter of Instructions which defined American policies and intentions. These policies enabled the Filipinos to acquire cultural and economic progress and learn self-government. In their ultimate consequences, they would logically and inevitably lead to national independence. It will yet prove one of the most important documents in the history of international relations.

This remarkable document outlined the process of transforming the military government, which had been established by the American army to administer the territories it wrestled from us, into a civil government. It vested in the Commission the legislative authority over the country effective September 1, 1900 and the executive power effective July 4, 1901. The Commission was to establish municipal and provincial governments and a civil service system primarily for and by Filipinos.

"In all cases," the Instructions stated, "the municipal officers . . . are to be selected by the people, and   wherever officers of more extended jurisdiction are to be selected in any way, natives of the Islands are to be preferred.   It will be necessary to fill some offices for the present with Americans, which, after a time, may well be filled by natives of the Islands."

The Taft Commission was directed to investigate the titles to the big landed estates which had bred the popular discontent that had erupted into the revolution against the Spaniards. As almost all the estates were owned by Spaniards, the vaster ones by religious orders, McKinley enjoined his Commission to abide by the due process of law and to respect "the separation between state and church which shall be real, entire and absolute."

Upon the recommendation of the Commission, the U.S. Congress in 1900 authorized the purchase of the bigger *haciendas* of the religious orders. To finance the purchase, the Commission was empowered to float bonds. The implementation of this policy took Taft to the Vatican in Rome to secure the authority of the Pope to the sale of the religious lands. As a result, the Philippine government embarked upon a policy of purchasing big landed estates to subdivide and sell to the tenants and other buyers. This policy is today still one of the major facets of the Philippines' program of social justice. The great amount of money needed to buy the private lands has however made the process slow and difficult.

Education was high in the Instructions' agenda. The Commission was to establish a school system based on free universal primary instruction.

"It will be the duty of the Commission to promote and extend and, as they find occasion, to improve the system of education already inaugurated by the Military authorities," the Instructions directed. "In doing this they should regard as of first importance the extension of a system of primary education which shall be free to all, and which shall tend to fit the people for the duties of citizenship and for the ordinary avocations of a civilized community. This instruction should be given, in the first instance, in every part of the Islands in the language of the people.

"In view of the great number of languages spoken by the different tribes," it added, "it is especially important to the prosperity of the Islands that a common medium of communication may be established, and it is obviously desirable that this medium should be the English language. Special attention should be at once given to affording full opportunity to all the people of the Islands to acquire the use of the English language."

The original plan had been to utilize the local dialects, at least in primary instruction. But officials and educators, American and Filipino alike, found a dearth both of teaching materials and of dialect literature. While the first was not insurmountable, the second posed a problem of utility and foresight. Once the Filipino became literate in his own dialect, it was pointed out, he would still be imprisoned within the narrow walls of his original linguistic jail. He would still find the doors of more modern cultures and civilizations than his own firmly locked. In any event, since English was the language of the new sovereign power, possesses one of the most complete literatures, and is one of the most widely spoken tongues in the world, it was finally decided to educate the Filipinos in English.

Education in English opened wide to the Filipinos the doors to the great literature of democracy. Under Spain only a few of us, like Jose Rizal and Andres Bonifacio, were ever able to read the histories of the American and French revolutions and only in Spanish translations. Now the younger generations could read in the English original not only these books but also the Declaration of Independence and the inspiring pronouncements on freedom of Jefferson, Lincoln and Webster and other great liberty-loving Americans. We who revolted against Spanish oppression, from Rizal to Del Pilar, came to demand our share of Western democracy largely for having had glimpses of it through reading of books written in Spanish. But we were a mere handful. Now the Filipinos as a people, through the medium of English, came under the inspiration of the great philosophers of democracy. They were also acquiring a comprehensive, first-hand knowledge of world progress. The schools and the Bill of Rights are truly the lifeblood of freedom.

For the Instructions also implanted in the islands the substance of the American Bill of Rights. It had been the lack of civil and political rights, especially the freedom of speech and press, aggravated by the fusion of church and state, which had made life under Spain unbearable. Now, in one stroke of the pen, in the altruistic American mood which superseded the transient imperialistic distemper, what we Filipinos had fought for in many revolutions and first proclaimed in our short-lived Constitution approved in Malolos, became ours at long last.

"Upon every division and branch of the Government of the Philippines," the Instructions enjoined, "must be imposed these inviolable rules: That no person shall be deprived of life, liberty, or property without due process of the law; that private property shall not be taken for public use without just compensation; that in all criminal prosecutions the accused shall enjoy the right to a speedy and public trial, to be informed of the nature and cause of the accusation, to be confronted with the witnesses against him, to have the assistance of counsel for his defense; that excessive bail shall not be required, nor excessive fines imposed, nor cruel and unusual punishment inflicted; that no person shall be put twice in jeopardy for the same offense or be compelled in any criminal case to be a witness against himself; that the right to be secure against unreasonable searches and seizures shall not be violated; that neither slavery nor involuntary servitude shall exist except as a punishment for crime; that no bill of attainder or ex post facto law shall be passed; that no law shall be passed abridging the freedom of speech or of the press or of the rights of the people to peaceably assemble and petition the Government for a redress of grievances; that no law shall be made respecting an establishment of religion or prohibiting the free exercise thereof, and that the free exercise and enjoyment of religious profession and worship without discrimination or preference shall forever be allowed."

These rights and liberties are, indeed, the foundation of true democracy. The freedom of expression through speech or press (including stage, screen, radio and TV) is, I think, the source of all other freedoms. For as long as the governed can criticize his governor, he possesses an effective weapon with which to protect his life and property as well as his other rights and liberties. Even the Spaniards themselves say, *Quien no llora no mama,* He who doesn't cry gets no milk. One cannot be oppressed provided he is vocal. Could but the Russians freely articulate their fears and pains, Communism would soon be talked out of existence.

For including a Bill of Rights, the Instructions has some times been called the Magna Charta of the Philippines. This claim ignores the fact that the Constitution we had adopted in Malolos had contained a complete Bill of Rights. It is not however entirely without justification. The English barons wrested the original Magna Charta from King John more or less by force. While the Malolos Constitution had been an act of the people, the Instructions came from the sovereign power above, in effect wrested through our struggles. Furthermore after having been in force briefly, the Malolos Constitution had lapsed, while the Instructions became the roots of the liberties developed under American guidance over nearly half a century, attaining full bloom in and becoming a permanent part of the Philippine Constitution.

Over and above the ordinary purposes and safeguards of government, the McKinley Instructions also set down certain ethical principles of conduct which were intended to make American rule light and easy to bear.

"In all the forms of government and administrative provisions which they are authorized to prescribe," it warned, "the Commission should bear in mind that the government which they are establishing is designed not for our satisfactions or for the expression of our theoretical views, but for the happiness, peace and prosperity of the people of the Philippine Islands, and the measures adopted should be made to conform to their customs, their habits, and even their prejudices, to the fullest extent consistent with the accomplishment of the indispensable requisites of just and effective government."

Not forgetting that good public relations is indispensable to an effective public administration, especially over an alien people, President McKinley included this directive: "Upon all officers and employees of the United States, both civil and military, should be impressed a sense of duty to observe not merely the material but also the personal and social rights of the people of the Islands, and to treat them with the same courtesy and respect for their personal dignity which the people of the United States are accustomed to require from each other."

The Instructions concluded in a penitential, ethical and prophetic tone which makes one wonder if McKinley did not after all receive that Divine Inspiration which he said had led him to decide on taking all the Philippines. The memorable last sentences of the Instructions read:

A high and sacred . . . obligation rests upon the Government of the United States to give protection for property and life, civil and religious freedom, and wise, firm, and unselfish guidance in the paths of peace and prosperity to all the people of the Philippine Islands. I charge this Commission to labor for the full preformance of this obligation, which concerns the honor and conscience of their country, in the firm hope that through their labors all the inhabitants of the Philippine Islands may come to look back with gratitude to the day when God gave victory to American arms at Manila, and set their land under the sovereignty and protection of the people of the United States.—*William McKinley.*

If McKinley breathed the spirit into and Root gave literary form to the Instructions, Taft gave it life.

In the gloomy atmosphere of Filipino hostility made darker even more by the deep and unreasonable resentments of his fellow Americans, this genial and understanding man from Ohio burst upon the Philippine scene like some overdue sunshine. His many attractive qualities soon endeared him to the Filipinos. At the same time, his evident liking for the Filipinos alienated him from his fellow Americans. But certain that he was doing that which, under the circumstances, best served the welfare, prestige and honor of his country, he seemed content to leave his acts to the verdict of time.

A huge elephant of a man with a full, benevolent face creased around the eyes by the crinkles of good humor and amiable temper, and given a venerable mien by a long, overflowing mustache, Taft was the friendliest American I have ever known. He was a federal judge in Ohio when President McKinley summoned him to become chairman of his Second Philippine Commission. He was therefore no politician. Yet, in Manila, he acted like a past master of the politician's common touch. He was, too, a consummate diplomat.

Nowhere were these qualities more evident than in his attempts to speak Spanish and to make native customs his own. He had been told that Filipinos were the embodiment of hospitality and generosity and that when receiving visitors, they were likely to offer everything they had in their homes. But he was also warned that it was part of good manners for a visitor, when offered hospitable considerations, to say, *Despues de usted,* After you. One day, as a guest in the home of a provincial politician of means and prestige, Taft was determined to show that he knew and accepted Filipino customs. When the host bade him go up the stairs first, he said, "After you." When he was next invited to proceed to the dining room for lunch, he offered, *Despues de usted.* Then, as is the habit of the country, he was invited after lunch to go to bed for the usual *siesta.* With all good intentions, he told his host, "After you."

Taft captured the heart of Manila's upper crust when, at a

banquet, he made a brief speech in Spanish. After he had been elaborately presented, he rose to his full six feet and 250 pounds and, caressing his enormous belly to indicate satisfaction with the repast, began: *"Despues de oir a los oradores eloquentes que me han precedido,* After listening to the eloquent orators who have preceded me, *yo me siento embarazo,* I feel embarrassed." An explosion of shouts and belly-laughs greeted him. He had meant to say *embarazado. Embarazo* happens to mean "pregnancy."

But while Taft was winning resounding applauses and approving laughters, he was also making the McKinley Instructions come to life, thus also capturing the people's hearts. Wrapping up the new American policy in a shining slogan of his minting, "The Philippines for the Filipinos," he proceeded to fill the Government with natives, in many cases replacing Americans. Schools mushroomed. Farms which two revolutions and a war had reduced to mudholes and weeds became once more yellow seas of ripening grains. Roads and bridges which repeated battles had wrecked were repaired and new ones constructed. The country's industries were once more humming. Peace and order were being restored to towns and villages once terror-stricken.

With the U.S. Supreme Court's decision in the Diamond Rings case, to the effect that the ratification of the Peace Treaty made the Philippines an American territory within the meaning of the American tariff act, Philippine-American trade began to gain impetus. Philippine goods were given by the U.S. Congress a 25 percent preference in the American market. Moneys collected as duties on Philippine exports were furthermore returned to the Philippine treasury. The upsurge in Philippine-American trade stimulated by these arrangements soon put the Philippines on the road to prosperity.

And Taft, both as Secretary of War and later as President, continued to work for additional privileges for Philippine exports in the American market until, in 1909, they were admitted free of duty within quota limits so generous that they were never actually reached.

It should be explained at this juncture that the American Constitution and American laws were not held applicable to the Philippines. As a consequence, the President of the United States had administered the Philippines under his war powers until such time as the U.S. Congress enacted special laws for its governance. Pending congressional action, President McKinley, solely as commander-in-chief of the armed forces, had directed the conquest of the Philippines and the establishment of the Military Government. In this capacity, he had constituted and sent to the Islands both the Schurman and Taft Commissions. The famed Instructions had been drafted and implemented under his war powers.

When in 1901 the U.S. Congress legislated on the Philippines for the first time in the so-called Spooner Amendment, it put Philippine natural resources and utility business under lock and key. In the same act, it also confirmed the previous steps taken by the President under his war powers affecting the Philippines and gave him authority thenceforth to direct its administration in his civil capacity. The act thus opened the way for the establishment of Civil Government.

The Spooner Amendment in reality supplemented the far-sighted and generous spirit of the McKinley Instructions by laying the basis of America's enlightened economic policy in the Philippines. It directed that, until Congress could enact a more comprehensive law, "no sale or lease or other disposition of the public lands or the timber thereon or the mining rights therein shall be made." It provided that "no franchise shall be granted which is not approved by the President of the United States, and is not in his judgment clearly necessary for the immediate government of the islands and indispensable for the interest of the people thereof, and which cannot, without great public mischief, be postponed until the establishment of permanent civil government." It added that all franchises so granted "shall terminate one year after the establishment of such permanent civil government."

These clear congressional directives, whose spirit and intent were incorporated in every subsequent organic act enacted by the U.S. Congress for the Philippines, prevented speculative and exploitative activities involving public utilities and natural resources. Together with territorial and political integrity, economic integrity was thus guaranteed to the Filipinos. In carrying out this policy faithfully, however, Taft reaped great unpopularity among his countrymen.

For the understanding and courageous Taft, it was not a continuous path of roses and palm shades. The American Army was not happy over the liquidation of the Military Government. The brass did not relish any diminution of their importance, and the enlisted men reflected their displeasure. Taft's economic and appointment policies also aroused the ire of civilian Americans.

It was not long before the military clubs rocked with laughter evoked by the increasing number of jokes told at Taft's expense. Soon the army camps also rang with ribald songs needling Taft for his friendliness and protective attitude to the Filipinos. One ditty was to the effect that "the Filipino may be a brother to Billy Taft" but he was only a "pock-marked kodiac ladrone" to the men in khaki.

With money to spend and no rank or uniform to lose, the American business men were even more articulate against Taft. An American commercial firm went so far as to publish a Sunday-size advertising in one of the early Manila dailies, also owned and operated by Americans, consisting of a blown-up picture of Governor Taft above the caption: "This is the cause of our leaving the Philippines." As Forbes observes however, "Despite this declaration the firm continued profitably in business in the Islands."

Times had obviously changed. With the military in retreat and the carpetbaggers threatening to pack up, we Filipinos must at last have begun to win in peace what we had failed to win in war. And it worked both ways. The respect and cooperation of the Filipinos, which the Americans had failed to win in war, they were now also winning in peace.

But the American redemption had just begun; 46 more years had to elaspe before it would be fairly completed. And far from being a smooth, continuous progress, it was often forced to a halt or detour by politics, pressure groups and economic panic in America and shortsightedness, demagoguery and personal ambition in the Philippines.

CHAPTER XI

THE REPUBLICAN RECORD

THE REPUBLICAN PARTY certainly started in the Philippines with both feet in its mouth. In a moment of imperialistic lunacy, it went to war against the Spaniards and then against the Filipinos. Had it not been for this temporary derangement, the Republican record might have been almost perfect.

There is no excuse for the crime committed under Republican leadership of conquering and subjugating a people anew just when their own long and costly pursuit of freedom was about to be rewarded with hard-earned success. Yet, except for this false start and the excessive conservatism of its record the Republican Party and its administrations in Washington showed an underlying understanding of the Philippine situation and, through it, of the new twentieth-century international role of America.

The Philippines remained under American sovereignty for 48 years. Of this period, 26 years were under the administration of the Republican Party and 22 years under that of the Democratic Party. The Republican Party was in power when the Spanish-American War broke out in 1898. With Presidents McKinley, Theodore Roosevelt and Taft successively in the White House, it remained in power until 1912. The Democratic Party took over that year and remained in control for eight years, all under President Wilson.

Returning to power in 1920, the Republican Party under Presidents Harding, Coolidge and Hoover governed for 12 years. In 1932, the Democrats won again, electing and re-electing Franklin D. Roosevelt for four precedent-smashing terms. Dying early during his fourth term, Roosevelt was succeeded by his Vice-President, Harry S. Truman, who subsequently won a term of his own, thus staying in the White House until 1952. It was President Truman who proclaimed the Philippines an independent and sovereign republic on July 4, 1946.

Of the organic acts promulgated by the President or enacted by the U. S. Congress for the governance of the Philippines, Republican administrations were responsible for the McKinley Instructions of 1900 and the Philippine Bill of 1902; Democratic administrations, for the Jones Law of 1916 and the Independence Act of 1933.

In administering the Philippines, the G. O. P. proceeded on the basis of a well-thought-out and high-minded philosophy. The Filipinos would be trained for self-government through a program of gradually-expanding autonomy uninfluenced by partisan politics. "We accepted," the Party announced, "the responsibility of the Islands as a duty to civilization and the Filipino people   . The policy of the Republican Party has been and is inspired by the belief that our duty to the Filipino people is a national obligation which should remain entirely free from parties and politics . . . . The largest measure of self-government consistent with their welfare and our duties shall be secured to them by law."

Although the Republican program would logically result in home rule and, in its ultimate consequences, in independence, the Filipinos themselves would eventually have the free choice between remaining within the American hegemony and setting up a sovereign and independent nation. "If the time comes," the G.O.P. platform declared, "when it is evident to Congress that independence would be better for the people of the Philippines with respect to both their domestic concern and their status in the world, and the Filipino people then desire complete independence, the American people will gladly accord it to them."

I must confess that I was one of those who were most impatient with the slow, evolutionary Republican policy. I claimed and I continue to do so today, that, since the time we organized our Republic in Malolos, we had been ready for complete self-government. I even came to believe that the Party was deliberately concealing its scheme of empire behind a feigned sanctimoniousness. Its pose of a stern and conscientious father tenderly nurse-maiding a growing son struck me as un-American.

American children are supposed to learn self-reliance by being exposed early to the hard facts of life. Selling newspapers, shining shoes, attending at gasoline stations and other instructive and paying pursuits toughen them in body and mind. It may be true, nevertheless, that the Republican Party, laboring under an over-conscientious avuncular complex, felt its responsibility so keenly that it was afraid to make a mistake.

In believing that independence was not necessarily the best goal for the Filipinos, the Republicans may also have glimpsed the future trend of world history. The British Commonwealth of Nations was in the making; why not an American Commonwealth of Nations also? There is, I think, a definite advantage to its members and to the peace of the world in a group of associated nations maintaining a common loyalty to a common way of life. Alliances for mutual defense and common prosperity continue today as one of the most effective means of facing a common peril and of thus maintaining world peace. Witness the NATO, WEO, SEATO and others along the same line still being forged in various parts of the world.

Even within the existing unions or alliances of sovereign nations there are movements for closer cooperation, necessarily at some cost to national independence.

"It is all to the good," says Sir Norman Angell, "that the (British) Dominions should have secured their independence, for the government of one people by another is a hateful relationship. The right alternative to that relationship is not for both to be independent. It is for both to form a partnership. But a partnership in which the parties are completely independent is a mere contradiction of terms. Right and freedom, whether of men or of nations, are incapable of defense without surrender of minor freedoms in order to preserve greater ones."

And is not the United Nations, in its logical consequences, an attempt to limit national independence in favor of a supranational world government for the purpose of preserving international peace and security?

I was and I continue to be firm for Philippine independence. Yet, it may be that the Republican program, instead of being ultra-conservative, has been truly progressive and farsighted.

Indeed, with the American world military strategy of "instant massive retaliation" built around the Hydrogen Bomb and guided missiles, the Philippines acquires a new military significance. The crude precursor of this strategy was tried first in China in 1900 during the so-called Boxer Rebellion when America's participation in its quelling was mounted in Manila. The Republican Party itself acknowledged this fact in its 1904 platform saying: "By our possession of the Philippines we were enabled to take prompt and effective action in the relief of the legations at Peking, and a decisive part in preventing the partition and preserving the integrity of China."

In recent years, due to its occupation by allied forces, mainly American, Japan temporarily served a similar purpose, principally in the United Nations police action in Korea. But the Philippines continued to play its 1900 role in the American relief of Indo-China. In spite of Okinawa and Guam, in the years to come—until perhaps the intercontinental guided missiles with atomic warheads is a reality—the Islands will be the most strategically located and most hospitable staging area for the massive retaliation needed to bolster up the free Far East. I am aware that such a service to American global strategy may be the surest way of inviting a Russian hydrogen-bomb attack upon us. But can we deny this assistance to the defense of the free world?

In implementing its policy, the main concern of the Republican Party in the Philippines was the broadening of Filipino participation in the government, accompanied by the basic rights of democratic citizens. The inauguration and subsequent expansion of the essential government services was part and parcel of this program. But in its anxiety to spread American trade and prosperity to the islands, the Party created a serious economic problem which remains today the despair of the young Philippine Republic and which the present Republican Administration in Washington is, I think, consequently obligated to help solve with generosity and statesmanship. This problem is the so-far incurable dependence of the Philippine economy upon the American market.

When the Taft Commission, a Republican creation, began to function as the Philippine Civil Government in 1900, it found that the Military Government had already done much spadework. In Manila and in the nearby provinces, the latter had organized municipal and provincial governments, including courts and schools. Their executive heads known as provincial governors and municipal presidents were elected by the people. But the provincial treasurers and engineers were at first generally American as were many of the school teachers and practically all the principals, supervising teachers, superintendents and the national school officials in Manila. The Military Governor performed the executive and legislative functions of the central government. But he surrounded himself with Filipino advisers, and appointed six Filipinos, including the Chief Justice, as against only three Americans, to the nine-man Supreme Court.

Taking over the Government from the military—the legislative functions on September 1, 1900 and the executive on July 4, 1901—the Commission gradually expanded the Filipinos' participation in accordance with the Taft Instructions. It displaced American provincial treasurers, engineers and judges with Filipinos as quickly as the latter could qualify. It encouraged Filipino teachers to take over the school work, giving them the highest positions warranted by their training and experience. But since English was the language of instruction, the teaching of English, as well as of American History and other basic subjects, was entrusted as much as possible to Americans.

To replace many of the army officers and enlisted men who had been the first to be mustered into the educational work, the Commission, by an act of January 21, 1901, authorized the American general superintendent of public instruction to hire 1,000 American teachers. These soon came on army transports and were immediately deployed all over the country, many of them being the first Americans seen in many a Filipino community.

A companion measure to the law importing American teachers was shortly adopted. In August 1903, the Commission inaugurated a plan of sending promising Filipino students to America to obtain university education. The first batch was composed of 125 bright boys many of whom later became prominent in the government service and the professions, as did many of those who followed them. The plan soon encouraged hundreds of other young men to go on their own to America to study in American universities, many of them for graduate work. In effect, the Philippine school system became an extension of the American school system.

In reorganizing the Supreme Court upon recommendation of the Commission, the President of the United States reduced the original Filipino majority to a minority. The new Court was cut down to only seven members, four Americans and three Filipinos, although the Filipino Chief Justice, Cayetano Arellano, remained in this position. Under the Military Government the Court had included more Filipinos probably because of the shortage of qualified U.S. army officers.

One of the most significant early steps taken to expand the natives' share of the Government was the naming of Filipinos to the Philippine Commission itself. On September 1, 1901, on the first anniversary of the Commission's first legislative session, President McKinley appointed Messrs. Trinidad Pardo de Tavera, Benito Legarda and Jose Luzuriaga as commissioners to participate in the legislative, though not in the executive work of the Commission. This was possibly the President's last direct act on the Philippines. Only four days later, on September 5, he was shot by an assassin and died on September 14. The act marked the maximum extent of Filipino autonomy effected under the McKinley Instructions. The Instructions was soon superseded by the first Philippine enabling act enacted by the U.S. Congress, the Cooper Act of 1902.

The Cooper Act, named after Congressman Henry Allen

Cooper of Wisconsin and more popularly known by the queer title "Philippine Bill of 1902," became the second American document to serve as the supreme law of the Philippines. The debate on the bill in the U.S. Congress let loose a new wave of denunciations against our people. Highly-placed Americans and leading newspapers attacked the bill's new concessions of autonomy by accusing us of being "savages," "pirates," "a race incapable of civilization." Although this was many months after my capture, the wounds of war still rankled on both sides of the Pacific. There were, too, isolated bands of guerrillas that were still operating, and their supposed activities were often distorted by the depredations of plain bandits who used the guise of guerrilla to cloak their crimes

To pacify the opponents of the Bill in the House, Congressman Cooper finally resorted to narrating the life of Jose Rizal and declaiming an English translation of his "My Last Farewell," a heart-rending poem of parting which the Filipino patriot had written in his cell during his last night of life before the Spaniards executed him early the next morning. Calmed by the sad thoughts of the hero and touched to the core by his noble and patriotic hopes for his people, the Congress listened with respect to the speech of Cooper which followed.

"The story and poetry of Rizal did something to the house akin to a miracle," Cooper recalled years later, talking to a Filipino newspaperman. "Your great patriot made congressmen —as well as senators—forget the Philippine insurrection and remember only your people's travails. Rizal kindled a light by which, for the first time, Americans saw the Filipinos fighting for liberty and dignity even as their own forefathers had done in 1776." When, finally, the vote was taken, the bill obtained a commanding majority.

Its passage in the Senate, if less stormy, was also the occasion for repeating some of the war-inspired diatribes against us. But statesmanship finally prevailed, and President Theodore Roosevelt soon affixed his signature to the bill.

The Cooper Law contained the seeds of some of the most important economic and political advances made in the Philippines under the American flag. It limited the sale or lease of agricultural lands, timberlands and mines to small areas for the obvious purpose of preventing speculation and exploitation. It laid down the basis for the solution of the acute agrarian problem, which had been one of the principal causes of Spain's downfall, by authorizing the purchase of the friars' biggest landed estates for resale to the tenants in small parcels. The Act strictly regulated public utility franchises, also with a view to avoiding the creation of vested interests. The Philippine Government was authorized to mint new coins and remint the old Spanish money so as to eliminate the monetary confusion created by the use of both Spanish and American currencies.

The most important concessions to the Filipinos, however, were not effected until 1907 because the Act required as prerequisites the taking and publication of a census and the restoration of peace and order in at least the Christian provinces.

The main concession was the establishment of an elective lower house called the Philippine Assembly. Before this time, the Commission exercised both the executive and legislative functions, and only in the latter work did a Filipino minority, appointed by the American President, participate. The Commission now became the upper house while also continuing as the executive department (cabinet) together with the Governor General.

With the organization of the Assembly, the Filipinos gained complete control of one of the legislative houses. And its Speaker, by official announcement of Taft, then Secretary of War, who returned to Manila to inaugurate the Assembly, became the second highest official of the Government outranked only by the Governor General.

The establishment of the Assembly not only broadened representative democracy in the islands but also gave the Filipinos a decisive voice in legislation. Through the Speaker, who was henceforth regularly consulted by the Governor General, they also won a share in the formulation of higher policies. From the start, the Assembly was aware and proud of the fact that it was the only elective national body, since the members of the

Commission and the Governor General were appointees of the American President. Asserting itself respectfully but firmly under the fine leadership of Speaker Sergio Osmeña, and initiating a series of truly wise and farsighted legislation, the Assembly soon won the respect of Filipinos and Americans alike. Our people successfully hurdled the first substantial trial in self-government to which America subjected them.

The Cooper Act also provided for Filipino representation in the American Congress, thus meeting a long-standing native demand to restore their brief representation in the Cortes in Madrid which the Spaniards had denied. It authorized the two houses of the Legislature to elect from among their members a Resident Commissioner each to sit in the U.S. House of Representatives. Although the Resident Commissioners had no vote and their voice was heard only on matters affecting the Philippines, their presence in the U.S. Capitol gave our people enormous satisfaction. Through them, we expressed our complaints and grievances, hopes and ambitions before America's highest official forum. They voiced opposition against unwarranted legislative intentions as well as worked for the approval of legislation favorable to us. They gave us a sense of participating in the shaping of our destiny. If only as the safety-valve for pent-up Filipino nationalism, our representation in the U.S. Congress was an effective contribution to Philippine-American harmony.

Over and above the concessions in the Cooper Act, the President of the United States continued to increase the number of Filipinos in the Commission. On June 30, 1908, he appointed Rafael Palma as Commissioner without portfolio, the first to come from the new victorious Nacionalista Party which controlled the Philippine Assembly. Then, on July 1 of the same year, he named the first Filipino Commissioner with portfolio. He was Gregorio Araneta, former Secretary of Justice in our Republic in Malolos, whose portfolio was the Department of Finance and Justice. In 1913 President Wilson carried this trend further by giving the majority of the Commission to the Filipinos.

Because the Democratic Party won the presidential election in 1912 for the first time since the taking of the Philippines, the Republican program suffered an interruption which was to last for eight years up to 1920. When the Republicans returned to power—after World War I and the Harrison-Quezon regime under the Jones Law—they found their Philippine work like the china shop after the proverbial bull had done its worst. During the entire 12 years of their new regime they had their hands full of trouble-shooting which was made difficult by the break between Governor General Wood and Senate President Quezon. Their difficulty was complicated by the fact that, in that controversy, the racial and nationalistic considerations invariably nullified the reasonable, the logical and even the legal.

President Warren G. Harding began his administration of the Philippines by sending Major General Leonard Wood and former Governor General W. Cameron Forbes to investigate how the country had fared under the Democratic rule. In the light of the Republicans' 1898-1912 policy, the two investigators found many things wrong and even alarming. In effect they reported to the new President that the Filipinos were suffering from an acute indigestion due to an overdose of home rule and recommended that they be given sufficient time to assimilate it before they be fed again with the solid food of further autonomy.

The unfavorable report and recommendation were bad enough. But when Harding named none other than Wood as the new Governor General, he practically set the stage for a new Philippine-American War. Fortunately this time words sufficed. The freedom of expression is truly wonderful.

An excellent military man, Wood started on the job by trying to consolidate his position in three ways. He restored efficiency and honesty in the public service, tightened supervision from above, and retrieved the powers of the Governor General which had been absorbed by the Legislature and the extra-constitutional bodies which Harrison and the Filipino leaders had created, the Council of State and the Board of Control. Led by Quezon, the political leaders blocked and bucked him at every turn, publicly attacking him through platform and press.

Although Wood was supported by many Filipinos including myself and was eventually upheld by the courts, I believe that his trying ordeal in Manila finally cost him his life. In 1927 he went to America for rest and medical consultation, fully determined to return to his arduous task. Before 1912, he had had two operations for brain tumor and his physicians now advised him to undergo a third. On August 7 he died on the operating table in a Boston hospital, "a martyr," in the words of W. Cameron Forbes, "to his devotion to the public service."

The Council of State and the Board of Control became effective means of undermining the powers of the Governor General. Including among its members the Governor General himself, the Speaker of the House, the President of the Senate and the members of the Cabinet, the Council was both an advisory and an executive body. In many instances, the Legislature conferred upon it, instead of upon the Governor General, the function of executing the laws it enacted. The net result was to take away powers from the Governor General and confer them upon this extra-constitutional body.

The Board of Control was likewise a means by which the Governor General was made to share his heretofore exclusive control over the various commercial corporations owned by the Government. As it was composed only of the Governor General, the Speaker and the Senate President, the Chief Executive was reduced to a mere minority. General Wood soon abolished the Board by executive order while the Council disappeared when its Filipino members resigned en masse as a protest against the new Wood policies in general.

The Wood-Quezon controversy now reached the court. Quezon and his colleagues went to the Philippine Supreme Court to question the legality of Wood's act of abolishing the Board. Basing its decision on the principle of separate powers, the Tribunal upheld Wood. "The Legislature cannot make a law," it declared, "and then take part in its execution." Quezon appealed to the U.S. Supreme Court which confirmed the Philippine Supreme Court's decision, upholding Wood. Inferentially, the Council of State was for the same reason unconstitutional.

To me the basic issue in the Wood-Quezon controversay was simple. Either we accepted American sovereignty or we did not. If we did not, our only logical course was to take up arms as we had done at the turn of the century. But if we did, as we had promised to do when we had taken the oath of American allegiance and had accepted President Roosevelt's amnesty, then we were bound to abide by the laws promulgated for our governance.

The law involved was precisely the Jones Law for whose passage by the U.S. Congress Quezon had claimed credit and on the wings of which he rode to national popularity and power. Quezon claimed that even if the letter of the law might have been violated its spirit was not; but even if both letter and spirit had been violated, the Filipinos still had the right and the duty to reduce the powers of the Governor General extra-constitutionally if not illegally. This was an excellent nationalistic line; perhaps most of the people, influenced by the emotional considerations, applauded him.

But I could not. I felt that it was unsound political education for the people to be trained to live under a regime of laws yet be indoctrinated to violate those laws including the Constitution.

As a nationalistic expediency, Quezon's position was understandable. But in the long pull, it was to my mind wrong. Although his nationalistic stance was also good political posture it was bad constitutional training. It failed to build respect for the supreme law, an indispensable foundation of constitutional government. This proved true under the Constitution we ourselves later framed when Quezon, as President of the Commonwealth, engineered its radical amendment primarily to feather his nest. Although he died before he could carry out his plan, his attempt to insure himself the title of First President of the Republic by constitutional amendment further retarded the development of sound Philippine constitutionalism.

But, it should be added, the Wood-Quezon quarrel was not

without its blessing. Wood and those who supported him, whether Americans or Filipinos, afforded our people the opposite education. The public discussion of the issue of whether or not the Harrison regime had violated the Jones Law was itself a valuable practical lesson in constitutionalism. When the Philippine and American supreme courts finally repudiated Quezon's stand and upheld Wood's, many of those who had sided with the Filipino leader could not have missed the point. An admirable nationalistic leader, Quezon was not, for this very reason, conditioned to be a good constitutional president.

After Wood, the Republican Administration sent other Governors General—Henry L. Stimson, Dwight Davis and Theodore Roosevelt, Jr. They continued Wood's policies, although they managed through compromises to reestablish harmonious Philippine-American relations. Stimson, for instance, restored the Council of State. Although he enlarged its membership by inviting the majority floorleaders, in addition to the presiding officers of both legislative chambers, he deprived it of its former share of executive authority and limited it to a strictly advisory role. Like Stimson, Davis and Roosevelt merely marked time while the Filipinos went through a less conspicuous and less embarrassing period of adjusting themselves to Republican policies.

It must have been most distressing to the Republicans that even before the Democrats could fully take over the Washington administration in 1932 they rushed the first Philippine independence bill through Congress. They must, however, have found some consolation in the fact that, in the great Democratic haste, the bill still overtook Republican President Herbert Hoover in the White House. For, even if he could not turn back the agrarian tide behind the measure, he gained an opportunity to read a sermon to the Democrats.

In a long, blistering veto message dated January 13, 1933, Hoover pointed out that "the United States has a triple responsibility . responsibility to the Filipino people, responsibility to the American people and responsibility to the world at large." He declared that farm relief as the motivation of the bill was unworthy for it "does not fulfill the idealism with which this task in human liberation was undertaken."

He added that the expected relief to U.S. agriculture was more fanciful than real, since Philippine exports to America are but a small fraction of American total consumption. The expected boon of liberty to the Filipinos would soon be lost in a chaotic world, he said, because they would be deprived of the American market and they are promised no protection except through neutralization which could not possibly materialize if America maintained Philippine military bases as indicated in the bill.

The veto concluded as follows:

> We are here dealing with one of the most precious rights of man—national independence interpreted as separate nationality. It is the national independence of thirteen million human beings. We have here a specific duty. The ideals under which we undertook this responsibility, our own national instincts and our institutions which we have implanted on these islands breathe with these desires. It is a goal not to be reached by yielding to selfish interests, to resentments or to abstractions, but with full recognition of our responsibilities and all their implications and all the forces which would destroy the boon we seek to confer and the dangers to our own freedom from entanglements which our actions may bring. Neither our successors nor history will discharge us of responsibility for actions which diminish the liberty we seek to confer nor for dangers which we create for ourselves as a consequence of our acts.

But the Great Depression's Democratic Congress was determined. It overrode President Hoover's veto by votes of 274-94 in the house and 66-26 in the senate. When the law was in turn rejected in Manila at the instance of Quezon, the U.S. Congress quickly re-enacted it. Perhaps there was in the situation a certain historic justice which sharpened the sense of responsibility of the Republican Administration. For the economic situation, which finally became the impelling motive behind the law, had developed more under Republican than Democratic auspices.

The economic situation revolved around the free trade. It was a Republican Congress which, following the U.S. Supreme Court's decision on the Diamond Rings case in 1901, started the movement that finally resulted in the establishment of complete free trade between America and the Philippines.

A returning American soldier had brought with him fourteen diamond rings on which he had refused to pay the American duty on the ground that, by force of the Treaty of Paris, the Philippines had ceased to be a foreign territory within the meaning of the American tariff act. The Supreme Court upheld his contention. This virtually nullified the ten-year most-favored nation privilege accorded Spain under the Treaty and immediately forced Congress to address itself to the subject of Philippine trade. This led to the enactment of a series of acts giving certain preferences to Philippine exports.

Prodded by the Philippine Commission, the Congress was for giving Philippine exports a preference of 50 percent at first but reduced it to only 25 percent when the American sugar and tobacco interests vehemently protested. This rate lasted until 1909 when the ten-year most-favored nation Spanish privilege expired. That year, in the general tariff revision embodied in the Payne-Aldrich Law, Congress established virtual Philippine-American free trade by setting up liberal quotas for Philippine exports to America, except rice, which would be free of duty. American goods had, of course, been entering the Philippines duty-free even before the Diamond Rings decision.

This limited free trade—which in effect was complete since current Philippine exports were well within the quota figures—was not unopposed in the Philippines. The all-Filipino Assembly passed a resolution protesting the measure on two grounds; namely, that "the duty-free exchange of products between the United States and the Philippines in the long run would be highly prejudicial to the economic interests of the Filipino people and would create a situation which might delay the obtaining of their independence." Spelled out, this meant that the Assembly wished to collect duties on American goods in order to replenish the public treasury and feared that an increasing dependence of Philippine exports on the American market would mean an additional link to the chain binding the islands to the United States.

But Governor General Forbes in Manila and President Taft in Washington, in the paternalistic Republican tradition, decided that they knew better what was good for the Philippines than the Filipinos themselves and gave the go-signal to the Congress. In 1913, the Wilson administration abolished the quotas and established complete free trade. Both the 1909 and 1913 acts gave unprecedented impetus to the development of Philippine export industries, especially sugar, coconut, tobacco and hemp.

But the free trade made Philippine economy a mere adjunct of American economy. By 1934, when the Independence Law was enacted, 65 percent of Philippine imports came from the United States while 84 percent of Philippine exports went to America. The Philippine exports, furthermore, were produced by only a few industries. Stimulated or created by the free trade, they supplied raw materials to American industries and thus depended on the American market almost entirely. In 1934, for instance, 66 percent of all copra production, all but 9,000 of the 144,187 long tons of coconut oil output, and nearly all of the 1,500,000 long tons of sugar the Islands exported were sold in America.

The almost complete dependence of Philippine economy upon America becomes even more startling when it is remembered that the Philippine coconut industry employed about 4,000,000 men, produced 17 percent of all Philippine exports and paid about 15 percent of real estate taxes; that the sugar industry supported 2,000,000 families, accounted for 60 percent of the government's total income, 30 percent of the total national income, and 63 percent of the entire Philippine export, furnished the bulk of the freight business of public carriers, and incurred almost 50 percent of all domestic bank loans. Add hemp and cordage and tobacco products and their proportionally similar dependence on the U.S. market and importance in the Philippine economy, and the picture is complete.

The Philippine export trade, President Grayson Kirk of Columbia University stated then, was directly developed by the free trade

"solely for the American market, and its continued existence depends largely upon its ability to maintain a relatively free access to that market. Philippine export to America was from 85 to 90 percent of the total Philippine export, yet the American export to the Philippines was less than 3 percent of the total American export. Thus the scrapping of the free trade, which was the price of independence, meant very little to America but everything to the Philippines.

"It is indeed paradoxical, in all probability tragically so," Dr. Kirk added, "that, although the American government has constantly designed its political policies so as to confer upon the islands an ever-widening sphere of autonomy, it has, at the same time, through the operation of free trade, deliberately drawn them into an ever closer integration with the American economic system."

This economic anomaly persists in about the same form today, a decade after the restoration of the Republic of the Philippines. Tackled only in a makeshift manner by the Democratic Roosevelt and Truman administrations in Washington and the Roxas and Quirino governments in Manila, it has come back to roost on the Eisenhower and Garcia administrations. Being mainly a Republican creation, it should, however, be susceptible to a Republican solution.

CHAPTER XII

THE DEMOCRATIC PARTY AND THE PHILIPPINES

IN A FREE SOCIETY larger than a Greek city-state unanimity is improbable. The American people naturally disagreed on what policy to follow in the Philippines and thus converted the fate of the Filipinos into a political issue. Being in power when our country came under the American flag, the Republican Party became known as the party of imperialism. The Democratic Party, taking the opposite view, championed Philippine independence. Once the battle was joined, the Philippine issue lasted as an American political football in and out of season during half a century.

The Democratic Party's Philippine record, if it proved anything, proved that a political party often serves the nation better when it is out of power than when it is in. Out of power, the Party was the great defender of the American Constitution and American Civilization as well as the champion, if sometimes scornfully, of a weak and struggling race. Its righteous and sanctimonious fulminations shamed the American conscience and encouraged the Filipinos to demand freedom. In power, the Party assumed a different guise. It put its humanitarian mantle in mothballs and donned the hood of expediency.

Personally I am deeply grateful for the vocal sympathy of the Democratic Party before and during the fateful Philippine-American War. It must have taken courage to spurn the apparently popular approval of McKinley's Philippine policy, and greater courage still to plead the justice of our cause even after the outbreak of hostilities. It is nevertheless my opinion that, with respect to the Philippines, the Democratic Party led off with the wrong foot.

It can perhaps even be said that William Jennings Bryan put

161

his foot in his mouth when he rushed to Washington to urge
Democratic senators to save the Treaty of Paris from defeat.

All indications had shown that the administration could not
muster the two-thirds vote required for ratification. Even after
the start of the war in the Philippines, a survey by Senator Lodge
showed that "the line of opposition stood absolutely firm." "I
thought," he regretfully reported, "the news from Manila would
have shattered it, but it did not." Two votes were still lacking to
complete the required two-thirds. It was shortly before the war's
outbreak that Mr. Bryan, who had been the unsuccessful Democratic standard-bearer in 1896 and expected to be his Party's
candidate for President in 1900 again, succumbed to a brain-
storm.

The Democratic leader thought that if the Treaty were ratified,
the issue of imperialism against the Republican Party would be
preserved as in a deep-freeze. And if we Filipinos were to go to
war against America as a result of the ratification, an eventuality
of which he was fatalistically certain, the issue would be more
than preserved. It would also be, as he said, paying twenty
million (the treaty provided for the payment of this sum to
Spain) for a revolution, a stupidity more than sufficient to defeat
any party.

Walter Millis describes the curious situation succinctly thus:
"Mr. Bryan himself had been among the first to see the useful-
ness of the anti-imperialistic issue, and the Bryanite wing in the
Senate was strong enough to have defeated the treaty. But Mr.
Bryan now proceeded to undertake a vigorous lobby among his
surprised supporters in the Senate to induce them to give their
votes for ratification. He told them that the Democratic Party
could not hope to win the next Presidential election upon the
silver issue, and that they must therefore preserve the issue of
imperialism for use in 1900. To do this, he argued, it was necessary that the treaty be ratified, so that we should be in possession
of the islands and the troubles they promised to bring with them
when the election came around."

Bryan's whirlwind lobby netted three votes—two to complete

Some of Aguinaldo's ranking officers are in this group. Although they themselves were well-educated and intelligent, they usually had no military training and no experience in commanding big bodies of men.

Gen. Pio del Pilar, one of Aguinaldo's more prominent general officers. He was a brother of Gen. Gregorio del Pilar, the greatest Filipino hero of the Philippine-American War.

the necessary two-thirds, and one to spare. But if the Administration had managed to put the treaty through because of Bryan, Bryan did not win the 1900 election in spite of imperialism. He lost it, as he had himself feared, on the silver issue.

In the 1900 presidential campaign, the two major American parties came before the people for the first time to submit to their verdict at the polls their respective records on the Philippines.

The Republican Party naturally justified in its platform what it had already done. "No other course was possible," it declared, "than to destroy Spain's sovereignty throughout the West Indies and in the Philippine Islands. That course created our responsibility before the world and with the unorganized population whom our intervention had freed from Spain, to provide for the maintenance of law and order, and for the establishment of good government, and for the performance of international obligations. " The Republican platform writers conveniently ignored the fact, which was nothing less than an earth-shaking event in all Asia, that we had established the first Republic in all the East in Malolos, Bulacan. But parties must, of course, be partisan.

Having waited for nearly two years to unleash its secret weapon, the Democratic Party now hit the Republicans with all the force and potency of the Republican error of forcing the Philippine-American war. "We condemn and denounce the Philippine policy of the present administration," its platform shouted. "It had involved the Republic in unnecessary war, sacrificed the lives of many of our noblest sons and placed the United States, previously known and applauded throughout the world as the champion of freedom, in the false and un-American position of crushing with military force the efforts of our former allies to achieve liberty and self-government."

We could not but warmly applaud this declaration. The Philippine program it outlined also pleased us. "We favor," it stated, "an immediate declaration of the nation's purpose to give to the Filipinos, first, a stable government; second, independence; and, third, protection from outside interference, such as has been given for nearly a century to the Republics of Central and South America."

The Party concluded its Philippine plank with a wall-eyed declaration which, keynoting the campaign, led to inevitable defeat: "The importance of other questions now pending before the American people is in no wise diminished, and the Democratic Party takes no backward step from its position on them; but the burning issue of Imperialism growing out of the Spanish war involves the very existence of the Republic and the destruction of our free institutions. We regard it as the paramount issue of the campaign."

Most important of the "other questions" was the issue of free silver. A natural-born orator, Bryan had won the 1896 Democratic presidential nomination by swaying the convention delegates with his famous "Cross of Gold" oration. The campaign had then been fought with Bryan and his party advocating the free and unlimited coinage of silver as a remedy to the ills of the workers and farmers. McKinley, the Republican candidate, had won the election largely because the American people had refused to accept a dangerous and unsound currency system. In 1900, to avert another disaster, the Eastern and gold Democrats tried to persuade Bryan to drop the ill-starred free silver issue. But he offered a compromise and prevailed: free silver would remain in the platform but imperialism would be "the paramount issue."

Imperialism had cut across party lines. Senators Hoar and Bacon, its most vocal enemies, were Republicans as were many others. With the imperialism fever subsiding fast, the Democratic Party might have been able to rally around itself, in such overwhelming numbers as to win the election, the Republicans and independents eager to atone for a mistake already demonstratedly expensive in blood and gold and gnawing at the national conscience. But when the showdown came, the free silver issue was paramount in the minds of American voters. While the fate of an alien race half way around the world could cause only a dull pang of conscience, the fate of America's currency—and of every American's pocketbook—was an immediate and urgent personal concern of all. The Americans voted for gold and the Republican Party.

Another confusion lurked in the Democratic plank, one which forever afterward conditioned Democracy's handling of the Philippines.

"The Filipinos," it announced, "cannot be citizens without endangering our civilization . . . and as we are not willing to surrender our civilization . . we favor   independence . . ." This nose-pinching attitude was even more emphatic in the pronouncements of the Party in the 1904 presidential campaign. "Whenever," its platform declared, "there may exist a people incapable of being governed under American laws, in consonance with the American Constitution, the territory of that people ought not to be part of the American domain. We insist that we ought to .   set the Filipino people upon their feet free and independent to work out their own destiny."

Considering the Filipinos as a sort of second class humanity, how could the Democratic Party promote their welfare with sincerity? It could not. In consequence, when the Party took over the Washington administration in 1912-1920 and again in 1932-1952, its performance on the Philippines was inconsistent, confused and unconscionable.

Fourteen years of American rule and partial Filipino self-government had elapsed when the Democratic Party came to power in 1912. During at least 10 of those years we had had a stable government. In three presidential elections, including that year's, the Party had advocated Philippine independence preceded by a stable government. But during its own administration of eight years under Woodrow Wilson it merely broadened Filipino self-government, then extended its promise of independence like an unpaid account. To be true to its promises the democratic administration should have widened Philippine autonomy during its first four years of power and granted independence during its second term.

The Clarke Amendment would have been a faithful fulfillment of Democratic promises. Introduced by the Senator from

Arkansas, it provided for Philippine independence in not less than two and not more than four years after its enactment. It was believed to have won the support of President Wilson after it had been approved in the Senate with the help of the deciding vote of Vice-President Marshall. In the house where it was put to a vote on May 2, 1916, exactly eighteen years and one day after the Battle of Manila Bay, it was lost because twenty-eight Democrats bolted to vote with the Republicans.

"These bolting members," Francis Burton Harrison reported later, "were virtually all members of the Roman Catholic Faith, and it is understood that their attitude was the result of intervention by Cardinal James Gibbons of Baltimore, acting, it is supposed, at the instigation of the ecclesiastical authorities in the Philippines."

Had the Clarke Amendment been approved, Philippine independence would have taken place between 1918 and 1920, after only about two decades of American tutelage. Our Republic would have emerged shortly after World War I and would have had two decades of life before World War II. Earlier Philippine independence might have meant earlier freedom for Indonesia, India, Pakistan, Burma, Ceylon and others. The rise of Eastern democracies might have made the rise of anti-democratic ideologies—Fascism, Nazism, and Communism—more obviously and shockingly anachronistic, evoking earlier countermeasures to deter their rambunctious and cancerous growth. World history might have veered away from World War II.

But the Democratic Administration enacted only the Jones Act of 1916. True, the law completely "Filipinized" the upper house of the Legislature, like the lower house which was already elective and all Filipino, and created a cabinet composed of Filipinos save the Secretary of the Department of Instruction. It had the additional merit of embodying in its preamble the declaration that "it is and has always been the purpose of the people of the United States to withdraw their sovereignty over the Philippine Islands and to recognize their independence as soon as a stable government can be established therein."

This was the first promise of independence made by the

American Government. But it also raised the issue of "stable government," a condition in political evolution as hard to determine as the question of which is first, the egg or the chicken. "The basis is thus laid for a quarrel of increasing intensity," pointed out Harrison, "permitting as it does the free expression of opinion upon the capacity, character, and ability of a whole race of people."

The Jones Law was certainly far from equating with Democratic Party promises. It embodied only the very minimum concession which the Wilson Administration had to make to save its face. Yet, just because it happened to have been enacted while Manuel L. Quezon was the senior Philippine Resident Commissioner in the American Congress, the Filipino people acclaimed him as a national idol. He was soon able to replace Sergio Osmeña, the House Speaker, as head of the ruling party and the acknowledged leader of the Filipinos. But heroes are indeed often the products of circumstances rather than the shapers of them.

Then, when the Law was implemented in Manila by the team of Quezon and Harrison, it made the people temporarily happy but also gave them an entirely wrong training in constitutionalism. The latter's repercussions gave a wrong direction to the subsequent constitutional development of the Philippines.

Harrison had been a congressman from New York, a ranking member of the Committee on Ways and Means. He and Resident Commissioner Quezon, having many characteristics in common, had struck off an intimate and loyal friendship. When President Wilson looked around for a new Governor General to send to Manila and consulted Quezon, the latter immediately recommended his congressional crony. Quezon himself, after the passage of the Jones Act, returned to the Philippines, ran for the new Senate and became its President.

The story of the Philippines during the next four years was largely the story of the two friends' meeting of minds.

The key to Harrison's performance is his postmortem statement that "the spirit as well as the letter of the Jones Act was to turn over to the Filipinos most of the powers of government of their own internal affairs." That to Quezon's own performance was in his declarations, "Our aim is to make the Governor General a figurehead," and "A government run like hell by Filipinos is better than a government run like heaven by Americans." These sentiments endeared the two men to the people but also set them on the wrong constitutional path.

I hasten to state that we Filipinos had been ready to run our own government for a long, long time. I therefore always fully approved the turning over to us of the widest governmental powers including independence at the earliest possible time.

If, as General Wood and Governor Forbes subsequently reported to President Harding, during the Harrison regime "the efficiency of the public services has fallen off, and they are now relatively inefficient, due to lack of inspection and the too rapid transfer of control to officials who have not had the necessary time for proper training," then such transfer was more than justifiable. The only way to learn is to try and learn.

Harding's investigators said about as much. "We feel that the lack of success in certain departments should not be considered as proof of essential incapacity on the part of the Filipinos," they explained, "but rather as indicating lack of experience and opportunity, and especially lack of inspection." The "lack of inspection" was an attempt to bolster up their recommendation that the Governor General be given "authority commensurate with his responsibility." What the Filipinos needed most was experience and opportunity, and these Harrison gave to them.

I dare say that Harrison, unlike his superiors in Washington, was bent on making good the promises of his Party to the fullest measure. Against that, we Filipinos could have no complaint. I also recognize that Quezon's contribution in subverting the Jones Act and absorbing for the Filipinos some of the powers of the American Governor General constituted brilliant nationalistic leadership.

But the same leadership, when subsequently exercised under the Constitution which the Filipinos had themselves drafted, produced a government of men and not of laws. It was this leadership, together with the wrong constitutional training of the people under the Jones Law, that led to the questionable amendment of the Philippine Constitution in 1940. As the late Professor J. Ralston Hayden of the University of Michigan, a former Philippine Vice-Governor, pointed out, the amendment was primarily to enable Quezon to become the first President of the Philippine Republic in 1946.

The Constitution has since suffered many other amendments. Such a treatment has prevented the people from building a tradition of reverence and respect for it and of regarding it, in the manner the British and the Americans regard theirs, as the supreme law whose relative permanence guarantees the government's stability. On the contrary, it is seldom remembered except in connection with some further changes. The observance of its anniversary invariably evokes addresses which are notable mainly for vying with each other in advocating further radical constitutional amendments.

More as a face-saving gesture than as a serious and conscientious effort to fulfill the Democratic pledge, President Wilson for the last time addressed himself to the Philippine question just before leaving the White House. In December 1920, when the Republicans had won control of the Congress and he himself was soon to give way to President Harding, he told the Congress in his annual message, ". . . it is now our liberty and our duty to keep our promise to the people of the Islands by granting them the independence which they so honorably covet."

Prophetic was the error of a news editor in Manila, which nearly cost him his job, of burying the *Associated Press* report on the message deep inside his paper. For nothing came out of the gesture. "Naturally," President Grayson Kirk of Columbia University concludes his survey of the Wilson Administration, "no congressional action was forthcoming, and the Democratic administration completed its eight years of office without carrying into execution the long-standing pledge of the Party."

Wilson, of course, was not Bryan. An outstanding political scientist and scholar, he did not, I suspect, quite relish the promise his Party had made long before he entered politics. As a university professor unshackled by political expediency and exercising full academic freedom, he had declared in a lecture at Columbia University that self-government can be acquired only through practice over a long period of time.

"Self-government is not a thing that can be given to any people," he had said, "because it is a form of character and not a form of constitution. . . . Only a long apprenticeship of obedience can secure them the precious possession, a thing no more to be bought than given. . . . Having ourselves gained self-government by a definite process which can have no substitute, let us put the people dependent upon us in the right way to gain it also."

If the performance of the Democratic Party in 1912-1920 fell far short of its promises, in 1932, when it returned to Washington after twelve more years of Republican control, it completely reversed its record. The new Democratic-controlled Congress, as soon as organized, rushed a Philippine independence bill through. Even after President Hoover had vetoed the bill, the Congress passed it over his veto. Even after the Philippine Legislature had rejected it in turn, the U.S. Congress reenacted it, so determined it was this time to set the Filipinos adrift.

Known as the Hare-Hawes-Cutting Law, the original independence act authorized the Filipinos to frame a Constitution and set up a transitional government of ten years called the Commonwealth, upon the termination of which the Philippines would be proclaimed a free and sovereign Republic. But the active motive behind the law was the desire of powerful sectors of U.S. agricultural interests to terminate the Philippine-American free trade. Confused and panic-stricken by the Great Depression, then at its worst, the American dairy, sugar and cotton farmers and cordage and tobacco manufacturers, together with their great organizations and elaborate lobbies, came to believe that the competition of duty-free Philippine exports to America was responsible, at least partly, for their plight.

And they could point out superficial evidences. Since money was scarce, many American housewives switched from creamery butter to oleomargarine made from coconut oil. The dairy farmers, thus deprived of a great part of their domestic market, blamed the "coconut cow" and the Philippines. Some such rationalizations created corresponding nightmares for other harassed American farm interests affected by the other duty-free Philippine exports. The farm bloc in Congress eventually translated the fear of these interests into the Hare-Hawes-Cutting Bill, and the Congress promptly approved it. An act providing for Philippine independence, it was in effect a relief measure intended to mitigate the acute economic crisis, at least for American farmers.

President Hoover swiftly vetoed the bill. He accompanied his veto with a message to the Congress which was at once a lecture on national and international responsibility and an updated definition of the Republican Party's Philippine policy. But, by overwhelming votes in both houses, the Democratic Congress as quickly overrode his veto. In this finally successful attempt to place the Philippines outside of the American political and economic orbit, the winning votes in the two houses were practically non-partisan. With the Democrats lined up Republican Senators and Congressmen from the so-called farm belt.

In the Philippines, the battle lines followed different motives and strategies.

Even before Senator Osmeña and Speaker Roxas, who had gone to Washington to help push the act through Congress, came home with it, Senate-President Quezon had announced his opposition and begun the campaign to reject it. He alleged four objections; namely, the "unfair trade provisions," the "offensive immigration restrictions," the "indefinite powers of the U.S. High Commissioner," and retention by America of military and naval reservations and bases. It was the last which he most emphasized, declaring that with portions of the Philippine territory retained by the United States, independence would be nothing but a joke.

There were also those who felt that Quezon's decision to reject the Act was dictated by personal considerations. He himself had gained national acclaim to the extent of overshadowing his chief, Sergio Osmeña, by bringing home the Jones Law. Now, he feared that the team of Osmeña and Roxas, having brought home no less than the Independence Act, would turn the table on him and completely eclipse him in the national esteem.

In any event Quezon, who knew American politics far more than any of his colleagues, having sat for years in the U.S. Congress, must have been certain of the depression-born American determination to liberate the Philippines. Having had the Legislature reject the Act, he rushed to America to obtain a substitute measure. As he had expected, the Congress was receptive. What is more, Hoover had been succeeded by President Franklin D. Roosevelt, who shared the temper of his Congress and was cooperative. The result was the Tydings-McDuffie Law. It was exactly the Hare-Hawes-Cutting Act re-enacted, save the modification of the provision on military bases which made the matter subject to future negotiations. The new law was accepted in the Philippines. Thus it was finally Quezon who came home with the Independence Act to a new national acclaim. No one, but no one, was more clever than Quezon.

Yet even during his short remaining lifetime, he had to eat his words.

Together with General MacArthur, Quezon had believed that the Philippines could defend itself alone against aggression, including Japanese. This was his justification for his opposition to U.S. bases in the Philippines. The Pacific War proved the contrary, and World War II made patent the fact that even the world's most powerful nations must seek alliances or perish. Even as the war raged, and the Philippines was occupied by Japan and the Commonwealth Government under Quezon was in exile in Washington, the U.S. Congress passed a resolution authorizing American military, naval and air bases in the Islands. Quezon accepted it.

Such is the Democratic Party's record up to the war. It is a record obviously dictated more by American conditions and wishes than the needs and desires of the Filipinos themselves. It is without intimation of the immediate American future, especially the economic and military power and the moral stature that would inevitably invest it with world responsibility and leadership. It is characterized by a day-to-dayness devoid of that vision and imagination which gave unity and consistency to the Republican record. And it lacked the broad conception and deep humanitarianism which were the shining jewels of McKinley's Instructions.

In justice to the Democrats, it should be stated that Wilson, while only superficially interested in the Philippines, showed deep understanding and concern of world affairs. The first American President to play the role of world leader, he was, however, frustrated in this attempt by the rejection in the U.S. Senate, led by none other than Henry Cabot Lodge, of American membership in the League of Nations. It was not until Franklin D. Roosevelt was catapulted to the same role by World War II that courageous and cosmopolitan American world leadership became an effective reality.

Whatever was the motivation behind the Democratic sponsorship of Philippine Independence and the Independence Act, however, we Filipinos did not much care. We desired freedom and sovereignty, the Democratic Party gave us effective support, so we justly regarded the Party as our sponsor and champion. The end we sought was everything to us; the motives of the Democratic Party were secondary. The Party's Philippine record after World War II, when America had emerged as the world's leader nation, was however a decided improvement.

But before we Filipinos could know and savor the new postwar Democratic policy, which the present Republican administration not only continued but also improved upon in many ways, we went through the terrible ordeal of war and enemy occupation. Even the independence which was to be placed in our hands in a planned and orderly manner came at the most inauspicious time, economically and psychologically. But militarily, it was perhaps the best hour. The concept of war and peace had changed; the United Nations had been established, and the United States had at last found and accepted her destiny as the world's peace-maker.

CHAPTER XIII

WAR, LIBERATION AND INDEPENDENCE

Most of the decisions of democracy are compromises. They are forged in debate and dissent, every contention and every argument leaving some mark of its impact. Because the fact is often only gradually discovered through many-sided and prolonged disquisitions and inquiries, no leader of government or of opinion is ever in possession of the complete and ultimate truth nor certain of being finally right. And because no government administration is perpetually in power, no public policy is ever permanent.

Philippine independence is a compromise. In its final form it is a synthesis of Filipino nationalism, Democratic pragmatism and Republican idealism, together with all the various human frailties and wisdom, machinations and pressures, defeats and triumphs which make up public opinion. It embodies, even if belatedly, the ideal of the Filipinos of an independent nationality. It fulfills, if also tardily, the American independence promises from Dewey's to the Democrats'. And it includes some of the important ideas of the Republicans such as a long period of preparation and an opportunity for the Filipinos to decide for themselves whether to remain in association with America or go it alone.

Even the post-independence relations between the Philippines and America can be said to be a compromise. When we ourselves first thought of the kind of relationship we might have with America, we envisioned U.S. protection, at least at the start. Quezon, however, appeared at first to have considered the military problem of little importance. But in the 1930's when independence seemed imminent, he maintained with General MacArthur that the country could be prepared to resist foreign aggression successfully and alone. In this belief, he opposed the original American plan to keep and maintain military bases in the islands. It took defeat and Japanese occupation to convince him that it was wise after all not only to allow American bases but also to enter into a military alliance with the United States.

The Democrats, apparently coinciding with our position, always advocated American protection of an independent Philippines. And one of the chief worries of Republican administrations was the safety of the country once it would be cut off from America. The present military alliance between the United States and the Philippines seems to satisfy all these various confluent anxieties. It apparently dovetails, furthermore, with the general American world strategy calculated to meet all possible eventualities in a hot or cold war against Communism. The provision of the Independence Act requesting the U.S. President to negotiate with foreign powers a treaty for the perpetual neutralization of the Philippines was abandoned as impractical after the war.

The final Independence Law was approved March 24, 1934. It authorized the Filipinos to write a Constitution for a transitional Commonwealth Government of ten years, upon the termination of which the Philippines would be proclaimed free and independent. The Law was subject to acceptance by the Philippines; the Constitution, to the approval of the President of the United States and the Filipino people in a plebiscite.

"If a majority of the votes cast shall be for the constitution," the act provided, "such vote shall be deemed an expression of the will of the people of the Philippine Islands in favor of Philippine independence." This met the Republican insistence that the Filipinos should have the opportunity to decide their fate, although the Party had favored the taking of such a vote after the Commonwealth period and not before.

Being at the same time an agricultural relief measure, the provisions of the law on Philippine-American trade were most detailed. Effective on the inauguration of the Commonwealth Government, it placed the principal Philippine exports to America on a quota basis—50,000 long tons for refined sugar, 800,000 long tons for unrefined sugar, 200,000 long tons for coconut oil, 3,000,000 pounds for cordage, twine and yarn.

Within these quotas, Philippine articles would enter the American market free of tariff duty; quantities in excess would pay the full duty. Upon the proclamation of independence, all Philippine exports to the United States would pay the full American duty.

At the same time, the law provided for the collection by the Philippines of export tax whose proceeds would be set aside for the payment of the country's bonded indebtedness. Beginning on the sixth year of the Commonwealth, it would be 5 percent of the corresponding American duty and would increase by 5 percent yearly up to 25 percent on the ninth year. The Philippines "shall place all funds received from such export taxes in a sinking fund, and such funds shall, in addition to other moneys available for that purpose, be applied solely to the payment of the principal and interest on the bonded indebtedness of the Philippine Islands, its Provinces and Municipalities, and instrumentalities, until such indebtedness has been fully discharged."

The concern of the U.S. Congress over the public debt was understandable; the bonds were guaranteed by the American Government and the holders were, in the main, Americans.

The ten-year pre-independence period was to be utilized by the Philippines for final preparations, mainly military and economic. The military job was entrusted to General MacArthur who forthwith instituted a program to build a citizen army like that of Switzerland. His plan called for the training of 100,000 young men each year so that in ten years the trained manpower would be 1,000,000. With this defensive force, MacArthur believed, an invader would need a force about ten times bigger in order to win. And, he said, no power would care to conquer the Philippines at such a tremendous cost. It would not pay.*

To advise on the economic preparations, a National Economic Council was organized with Manuel Roxas as chairman. It recommended crop diversification, electrification, easier credit, and an increasing government participation in business, especially in the distributive and manufacturing phases. The main objectives of these activities were to wrest for the Filipinos a

* For the historical support of MacArthur's theory, see Chapter 6.

greater portion of the retail and wholesale trade, which was controlled by foreigners, and to develop the economy from agricultural to industrial.

There was, however, no compulsion created, outside of the quotas and scheduled export tax, for the sugar, coconut and other export industries to adjust themselves to the impending loss of the American market. They were not stimulated or encouraged to diversify into other industries or markets or to reduce production costs so as to be able to hurdle the U.S. tariff wall.

When the Constitution had been approved by President Roosevelt and accepted by the Filipinos and the election of the first President and other officials scheduled, I yielded to the pressure of my friends to run for President against Quezon and Bishop Gregorio Aglipay, head of the Philippine Independent Church. But not without considerable reluctance. Having scrupulously kept out of politics since my capture by the Americans and being already 66 years old, I lacked the well-knit and well-financed organization and perhaps the youthful vigor which the occasion demanded.

But my people were insistent. They pointed out that, while the independence of which the Commonwealth was to be the immediate prelude had been won by the combined work of Americans and Filipinos, our war and diplomacy with both Spain and the United States had really been the decisive factors. In their opinion, the liquidation of Spanish imperialism in the Philippines had been at least as much our work as that of the United States. In addition, they claimed, we not only resisted the upsurge of American imperialism until it disillusioned the American people, but our resistance also hastened the birth of the subsequent American policy of altruism.

If this is the case, they concluded, the McKinley Instructions and the Philippine Bill of 1902 and both the Jones Law and the Tydings-McDuffie Act, on which Quezon had ridden to power and popularity, were really the fruits of the seeds we had planted with out bayonets and watered with our blood.

While I am not one to regard public office as a reward for

past services however invaluable, I allowed myself to be per-
suaded on the additional consideration that, in my opinion,
Quezon would not make a good constitutional president.

This Spanish-Filipino politician had been in the public service
since the tender age of 27. Although his highest legitimate salary
had never at any time exceeded 12,000 pesos a year, he had
managed to amass considerable wealth. It was evident that his
attitude to public office was not one of service and sacrifice. And,
indeed, his continuous exercise of power since 1922, when he
replaced Osmeña as the highest Filipino leader, had apparently
given him a prescriptive attitude not only to the particular office
he held but also to the all-powerful Nacionalista Party as well as
to the entire Legislative Department which he headed.

This possessive attitude was even more evident years later
during the war in Washington. By operation of the amendment
to the Philippine Constitution which he had himself engineered,
limiting the President's term of Office to eight consecutive years,
he should have stepped out of the presidency of the refugee
Commonwealth Government in 1934 in favor of Sergio Osmeña,
the Vice-President. The prospect of retirement seemed to aggra-
vate his tuberculosis, however, the Quezon family began to look
upon Osmeña not as a constitutional successor but as an unwel-
come interloper. Osmeña, ever the gentleman, had finally to request the U.S. Congress to set aside the constitutional provision
and allow Quezon to remain in office indefinitely.

My decision to run in 1935 was perhaps influenced more than
anything else by an observation I had made during the Wood-
Quezon quarrel, in which I had supported the Governor General.
At that time, I convinced myself that Quezon's long nationalistic career had made him an advocate and practitioner of government of men and not of laws, unfitting him for the necessary
and primary task under the Commonwealth of educating the
people in constitutionalism.

But Quezon won the election. He had behind him a well-oiled
political machine which had won every election since 1907 and,
in its determined stride, had killed or absorbed every opposition
party. The latest gorging came about precisely as an incident of

the fight over the first independence act, the Hare-Hawes-Cutting Law. In opposing the law, Quezon once more split the Nacionalista Party wide open. He led one wing, and Osmeña and Roxas, who had brought home the law from Washington, the other.

The other major party, the Democrata, feeling constrained to take sides in this new and certainly most important issue, also split up. One faction joined Quezon and the other the Osmeña-Roxas group. When Quezon had the Act rejected in Manila and replaced in Washington with the Tydings-McDuffie Law, and Osmeña and Roxas immediately decided to support the new act since it was indeed the Hare-Hawes-Cutting Law re-enacted, the two Nacionalista wings once more reunited. In the process the Democrats were assimilated. The reunited and reinforced Nacionalista Party then elected Quezon as President and Osmeña as Vice-President of the Commonwealth. It also elected all the members of the Legislature.

As my makeshift party and that of Bishop Aglipay's presently disintegrated—for I returned to my Elysian retirement and Aglipay to his Church—Quezon presided as the head of a one-party government. And so completely confident did he feel after a while that he proposed the abolition of his own party in order to institute what he called "a partyless democracy."

A party glutted with power, like the Nacionalista Party, is likely to break up into two at any time. While this may endanger the party's supremacy, it returns the country to a government by public opinion. But where there is no party, the man already entrenched in power can perpetuate himself as a dictator. People, in fact, called Quezon just that—a dictator.

He did not quite get around to abolishing his party, but once he was president he abolished my life pension, granted under the American Governors General, upon his own initiative, of 12,000 pesos a year. And while he was at it, he also had a parcel of the former friar lands I was buying on installment and cultivating at great expense repossessed by the Government on the ground that I was in arrears. This was part of the vast landed estates of the religious orders for which we had fought the Spaniards and which had been purchased and sold in smaller parcels by the

Government under a plan embodied in the Philippine Bill of 1902. Truth to tell, there were many other purchasers who were in arrears like me—but then they had not run for President of the Commonwealth against Quezon.

I should have wished to see the entire period of the Commonwealth uninterrupted by the Japanese invasion. Perhaps without this interruption, the preparatory work envisioned by the U.S. Congress, including the radical overhaul of the economy, might have been successfully accomplished. As it was, the highest pre-war achievement of the Commonwealth seems to be only the radical amendment of the Constitution in 1940, when public opinion had been reduced to a whisper under the one-party Government, primarily to enable Quezon to be the first President of the Republic scheduled to be inaugurated in 1946,* just as he had managed to be the first President of the Philippine Senate in 1916 and first President of the Commonwealth in 1935. But this was not to be. The preparatory program for independence was wrecked in mid-passage by World War II.

The timing, somehow, was wrong. The scheduling of independence seems to have been understood by Japan as a notice of final American withdrawal from the Far East. If this notice did not by itself inspire Nippon to dream up the Pacific War and Greater East Asia Co-Prosperity Sphere, it at least contributed decisively to their motivation and attempted consummation. The power vacuum apparently being left by America had to be occupied by someone else, and the only logical candidates for successor were the two old rivals in Asia, Russia and Japan. As

---

* The amendment was ingeniously worded so as to fit exactly the political situation of Quezon. He had been elected in 1935 under the original constitutional provision which provided for a six-year term but prohibited re-election. The 1940 amendment provided that the presidential term should be four years and that no president should serve more than eight consecutive years. Then, it was made to apply retroactively to 1935. Therefore, when the 1941 election came around Quezon was still qualified to serve two years. So he ran for re-election and was re-elected. His plan was to surrender the presidency to Sergio Osmeña, his Vice-President, in 1943, in compliance with the "eight consecutive years" requirement. But in the election of 1945, he would run again and thus be the first President of the Philippine Republic when it was proclaimed in 1946 as scheduled. Under the amended Constitution, his retiring for two years in 1943-1945 would have qualified him for another term of not more than eight consecutive years.

at the time Russia was pinned down in Europe by German aggression, Japan naturally believed that the iron would never be so hot again and struck in Pearl Harbor the blow that was heard around the world. In the midst of its final preparations for nationhood, the Philippines was invaded, occupied and subjected to three long years of frantic Japanese anti-American propaganda and ruthless military rule.

The history of the war in the Philippines is now a well-known epic tragedy. Although about 100,000 of MacArthur's raw trainees were integrated with the token American forces scattered in the Far East, the resulting USAFFE proved no match against the Japanese. Within two weeks of Pearl Harbor, MacArthur abandoned Manila and ordered a general retreat to Bataan and Corregidor, taking with him to the latter the now-refugee Commonwealth Government in the person of Quezon, Osmeña and a few others. Reinforcement was impossible because the entire American Pacific fleet had been wiped out in the sneak attack at Pearl Harbor. The remnant of the U.S. Asiatic fleet had fled to Australia. The resistance in Corregidor and Bataan became a mere delaying action, especially after the air and naval supports had been annihilated.

But it lasted until the defenders were almost without food and ammunition and on the verge of physical exhaustion. Tying up many Japanese divisions, together with supporting air and sea forces, they upset the Japanese schedule of southward conquest and saved Australia for MacArthur to use as the safe staging ground for his return. The valiant resistance, together with the subsequent guerrilla action, also proved to the world in the ultimate terms that America had earned the abiding loyalty of the Filipinos. Even in tragic defeat, the United States won epic vindication.

Japanese propaganda, backed by barbaric military ruthlessness, nevertheless created confusion among the people. Seizing Filipino nationalism, just limbering up in expectation of independence, as an ally, the Japanese dazzled the Filipinos not only with their early military successes but also with their swiftness in setting up a so-called Philippine Republic. They succeeded in getting the cooperation, sincere or otherwise, of most of the prominent political leaders, and using them as fronts, they launched a frantic campaign of hate to alienate the Filipinos from the United States.

But the farce of the situation must have been apparent, especially to the experienced public men they herded about as collaborators. The Constitution written for the puppet republic at the dictation of the Japanese military, though embodying most of the democratic features of the American-sponsored Philippine Constitution, included provisions which nullified them.

Representative government disappeared; election of public officials was not by the people but by the members of a Japanese-controlled political party called *Kalibapi*. Individual freedom was lost; the legislature was authorized upon its discretion to set aside the Bill of Rights. Imperialism in its worst form returned; the puppet president was empowered to conclude a treaty with "a foreign country," which could not be any other than Japan, for the thorough exploitation of the country's natural resources. Here was the intended key to the transformation of the Philippines into another Manchukuo.

There was no way of knowing what the exact motive was of those who collaborated with the Japanese, whether sincere or feigned. Perhaps, fear entered into the situation, for the Japanese were cruel and sadistic and did not spare life or property in order to impose their will or get what they wanted. Perhaps there was, too, ambition and love of power. And it was possible that the easy initial military successes of the Japanese convinced still others that Japan would win the War and, like my friends who deserted us in Malolos, decided to climb up the winner's bandwagon early.

I was one of those who were helplessly misused by the Japanese. Perhaps banking on my old forgotten feud with the Americans, they expected me to be their natural friend. They ghost-wrote speeches for me to read over the radio and articles to publish in newspapers and magazines. They had me hoist the Philippine flag at the inauguration of the puppet republic. It was one of the penalties of the fame and prominence with which, rightly or wrongly, history has honored me, that I could not, like most of my countrymen, lose myself in the multitude beyond the recognition and reach of the enemy.

Of the war-time chores I could not escape, my having to address a radio appeal to General MacArthur, then fighting in Bataan and Corregidor, to surrender was one of the strangest. It was most strange because I, who had led two revolutions against Spain and a war against America, each time against the heaviest odds, found myself pleading to the American general not to sacrifice the youth of my country uselessly. I told him that, in his precarious position, he could never win, that prolonged resistance was useless, that the further sacrifice of life had no further purpose to serve.

Yet I must admit that I also felt that my appeal was not entirely insane. The remnants of the USAFFE were hopelessly bottled up in Corregidor and the Bataan Peninsula without hope of reinforcement.

On the other hand, the Japanese forces had complete control not only of the rest of the Philippines, the seas around it and the air above it but also of all the Pacific west of Hawaii and of all East Asia north of Australia. The lines of communication and supply from Japan to all this area, including the Philippines, was well-established and secure.

It was also my hope that the rest of our forces which had not been able to reach Bataan before the Japanese slammed the gates close, as well as those to be released from Bataan, might continue to fight as guerrillas either by splitting up and deploying to strategic points or joining the guerrilla bands which even then had started to harass the enemy.

Strangest of all was the fact that, as he records in his autobiography, *The Good Fight*, Quezon in Corregidor was thinking as I did: that, in his own words, "the struggle on the part of the American and Filipino armies was heroic, but in a sense it was a futile one," that the "larger question" was "the possibly useless sacrifice of the Philippine army."

Pursuing this thought, he sent a cable to President Roosevelt suggesting that, in order to extricate and isolate the Philippines from the raging war, the American Government should take or agree to the following steps: First, immediately declare the independence of the Philippines; second, immediately sign a treaty with Japan neutralizing the Philippines; third, both countries forthwith withdraw their forces from the Philippines; fourth, the Philippine army be demobilized; and fifth, American and Japanese civilians who wished be evacuated with their forces.

I never heard from MacArthur during the war. On the other hand, Quezon did hear from Roosevelt through MacArthur to whom the American President sent a long message. "I thought I could read between the lines more than what the President had actually said." Quezon confesses in his book regarding the Roosevelt cable. "I suspected that he had gone so far as to tell General MacArthur that if the Filipinos desired to quit, which they did not, no obstacle should be placed in their way; that the President of the Philippines with his whole Government and his army could surrender if they wanted to . . ."

Even so, Quezon devoted an entire page to a bitter criticism of my own radio talk. To him, it was unpatriotic for me to publicly urge MacArthur to surrender and plead against the sacrifice of the flower of my country's manhood. But it was patriotic for him to urge virtually the same thing upon President Roosevelt. As I have said, the whole thing was most strange.

One of the early acts of the Japanese was to bring back from Japan one of my former generals, Artemio Ricarte, to contact me and other former colleagues still living in order to try to rally us behind the Japanese. Ricarte made it brutally plain that the Japanese would not stand for evasions, that it was a do-or-die proposition. He boasted that he was himself to be set up as head of the government and that he would, as such, know how to square accounts. Brandishing a *samurai* sword which he claimed Premier Tojo himself had given him "with which to cut the American chain off my dear motherland," he talked in terms of threat and blackmail.

I could not but look upon Ricarte with mixed pity and contempt. In his youth, he had been fanatically courageous. Instead of surrendering to the Americans and swearing allegiance after our defeat in 1901, he had escaped to Japan. There, ignored by the Japanese, he lived in want and disillusionment. To support himself and his family, he had performed odd jobs and, in later years, had taught Spanish in a school in Tokyo where he had earned about 80 yen a month. To do this, he had commuted daily from Yokohama where he had rented a modest house across the street from a foul-smelling public market.

On the ground floor, Mrs. Ricarte had run a restaurant of sorts whose only customers had seemed to be Filipinos visiting or passing through Japan. It had soon become a tradition among our traveling countrymen to stop there and dine on native Filipino cooking, then on top of paying the bill, leave a cash donation for the exiled patriot.

When the Japanese flew him from Tokyo about January 1942, Ricarte saw the Philippines for the first time since 1901. How he must have regretted having lived away from so much economic and cultural progress in his own country under the American flag! For much of it was still evident in spite of the virtual paralyzation of normal activities under the early Japanese rule.

Ricarte met his sad end when, upon the retaking of Manila by the Americans, he retreated to the mountains with the Japanese. He is said to have perished somewhere in the wilds of Northern Luzon together with a few other Filipinos who chose to remain on the side of the enemy to the grim and bitter end.

My experience with the Americans in 1898-1901 immuned me against the dazzle of the early Japanese victories. I had learned that in war the Americans are slow starters but terrible finishers. Having secretly prepared for war for at least ten years, the Japanese were in top form at the start while the Americans were caught with their pants down, so to say. But I knew, because I had myself learned it as a very hard lesson, that the giant that is America would gradually unlimber and then deliver a massive knockout blow. I had not foreseen the atomic bombs dropped over Nagasaki and Hiroshima—as who had, except perhaps the late Albert Einstein?—but I had fully expected America to overwhelm Japan completely in due time.

I was already in my 70's and I no longer possessed the hardiness and strength to run up the mountains. I had to remain in my house in Kawit. Through half a century of accumulating relics and souvenirs, I had converted it into a sort of museum of the wars we had fought. Unfortunately this gave the Japanese an excuse to frequent the place. I was a virtual prisoner.

As President Sergio Osmeña accurately observed upon returning with General MacArthur, under the Japanese the whole country had been a prison camp. A man had to give in to them to a certain extent to buy some degree of day-to-day security for his family and himself. The number of people the enemy imprisoned, tortured or killed on suspicion of being anti-Japanese or pro-American was great and well-known. The Japanese created a general reign of terror.

Conspicuous Filipinos whose names and prestige the Japanese wanted to exploit had no resort to the safety of anonymity. They had but one of five alternatives: to resist and risk death, to comply to a degree sufficient to buy relative saftey, to feign conformity as a cloak for sabotage, to flee to the mountains, or to seek escape in suicide. And, Major General William F. Dean, who has announced that he would carry a suicide pill the next time he goes to war, seems to imply that suicide is the easiest way out. Trying to fool the enemy was certainly as risky as resisting him frontally.

Apropos is the talk delivered by one of Admiral Chester Nimitz' briefing officers to American airmen poised to hit Rabaul with 320 planes. As related by James A. Michener, the following was the heart of the talk in the officer's own words:

" . . Some of you will probably go down. Some of you will be captured. And if you are so stubborn that you give the Japs only your name, rank and number you will be shot within ten minutes of your capture—if you're lucky. If you are unlucky you'll be tortured to death. . Admiral Nimitz has decided that in dealing with the Japs we must throw the book away . . . as soon as they start to muss you up, make believe that you've turned yellow. Give them little bits of news. Cry a little.

Tremble. Then give them a little more. When they see you're a coward they won't shoot you. . . . Do anything in your power to get past that first gang. They're the ones who shoot you or slice your head off.

"When you get back to civilian interrogators, continue to betray small things, niggardly, one by one. Above all, tell the truth, because they can check on you. Stay alive the first night. If you can do that, they may send you to a rear area where your chances of living are 50-50.

"Is this being a traitor? If you are caught betraying your country you'll be tried and there'll be no good shouting for Uncle Chester. You've got to sweat that part out yourself. But just between us, Nimitz wants you to stay alive."

Civilians who fell into the hands of the Japanese had to play some such game too in order to keep their heads. The more conspicuous they were politically and intellectually, the harder they had to play. It was a dirty necessary game.

I was not one of those few who could say that they had received instructions from President Quezon as to how to deal with the Japanese. I did not receive any directive or advice from him or any one else. But even if I had, it wouldn't have done me or anybody else any good.

If Quezon had left any instructions at all, the most likely recipients were Jorge Vargas, whom he had appointed mayor of Greater Manila to receive the Japanese; Manuel Roxas, who had served as his secretary and adviser in Corregidor and whom he had reluctantly left in Mindanao when he was flown to Australia, after having designated him as rightful successor to the presidency should he and Osmeña perish; and Jose Abad Santos, Chief Justice of the Supreme Court and, in Corregidor and later in Cebu, also Secretary of Justice. If they had had any instructions from Quezon, these should have been more or less uniform in purport.

Yet, when each was confronted separately by the brutal demands of the Japanese for cooperation, he behaved in his own way—and differently from the others. Vargas, a lawyer educated in the

University of the Philippines, became chairman of the executive commission, the first so-called Filipino governing group, and, later, under the puppet republic, ambassador to Tokyo.

Roxas, also a lawyer who had studied in the St. John College in Hongkong and the University of the Philippines, led a guerrilla band in Bukidnon, Mindanao, but falling ill almost immediately, surrendered to the Japanese. In Manila, he continued to malinger whereupon the Japanese brought three specialists from Tokyo to treat him. Soon, he accepted membership in the commission which drafted the puppet constitution and, later, a position in the cabinet of the puppet republic itself.

Abad Santos, a lawyer trained in Indiana University, U.S.A., when captured in Cebu, was asked by the Japanese to cooperate. He said no—firmly. They shot him.

MacArthur did return. But he returned with an entirely new force. He had better guns, better planes, better warships—new weapons altogether. The technical and scientific lag resulting from the isolation of centuries had just been about bridged by Japan when its militarists became over-confident and ambitious and went to war. And of all things, they picked as main target precisely the very nation which had forced them to abandon their isolation. While American technical and scientific know-how went to work and produced the proximity fuse, the flying fortress, the electronically-guided bombsight and gun, the radar and the atomic bomb, the Japanese could conceive no new tricks and were left behind standing still. MacArthur found the enemy practically where he had been three years before. Confronted by the new massive strength of America, the Japanese, in final desperation, resorted to the *kamikaze,* a martial adaptation of the *harakiri.*

MacArthur's victory over Japan is one of the greatest in military history. Nothing that can be said, not even the mention of the failure to protect airplanes in Clark and Nichols fields in Luzon after the Pearl Harbor warning, can ever detract from its epic magnitude. The Filipinos are grateful for their liberation from the Japanese terror and consider MacArthur one of their great martial heroes. Even the loss of their fathers and brothers and sons and wives and daughters and the ruin of their homes and farms and factories and public buildings cannot dampen the ardor of their admiration for MacArthur and gratitude to America. But it is a fact, which I must mention, that MacArthur's treatment of the so-called collaborators of the Japanese created a flaw in the new Filamerican friendship dearly forged in war.

The Philippines having been liberated, the Commonwealth Government was reconstituted in February 1945 under President Osmeña who had succeeded Quezon in the presidency upon the latter's death in 1944. As provided by law, the third and last election under the Commonwealth was held early in 1946. And, as scheduled, independence was proclaimed on July 4 that year.

In the 1946 election, the candidates for President were Osmeña to succeed himself and Roxas. Then MacArthur announced that all those who had given aid and comfort to the Japanese would be tried and punished as traitors. When he thus raised the issue of collaboration, Osmeña really lost the election. For it split the Nacionalista Party all the way through once again.

Roxas took the defense of those who had assisted the Japanese, nearly all of them members of the Party, declaring that they might have committed a mistake of the mind but not of the heart. Collaboration was a myth, he declared. Osmeña tried to take the middle ground. Upon landing in Leyte with MacArthur, he declared that the mere act of collaboration would not be taken as treason but that the motives, the intentions and the circumstances would rule. Roxas, nevertheless, became the hope of those who faced prosecution for treason, and among them were most of the powerful political leaders.

But Osmeña faced other handicaps. The men who had returned with him to Manila, either from the mountains or from the sanctuary of the United States, considered themselves the heroes of the hour and acted high and mighty. One of them, while denouncing collaborators wholesale at a political meeting in Malacañan, was stopped by the man who was soon to run for Vice-President on Osmeña's ticket and is today the President of the Senate. "Take it easy, son," Eulogio Rodriguez, Sr. advised him, giving him a fatherly pat on the back. "Had you been here, you might have been the Japanese's editor-in-chief." But he and his brother heroes had already alienated many potent political figures from Osmeña.

Osmeña was also too sincere and too sick. He was absent abroad for medical treatment when the Congress voted to its own members, cash backpay corresponding to the three years of Japanese occupation. Informed by his office, he cabled his approval of the proposed raid on the empty Treasury, basing it on the separation of powers.

Later, at the height of the presidential campaign, thousands of government employees massed before Malacañan, the President's residence, and their spokesman asked Osmeña pointblank if he would approve backpay for them too. What is sauce for the goose, they argued, is also gravy for the gander. Osmeña told them frankly and truthfully that the treasury was empty, that it was problem enough to raise their current salaries, and that paying them the equivalent of three years' compensation was impossible. Disappointed and openly angry, they next marched to the headquarters of his oppenent to ask him the same question. With alacrity, Roxas promised to give them full backpay if elected.

From that moment, Osmeña lost their votes to Roxas, even if it took Roxas' successor, President Elpidio Quirino, to pay them—with ten-year certificates. But Osmeña was too sick to argue. He made just one public speech during the entire campaign, a very brief one in which he simply stated, among a few other things, "The people know my lifelong record of public service; I have faith in their judgment."

The release by Mrs. Quezon of a letter her husband had written to General MacArthur in which he had praised Roxas to the skies was one of the decisive if strange literature of the campaign. The rumor had apparently reached Washington that the Japanese had asked Roxas to cooperate, that he had refused, that they had imprisoned and very likely had shot him. It was evidently a garbled version of the ruthless killing of Jose Abad

Santos. At any rate, it moved Quezon to write a letter to MacArthur asking him to promote Roxas to major general posthumously.

"But, oh, how proud I am of him," the letter read in part. "I almost envy him for he had occasion to do just what I wanted to do myself. . He is the greatest loss that the Filipino people have suffered in this war. He cannot be replaced and I don't know how long before the race will produce another Manuel Roxas. He saved his people from eternal ignominy. Had he accepted the offer, Japan might have already established a Manchukuo or a Nanking regime in Manila . . . and see how well informed those Japanese are as to who is who in the Philippines! They did not offer the presidency to Vargas or Laurel or Aquino or Yulo or Paredes—only to Roxas."

The effect of this letter, written on the basis of an erroneous rumor was to indicate to the electorate that Quezon had looked upon Roxas as his political heir. Roxas won.

Independence came to the Filipinos when they were profoundly divided by the touchy issue of collaboration, when they were in rags, when their country was prostrate and bleeding. But it was to the eternal credit of America that, instead of inquiring, like Shylock, if it was so nominated in the Independence Law, she forthwith proceeded in full good will to assist the young Republic to rise from the ruins of war. This labor still remains unfinished.

CHAPTER XIV

THE ULTIMATE ALTRUISM

IF IN 1898 America welched on the promises made to me by her accredited consular and military representatives, in1945 she reached the ultimate in altruism in her treatment of my country. This time she liberated the Philippines from another foreign yoke. Then she gathered the starved, naked and bleeding Filipino in her arms and nursed him to health and strength.

Since 1917, it is true, America has been extending military, economic and technical assistance to virtually all the world. She started during World War I with advances and loans to European countries amounting to over $17 billion. None save a small portion was ever paid back. After that war, she undertook a vast relief program, administered by Herbert Hoover, which cost $1.5 billion more. But these gifts only blazed the trail for more massive American philanthropies during and after World War II and up to the present.

During World War II, her net expenditure through lend-lease, grants and credits extended to some 40 nations was $48.9 billion. Over $11 billion of this went to Russia. In the vast foreign grants through the Marshall Plan, ECA, MSA, FOA, now ICA, and other agencies, America gave to 93 countries $89 billion. About $10.8 billion of this also went to Russia. This is not to mention about $15 billion given in foreign loans. Appropriated American foreign assistance from April 1917 to July 1954, reached the dizzy total of $152.7 billion. Some $14 billion was however, undisbursed as of July 1, 1954, and about $4 billion had been received in repayments. The net American philanthropy was therefore $134.7 billion.

The Philippines' share of the vast American largess since the liberation up to June 1956 was approximately $2,490,701,000. This included a special war damage payment plan which cost

$620,000,000. The cash aids were supplemented by the exten-
tion of the free trade between the Philippines and the United
States which should otherwise have terminated in 1946 upon
the grant of independence.

American assistance to the islands has been of two categories.
One category has included the standard American aids given to
all friendly nations after World War II mainly for the purpose of
giving impetus to their postwar rehabilitation. In this bracket,
the initial tide of aid took the form of swift relief extended by
the United States armed forces to hundreds of thousands of
Filipino civilians who had been displaced, rendered homeless,
or otherwise destitute. The other kind comprehends forms of
assistance, both direct and indirect, which have been especially
devised to meet the Filipino's particular needs. They are over
and above the usual American aid to foreign countries.

The three years of Japanese occupation, together with the
battles which opened and closed the terrible period, had para-
lyzed the production and importation of food, clothing and other
necessities and had left the people half-starved and half-naked.
The Japanese had lived on the fat of the land and had com-
mandeered or bought with worthless war notes most of the
available food. The average wardrobe of the Filipino had been
worn down to a change of old, frayed clothes and a pair of
wooden clogs. His diet had been reduced to skimpy meals of
rice gruel and *kangkong* leaves. His home had been either razed
by fire or shattered by bombs or, having escaped these fates, had
half crumbled from disrepair. Most of the remaining houses,
together with the residue of foods and other goods under their
shelter, had either been put to the torch by the Japanese when
they had retreated, or been looted by starved and desperate
hordes let loose by the brief interregnum.

The PCAU, Philippine Civilian Administration Unit, of the
United States Army, was the spearhead of routine American aid.
As soon as the Army had liberated an area from the Japanese,
PCAU teams rushed in and immediately set up centers for
distributing food, medicine and clothing.

The food was doubly welcome because it appeased the hunger of years—and it was American. For three years the Filipinos had missed the American preserved and canned foods and fresh fruits which had become part of their diet as American nationals. Now the PCAU was giving them their first taste of them in three years, and it was a banquet! The food items even included a few things they had never known before the war, and the novelty added to their satisfaction. That they tired of army rations, Spam and powdered egg after a while is only proof of their first state of satiation in years.

Many who had been in rags during the last year of the occupation presently blossomed in American clothing, either new or second-hand, as well as in newly-sewn dresses made out of materials obtained from the PCAU stations. The fact that the clothes were sizes too big or too small in many cases did not matter. The enemy occupation had atrophied their sense of fit and style. To be dressed somehow had become their only concern.

After a week or so of a PCAU's appearance in an area, the change in the Filipinos became marked. Eating California rice and fruits, Alaska salmon and Texas beef, and wearing better clothing, they not only looked healthier and neater; for the first time since Pearl Harbor, they were also happy and hopeful. The U. S. Government spent about $48,000,000 in this fine relief work. The returning American Army was hailed as a liberator; with its inevitable PCAU's, it was also acclaimed a benefactor. The Filipinos' welcome to the returning Americans could not have been more complete.

In the wake of the Army and the PCAU, came the UNRRA, United Nations Relief and Rehabilitation Administration. It distributed tons upon tons of food, clothing, shoes, medicine and other much-needed articles. The American contribution to the UNRRA's generosity was $7,700,000.

Soon, most of the male population in each Philippine community were wearing GI khaki suits, replacing the less serviceable PCAU and UNRRA issues. The GI uniforms became available first from individual GI's who traded them for various

Gen. Tomas Mascardo, who was regarded one of the most brilliant officers of Aguinaldo. A native of Cavite and a former school-teacher, his intelligence and energy brought him a great prominence.

Gen. Mascardo and staff reviewing Filipino forces near Calumpit, Bulacan. As shown by the mixture of uniforms, various companies were integrated as a result of losses to the Americans.

This is a representative group of Filipino prisoners of war captured by the Americans. It is composed of Filipinos from all regions. The men with long hair are Macabebes, a few of whom joined Aguinaldo. Traditionally, however, Macabebes served in the Spanish forces and later in the American army. Out of selected Macabebe soldiers who joined the U.S. Army, Col. Frederick Funston formed a company to employ in his ruse which resulted in the capture of General Aguinaldo in Palanan, Isabela.

favors, like bottles of homemade whisky. The women, too, sported ready-made dresses, some hand-me-downs, but some new with well-known New York Fifth Avenue, Broadway and 14th Street labels. Later on, surplus goods glutted the local market with every conceivable American military article from steel helmets to jungle boots, clothing to tents, jeeps to tractors.

Meanwhile, the reconstituted Philippine Government, finding an empty treasury* and as yet reluctant to collect taxes from a people just reviving from near-total prostration, had to operate on American grants and loans which, during the first year after the liberation, amounted to $36,700,000.

While the assistance in dollars, clothing, medicine and other articles lasted only during the first months after the liberation of each area and was intended only as a day-to-day relief, America soon devised a formula of aid calculated to be lasting in result. This aid was mainly channeled through the ECA, Economic Cooperation Administration, later the MSA, Mutual Security Administration, still later the FOA, Foreign Operations Administration, and currently the ICA, International Cooperation Administration. Through these agencies, America had spent in the Philippines up to June 1956 the sum of $127,100,000.

American economic aid to the islands is described by ICA's Manila Director, Mr. Harry A. Brenn, as "a partnership program." He enumerates five ICA objectives in the islands as follows:

"1· Formulate and execute a coordinated economic program designed to improve the country's balance-of-payments position, increase private participation in national development, broaden economic opportunities, and increase the per capita real income.

"2· Strengthen the foundations of democratic economy by improving the status of the farmer and laborer.

"3· Encourage private investment, especially in small and medium-scale enterprises.

"4· Improve the effectiveness of public administration,

* No accounting of the considerable funds of the Commonwealth Government at the outbreak of the war has yet been rendered.

especially of fiscal operations and revenue collections, to permit more adequate and effective appropriations for defense, essential public services, and economic development.

"5· Increase and diversify agricultural production, particularly food crops."

By early 1956, the ICA headquarters in Manila could summarize the economic program as follows:

"Under the program the economic health of the country has been vastly improved and Filipinos in practically every walk of life have been benefited by it . . . . commodities and technical assistance have expanded agricultural production, provided industrial machinery, taken health services to the barrios (villages) for the first time, rehabilitated and equipped agricultural and industrial vocational schools, given pure drinking water to hundreds of thousands, irrigated vast tracts of lands, constructed roads to open new lands to cultivation, improved government services to the people in all fields of activity, and made notable progress in solving age-old rural problems through extension of credit, easing of landlord-tenant relationships and opening new lands for settlement."

Programs utilizing ICA funds are joint undertakings of the Philippine and American governments. As a rule, American dollars are used for the purchase abroad, mainly from the United States, of the tools and materials, mainly capital goods, called for by the programs. The Philippine Government furnishes the counterfund—pesos to be expended for their utilization and operation. Some times, such financing is negligible, like the nominal cost of distributing ICA-imported fertilizer to farmers. Some times it entails much more than the cost of equipment, as in road-building in which $1 million worth of ICA machinery may cost $5 million a year to operate.

U. S. aid through ICA and its predecessors might have been considerably more had the Philippine Government been able to shake off its postwar lassitude earlier. In spite of the American commitment under the Quirino-Foster Agreement of 1950 to make $50,000,000 available yearly for five years, ICA expenditures have been considerably less, being about $47,000,000 in

1951-1952, and only $17,929,000 in 1955. The Philippines has lagged both in the initiation of acceptable projects and the appropriation of peso counterfund to guarantee that ICA goods, mainly machines and other equipment, do not rust in the wharves or rot in warehouses but are utilized promptly and fully.

"The total magnitude of each year's program," ICA headquarters explains, "is determined by the programs presented by Philippine Government agencies to the National Economic Council, which, after screening the requests, forwards them to the U.S. International Cooperation Administration for approval and appropriation of necessary funds by the U.S. Congress."

American technical assistance is extended through two channels, direct assignment and contract. Technical men on the ICA's staff are directly assigned to assist Philippine Government agencies, especially those concerned with finance, trade and industrial development, agriculture, public health, education, labor, public works, public administration, mining and information. Through the contract channel, ICA finances the technical assistance extended by various American groups, usually private. The current operating contract types of technical assistance are the following:

1. University of the Philippines contracts with Cornell University to assist its College of Agriculture; with Stanford University to assist its colleges of Education, Engineering and Business Administration; with the University of Connecticut for the development of a Labor Education Center; and with the University of Michigan for the establishment of an Institute of Public Administration.

2. Budget Commission contracts with Louis Kroeger & Associates for assistance in a complete survey and reorganization of the executive machinery of the Government and in conducting a wage and position classification survey of all Philippine Government employees; and with Booz, Allen & Hamilton for assistance in the modernization of the Government's budget and accounting procedures.

3. Department of Agriculture and Natural Resources con-

tract with Booz, Allen & Hamilton for the modernization and streamlining of the Bureau of Lands.

That the ultimate objective of American assistance is to enable the assisted country to stand on its feet permanently—self-respecting, prosperous and freedom-loving—is evident in the following statistics of accomplishment in the Philippines listed by Mr. Brenn in September 1954:

1. A total of 205 farmers' coops with 85,000 members organized, 174 of them in 1954.

2. A total of 14 warehouses constructed to store 494,000 cavans of rice; 130 more under construction or planned.

3. Loans to assist farmers total $2,250,000 of which all but $227,645 was accomplished in 1954.

4. Rice production has increased from 2.8 million metric tons in 1952 to 3.2 million metric tons in 1954.

5. More than 7.6 million animals are being vaccinated against disease in 1954 as against 3.4 million in 1951.

6. Enrollment at the Government's College of Agriculture in Los Baños has jumped from 851 in 1952 to 2,700 in 1954.

7. Reconnaissance soil surveys have been made in four provinces covering 2,435,000 hectares; two new soil conservation stations have been established and two old ones reactivated.

8. About 551,364 hectares of land have been subdivided into 63,800 farm lots up to 10 hectares each.

9. In fiscal year 1951, only 3,806 titles were issued by the bureau of lands; the goal for 1954 was 15,000 and it was exceeded by 2,417. Since June 30, an additional 6,000-odd have been issued, and the bureau is certain to surpass 50,000 titles during fiscal 1955.

10. A total of 1,005,049 hectares of public land have been classified for forest, agriculture or other purposes, and 476,000 hectares have been released, mostly for agriculture.

11. A total of 1,240,000 houses have been sprayed with DDT, giving 8,200,000 man-years of protection against malaria; 264,000 persons have been treated with anti-malaria drugs.

12. A total of 81 rural health units have been established, each with a medical officer, a nurse, a midwife, a sanitary

engineer and a driver-clerk to bring medical care to the rural population.

13. About 45 provincial hospitals have been equipped and modernized.

14. A total of 30 vocational agricultural schools and 34 vocational trade schools have received dollar-purchasing equipment and put it to use.

15. A total of 54 irrigation pump systems have been installed, bringing controlled water supply to some 18,000 hectares of land.

16. Work has been accelerated on the Maga, Jalaur and Pampanga gravity irrigation systems; the Padada, in Mindanao is already complete and will benefit thousands of hectares. The $6-million Agno irrigation system will be in operation in 1956.

17. Not less than 262 kilometers of main roads and 81 kilometers of feeder roads are under construction in the Mindanao road development program, opening previously inaccessible areas to settlement; the target is 594 kilometers by June 30, 1958.

18. A total of 49 bridges are under construction, and 148 more are in the planning stage.

19. Nearly $8,000,000 worth of heavy equipment has been ordered for a vast highway improvement program; although less than half has arrived, 608 kilometers of road are already under improvement in nine provinces.

20. The nation's resources of coal, iron ore and strategic minerals are being surveyed; the areo-magnetic survey of iron ore has led five private mining firms to contract for similar surveys.

21. Industrial consultations have been initiated to assist Philippine firms in improving cost accounting methods, production scheduling, pricing, etc.

22. Blueprinting of a completely coordinated multiple-purpose public works project for the Marikina river basin to provide hydroelectric power, municipal and industrial water supply, flood control and irrigation.

23. At least 588 Filipino technicians have been or are being

sent abroad, mainly to the United States, for advanced studies at a cost to ICA of $2,200,600 and to the Philippine Government of $1,013,000.

Helpful as the various aids comprehended in the first category have been, totalling $210,500,000 in money value, the Philippines has derived perhaps even greater benefit from especially tailored American assistance without counterpart in American aids to other nations. These have consisted of tax refunds to the Government, backpays to Filipino enlisted men and officers in the USAFFE and recognized guerrilla groups, redemption of guerrilla currencies, disbursements by the U.S. Veterans Administration, payments for civilian claims against the American Armed Forces, military assistance in the form of equipment, material, construction and services, and direct payments for war damage under a special U.S. law. By the end of 1953, these different aids amounted to $2,271,201,000.

Involving no direct monetary consideration yet perhaps of greater material benefit to the Philippines, the Bell Trade Act was also enacted by the U.S. Congress on April 30, 1946, since modified in the so-called Laurel-Langley Agreement of 1955, mainly to rehabilitate Philippine-American trade and stimulate Philippine economic rehabilitation and development.

The tax refund of $89,500,000 came as a windfall to a penniless Government. This sum was an accumulation of processing and excise taxes collected by the U.S. Government before the war on certain Philippine exports like coconut oil. Its payment was a timely and badly-needed assistance to a Government "starting from scratch."

Backpay as a policy was both a joy and a headache. The sums distributed as such to members of the USAFFE and recognized guerrillas gave to almost a million men and their families a good start towards personal rehabilitation. Backpay had been promised them through radio announcements as part of the campaign to keep up Filipino resistance against the Japanese. America lived up to this commitment, disbursing no less than $186,600,000.

Yet, there were also unforeseen repercussions. Hundreds of

thousands of unrecognized and unpaid guerrillas could never be convinced that they had less claim to backpay than those who were recognized and paid. The insolvent Philippine Government, unable to squelch the increasing clamor for backpay among its civilian employees, largely encouraged by the American policy, finally had to give in at an eventual cost of over $200,000,000, to this date less than 50 percent redeemed.

Guerrilla units, imitating the Japanese, also issued their own currencies to finance their operations. When the United States Government recognized a guerrilla unit as having performed services helpful to the war effort and distributed backpay to its members, it also had to redeem its currency which, in effect, was composed of promissory notes. In this way $57,000,000 was additionally spent. While the holders of recognized guerrilla notes were indeed fortunate, the hapless owners of currencies issued by units which were refused recognition were left "holding the bag."

Disbursements of the U.S. Veterans Administration amounting to $240,601,000, up to the end of 1953 have also been very helpful to the country. Thousands of students are in school on veterans benefit. Tens of thousands of widows and orphans are able to make both ends meet due to monthly pension checks. With money appropriated by the U.S. Congress, the best and biggest hospital in the Far East was inaugurated near Manila in 1955. Consisting of several modern buildings and provided with the most advanced equipment, it is exclusively for Filipino veterans. How I wish my own veterans had had even only a small part of these unheard-of attentions and privileges!

Soon after the liberation from Japan, the Philippines and the United States entered upon a mutual military assistance pact. Under this Treaty the United States obligated itself to furnish the Philippine Armed Forces practically all their munitions and equipment.from tanks to destroyers, jeeps to airplanes.

The total U.S. military assistance to the Philippines up to the end of 1954, including the cost of materiel and payments for military personnel, construction materials and services, was $840,000,000. There are indications that future military assistance will be increased considerably as part of the build-up to strengthen SEATO, South East Asia Treaty Organization. The U.S. Army also paid cilvilian claims for materials and services amounting to $170,700,000, while the U.S. Navy disbursed $17,500,000 as missing persons benefits.

In addition, there is the JUSMAG, Joint United States Military Assistance Group, headed by a major general. Its mission is to channel American military aid and furnish technical advice in the development of the Philippine Armed Forces. No little of the success of the Philippine Army in liquidating the Communist-led Hukbalahap rebellion is due to JUSMAG advice and the arms furnished by Washington upon its recommendation.

Constituting perhaps the greatest expression of American good will towards the Filipinos are two 1946 acts of the United States Congress calculated to give direct impetus to individual and national postwar rehabilitation. One of them, the War Damage Law, had the two generous purposes of compensating individuals and corporations for damage suffered due to the war and of assisting the Philippine Government in the restoration and improvement of public properties and essential public services. In carrying out the latter objectives, the law enlisted the direct services of various U.S. Government instrumentalities including the Public Roads Administration of the Federal Works Agency, the Corps of Engineers of the U.S. Army, the Public Health Service of the Federal Security Agency, the U.S. Maritime Commission, the Fish and Wild Life Service of the Department of Interior, and the Administrator of Civil Aeronautics, the Weather Bureau, and the Coast and Geodetic Survey of the Department of Commerce.

The other law was the Bell Trade Act which also had the double purpose of reviving the all-but-wrecked Philippine export industries and of attracting American capital and American businessmen and technicians to assist in the tremendous work of postwar economic rehabilitation and development. Many of the provisions of this law, including those regulating commerce between the Philippines and America, were to continue in force

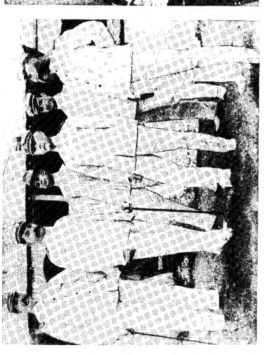

Left—At Fort Alfonso XII, Jolo, Sulu Island on March 11, 1900. Among those shown are Rear Admiral John C. Watson, U.S.N.; Maj. Owen J. Sweet, U.S. Infantry; Capt. Nichol, 23rd U.S. Infantry; and Executive Officer Lt. Com. Aaron Ward, Capt. William H. Sage and Flag Officer Frank Marble, U.S.N.

Right—American officers are shown here with the egendary su tan o Su u. In the front row are Hadji Cato Mohamad Sali, sword bearer to the Sultan; Hadji Mohamad Butu, Prime minister to the Sultan; Maj. Owen J. Sweet, 22nd U.S. Infantry and governor of Sulu; the Sultan; Prince Dato Rajah Mudah Mohamad Mualil Wasit, the Sultan's elder brother and heir apparent to the Sulu throne. Back row from left: Charles Schuck, interpreter to the governor of Sulu; Otto Basarudin fourth principal adviser o he Sultan; Abdu Uahab interpreter or he Su tan Cap Wm. H.

General Aguinaldo stands before the original Philippine flag which
he himself unfurled when he organized his own Government about
a month after Admiral George Dewey had brought him back from
Hongkong. The sword belonged to a Spanish general whom he had

until 1974, but they were modified by the Laurel-Langley Agreement of 1955.

The War Damage Act appropriated $400,000,000 for direct payment to private persons and corporations of Philippine or American nationality for damage or destruction to their properties from war action. It set aside an additional $120 million as direct assistance to the Philippine Government in the restoration of at least the most essential public services and the reconstruction or repair of war-torn public properties. To the Government it also transferred military surplus goods whose "fair value" at the time "shall not exceed $100,000,000." Through the War Damage Act, America directly helped about 1,000,000 individuals, corporations and institutions financially. It also rendered indispensable financial and technical assistance to the Philippine Government during its first postwar years.

In the distribution of payments, claims not exceeding $500 were given top priority and settled expeditiously. Only after the small claims had been satisfied were the larger claims also paid on the basis of $500 plus 53 percent of the balance of each claim. A number of the larger claims of commercial firms and educational and religious institutions are however still pending in Washington.

The $120,000,000 authorized as direct assistance to the Government was declared by the law "a manifestation of good will to the Filipino people." Part of it financed the activities of various trouble-shooting teams sent to the Philippines by different Federal Agencies. These helped to reconstruct roads, bridges, harbors and public buildings; rehabilitate the Department of Health and its various agencies; restore inter-island shipping, charter suitable U.S. vessels and re-establish inter-island airways operations; reopen and expand the weather service, revive and modernize the fishing industry, and continue the coast and geodetic survey work which, up to the war, had been in the hands of the U.S. Government.

Along with the direct assistance of Federal Agencies, the War Damage Act provided for the training and education of a considerable number of Filipinos either in schools established by the corresponding Federal agencies in the Philippines or in American universities, the U.S. Merchant Marine Cadet Corps, and the U.S. Merchant Marine Academy. More than doing only restoration work, the Federal agencies also made sure that when the American technicians withdrew, properly trained Filipinos would be ready to continue their work efficiently.

The training program is being continued with greater diversity. The ICA and its predecessors have devoted some of their funds to the financing of travel grants to carefully handpicked Filipinos in various pursuits and professions. Several hundred government officials, newspapermen, teachers and other professionals have each spent several months in the United States observing American life in government, industry, farm and home. The educational program has also resulted in the assignment to government colleges and universities and a few other non-profit schools, of American teachers and professors whose influence on campus has been most salutary.

In the University of the Philippines, a government institution, the program has resulted in the establishment of new colleges and the marked strengthening with American personnel of the faculties of important departments. In addition, the United States Educational Foundation yearly awards the Philippines' allotment of the Fulbright Travel Grants and Smith-Mundt Scholarships, also benefiting an increasing number of promising young Filipino scholars and professionals. The Foundation also secures scholarships for Filipinos in various American colleges and universities.

All in all, the educational program has expanded to such an extent that it has become a worthy successor to the "pensionado" system started by Governor Taft in the early 1900's. Under the Taft system, the most promising Filipino young men and women were sent each year to American schools for advanced studies at government expense. Unfortunately, many of its outstanding products perished during the war. They included educators, scientists, and professionals who had been educated in the best American colleges and universities, and military officers who had been trained in U.S. military and naval academies and colleges. They had either died in the battlefield or been deliberately killed by the Japanese as confined or released prisoners or plain civilians. This loss is being slowly made good with the American educational assistance.

Military surplus goods actually worth $1,121,400,000 at procurement cost were turned over to the Government. But through mismanagement, pilferages and corruption, only $80 million was realized from their sale. As the law did not specifically provide the manner in which it was to be spent, the money went to the general fund as miscellaneous receipts to meet ordinary expenditures.

In its Report to the President of the United States dated October 9, 1950, an Economic Survey Mission to the Philippines, headed by Mr. Daniel W. Bell, declared that "the Philippine economy did not secure the intended increment of machinery and equipment represented by the great stock of surplus property." The Report also said: "The property was disposed of without reference to its specific use for industries in the Philippines. Large blocks were purchased by private buyers at bargain prices and exported from the Philippines to other countries at enormous profits. The proceeds from these transactions were, in many instances, converted into dollars remitted to the United States." These remittances were for the importation of American goods which in those years reached one billion pesos annually, a high level unheard of before the war and doubly anomalous shortly after the liberation when Philippine export was almost nil.

The Bell Trade Act brought relief of another character. It extended the free trade between the Philippines and the United States which, according to the Independence Law, should have terminated upon the grant of independence on July 4, 1946. But instead of unlimited export of Philippine products to America, the leading articles, including sugar, copra and coconut oil, were placed on absolute annual quotas, above which they had to pay the American tariff duty. This limited free trade was to last until July 4, 1954, when it would be replaced by a formula of annually diminishing quotas and annually increasing tariff duties.

While the quotas would dwindle to zero by 1974, the tariff duties would increase at the rate of 5 percent annually to the full 100 percent by the same year.

Meanwhile, no ceilings were placed on American exports to the Philippines, although, between 1954 and 1974, tariff duties would also be collected on such goods at the same rates as those currently levied on Philippine articles in America. The extension of the free trade, limited as it was, stimulated the revival of the Philippine export industries and generally improved the country's economic situation. The progressive imposition of tariff duties was meant to habituate these industries to shoulder the U.S. tariff burden so as to be able to continue entry into the American market beyond 1974. Failing in this, they would either have to liquidate or seek other foreign markets. The first would be disastrous while the second, problematical.

The revival of the Philippine export industries, once the expected damage payments restored their credit and their free American market became available again, was rapid. During 1941, the last year before the war and considered a normal year, the total Philippine export was valued at $161,150,000, about 80 percent of which went to the United States. In 1946, the year the Bell Trade Act was enacted, the total export had dropped to only $64,200,000. This increased to $264,550,000 in 1947, $317,750,000 in 1948, $253,755,000 in 1949, $337,169,500 in 1950, $404,701,500 in 1951, $351,918,000 in 1952, and $392,458,500 in 1953. Typical of the share of the U.S. market of these exports are the following figures taken at random: Out of a total export of $253,755,000 in 1949, $181,886,500; out of $351,918,000 in 1952, $236,802,000; and out of $392,458,500 in 1953, $264,572,000.

The tax collection of the Philippine Government spiralled upward together with the exports. It was $48,463,500 in 1941, $88,270,000 in 1946, $158,151,000 in 1949, $200,221,000 in 1952, and $304,772,500 in 1953. Unfortunately, both the Philippines' foreign trade and national budget have so far failed to balance. Due to the acute need of the Philippines for capital and consumer goods, a natural consequence of the war, its annual imports have so far consistently been greater than its annual exports. The gigantic reconstruction and rehabilitation programs of the Government, together with new long-range undertakings like the building of hydroelectric power plants, have likewise made deficit-spending inescapable. Even the Magsaysay administration, which paved its way to power with the promise to balance the budget, has not yet been able to get out of deficit-spending.

Deficit-spending, unfavorable trade balance and the consequent depletion of the country's dollar reserves have been sources of worry since the war. This nerved the Government into seeking President Truman's approval of the application of internal regulations calculated to improve the situation even if they subverted the Bell Act. Approved by the President were import control to reduce foreign buying principally from the U.S., dollar allocation control to supplement import control and give Filipino businessmen a fighting chance against Chinese and Indian businessmen, and a 17 percent tax on dollar exchange to prevent the flight of capital abroad.

Although these regulations have added new and lucrative opportunities for graft and corruption, they have reduced the trade imbalance. Certain American export industries, particularly those producing toilet articles, medicine and motor vehicles, have also been induced to set up branch factories or assembly plants in the Philippines. At the same time, manufacturing industries unheard of before the war have been established. They have been encouraged not only by the import and dollar controls, but mainly by a new law exempting "new and necessary" industries from all taxes for a number of years. By January 1956, there were 422 such industries on which taxes amounting to $28,133,266 were waived in 1955. Many of them, however, are bottling, packaging and assembling plants for semi-processed American and other imported goods, and many of the rest are dependent on imported raw materials like steel, rubber, jute yarns and cloth, giving room for doubt as to their permanence.

Late in 1955, the basis of Philippine-American relations as

defined in the Bell Act was replaced by the so-called Laurel-Langley Agreement. The latter's main feature is its new trade terms. While in 1956 Philippine exports were to pay only 5 percent of the American duty, increasing by 5 percent each year, American exports to the Philippines started to pay 25 percent of the full duty, increasing every five years by 25 percent more. At the end of 20 years, the free trade would be completely liquidated and the export of each country would pay the full duty.

All in all, American assistance from 1945 to the present has had a vivifying effect on every level of life. In the Philippines, more than anywhere else, America has given final and definitive proof of her disinterested desire to help the needy part of mankind.

After the Philippine-American War, when my country had also been devastated by a long series of battles over a period of six years, 1896-1901, the Philippines was left equally ravished and shattered. But American assistance was limited to $1,000,000 which went into the repair of war-damaged public works.

Throughout the 50 years of American sovereignty indeed, the only expense America incurred was that for the maintenance of her armed forces stationed in the islands. The Philippine Government was completely self-supporting; domestic taxes paid for even the salaries and perquisites of American civilian officials. But no tribute was ever paid to the United States, while the free trade enabled the Filipinos to achieve a degree of prosperity unequalled in the Far East with the possible exception of Japan.

Its scheduled liquidation has, however, become the Philippine Republic's No. 1 nightmare.

CHAPTER XV

IRRITANTS IN PHILIPPINE-AMERICAN RELATIONS

BECAUSE I BELIEVE in the profound significance of Philippine-American friendship in our troubled world, I am deeply disturbed by the growing number of irritants in Philippine-American relations. That friendship is durable surely. Evolved out of the welter of gratitude and ingratitude, harmony and dissent, peace and war, it has survived the severest tests of human reason and emotion. It has become a touchstone by which all the East seems destined eventually to prove and accept the anti-imperialistic, anti-colonial, and anti-communistic leadership of the United States. And yet, just as water can erode the hardest granite, so misunderstanding can undermine the firmest friendship.

Some of the irritants have arisen out of a failure to understand the historic content of Philippine-American association. Others have been molehill-to-mountain affairs, inspired mainly by personal resentments, partisan politics or economic bias. Still others have stemmed from the exuberance of the promises and claims of psychological warfare and the often late and inadequate follow-up and fulfillment. But there are also genuine, even deliberate, causes of Philippine-American misunderstanding, ranging from racial and cultural snobbery to the arbitrary nature of military tradition and execution. And, quite naturally, surging nationalism and growing-up pains inevitably season the Philippines' attitude to anything foreign, including American.

The growing brittleness of Philippine-American relations has become evident in recent months. An opinion by the U.S. Attorney General that the United States had acquired ownership of the 22 bases it has leased in the Philippines seemed to have been sufficient to start a new round of denunciations against America and her acts and intentions in the Philippines by senators, congressmen, newspaper editorialists and columnists and others. It was quite natural for the Filipinos to regard the claim preposterous. It is treason to posterity for a people to allow permanent alienation of any part of its national territory without defending it to the last drop of their blood.

Smouldering anger over the claim led some people and newspapers to acquire a new interest in what was going on within the bases themselves. They soon found gratification in a serialized "expose" of native life in the naval base at Olongapo. According to the "expose," the naval authorities were tyrannizing the Filipinos in the reservation. They imposed arbitrary taxes, deprived them of their right to elect their own municipal officials, took control of their schools, denied the civilian courts jurisdiction over civilian offenders, placed military checkpoints along the national highways, thus interfering with the constabulary in its duty of regulating traffic. The President of the Philippines ordered an investigation of the charges, and the American authorities promptly made the necessary changes and adjustments.

The American bases now became regular news beats. As a result incidents which otherwise would have been ignored became hot news. They not only became front page materials but some of them inspired sizzling and biting speeches on the floors of the House and Senate. Sensationalism also came in. The trivial was exaggerated and the false foisted as truth, especially when their effect was to fan anti-Americanism and narrow nationalism.

A group of Filipino newspapermen accompanied our late President Magsaysay to Clark Field to receive in a formal turnover to the Philippine Government the first jet-planes under the Philippine-American military assistance pact. Upon entering the Auditorium grounds, the President was escorted through the front door but the newspapermen were led through a side door. They took their treatment for snobbery and said so in the columns of their newspapers.

An officer of the U.S. 13th Airforce appears at the Luneta in Manila. He measures distances with practiced eyes, moves about to calculate more accurately. He climbs the Independence Grandstand and sits himself successively at one wing, in the center, and at the other wing. The next day, some of the papers announce that the U.S. Airforce plans to stage an aerial mock war over Manila.

Rear Admiral Wendell G. Switzer invites members of the Philippine Congress to visit the Subic Bay Naval Base and omits newspapermen. Another snobbery. The admiral is forced to issue a statement explaining that "a naval base under certain stages of construction is not ready for visits from the press for security and other reasons."

The ever-vigilant Manila press got a real break, however, when American airforce authorities based in Camp O'Donnell in Capas, Tarlac, arrested a Filipino mining engineer and his crew and impounded his truck together with its load of manganese ore. They had been mining a claim in a district within the municipality of Capas. The American authorities asserted that the claim was within a U.S. military reservation, and mining operation by Filipinos was therefore illegal.

Once released, the engineer went directly to Senator Claro M. Recto, perhaps the Filipino political figure most critical of American policies and the leading critic of Mr. Brownell's claim of American ownership over Philippine bases, to seek his legal services. Not satisfied, he also engaged another senator, Lorenzo M. Tañada, president of the Citizens' Party and of the Civil Liberties Union. Together, the two bombarded the Department of Foreign Affairs with memoranda and the public with press interviews and speeches on the senate floor. The American authorities gave in. They returned the truck and its load of ore and announced mining operations in American bases would henceforth be allowed.

The recurring controversies involving the bases inevitably widened into a more general criticism of American politics. It was noted with bitterness that Philippine sugar was being punished in the American market because Philippine growers of Virginia tobacco opposed the further importation of American leaf tobacco.

The attempt in Washington to exclude Guam, where 16,000

Filipinos are employed, from the American minimum wage law providing for $1 an hour stirred up Filipino labor and politics. A congressional mission went to Guam to make inquiries on the spot and came home complaining that an American congressional committee had snubbed its members by not appearing in Guam as expected. It urged the bringing home of the 16,000 laborers unless they are allowed to enjoy American wage scales.

Surprised, the Washington committee made it known it had had no commitment to go to Guam and meet with the Manila committee. As for pulling out Filipino laborers in Guam, the Director of Labor in Manila indirectly squelched the idea by announcing Philippine unemployment had risen to 2,000,000 out of 7,000,000 employable men and women.

More serious charges and criticisms were still to come. No less than the Speaker of the House and the Vice Chief of Staff of the Armed Forces categorically declared that American military aid to the Philippines was "inadequate considering our military value to America." When Major General Wayne C. Smith, JUSMAG chief, explained that the Philippines was getting "a fair share" of available American aid, the Vice Chief of Staff replied that the military position of the Philippines was weaker than at the outbreak of the last war because America was not interested in furnishing arms for the reserved forces.

ICA assistance drew criticism on at least three scores. The American technical men, it was claimed, were overpaid and sometimes arrogant. The dollar assistance was insufficient. These are not as new charges as that of Representative Jose J. Roy of Tarlac who said of the direction of ICA aid: "They are trying to pin down our country to its agricultural economy and make Filipinos eternal distributors of raw materials and consumers of goods."

Then, no less than President Magsaysay himself announced that the Philippine Government had filed financial claims with Washington aggregating $860,000,000. "These claims," his *aide memoire* handed to Secretary of State Dulles on his last visit to Manila read, "represent the financial obligations incurred by the United States Government as a result of special relationship

that existed between the two countries and their joint prosecution of the last Pacific war. Some of them were contracted even
prior to Philippine independence in 1946."

Some of the amounts cover the claims of Filipino veterans as
well as claims of the Government for a share in the gold devaluation profit when the peso was on the gold standard together with
the dollar, for the refund of processing taxes collected on Philippines sugar and coconut oil, and for additional war damage.

A small group, of which the mayor of Manila is typical, has
become bitter. Early in April the mayor was reported in the papers
to have lambasted Filipinos "who by their actuations and utter-
ances would make America too sure of us and for which reason the
Philippines today gets less aid than former enemy countries such
as Japan and Germany." He added: "In Spain and Yugoslavia
the U.S. Government is dealing with fascistic and communistic
states respectively and yet there U.S. military authorities do not
claim ownership of bases as they do here. . . ." The mayor, like
the group he represents, also urges Philippine trade with Red
China and Russia.

These recent incidents and viewpoints have their origin in
events of earlier vintage. Just as Philippine independence became an American political football, so Philippine relations with
America became a perennial issue between Philippine political
parties. From 1907, when the first national election was held, to
1934 when the U.S. Congress enacted the Independence Act, the
Nacionalista Party won all the elections because it could clamor
for independence loudest and most convincingly.

After the war, the Philippines' post-independence relations
with America again became the favorite political issue. It was
not a clear-cut issue in the election of 1946, to be sure. But it
was definitely the paramount issue in 1949 when Elpidio
Quirino defeated Jose P. Laurel for president by branding the
latter a Japanese collaborator and claiming that he, as an advocate of friendship with America, would secure more American
aid. In the election of 1953, Quirino reversed himself and raised
the issue of subservience to America, and Ramon Magsaysay
won the election by advocating closer ties with Washington. In

the congressional election of 1952, Senator Recto ran for re-election by adopting Quirino's stand as his own and failed to get the most vote, as he did in 1941 under Quezon's banner, being only fifth among the eight successful senatorial candidates.

The partisan attitude to America is further colored by certain American policies and acts which are susceptible to misunderstanding and criticism. Among these are the Philippine-American free trade and the subsequent attempts to liquidate it.

In 1909, against the solemn protest of the Philippine Assembly, which was submitted to Washington as a Resolution and supported with vigorous speeches on the floor of the House by the Filipino resident commissioners, the U.S. Congress took the first long stride to free trade. It enacted a law exempting Philippine exports to America from duty within specified quota limits. At the same time, it allowed U.S. goods to enter the Islands duty-free without limit. When the Democratic Party took over in 1912, it lost little time in abolishing the quotas. Thus complete free trade was established in 1913.

The free access of Philippine export to the rich and protected American market stimulated the rambunctious growth of a few industries supplying raw products in demand in America. The sugar industry expanded and prospered to become the mainstay of Philippine economy, producing 60 percent of all exports, accounting for 60 percent of the total Government income, and furnishing the wherewithal of some two million families. The coconut industry developed to a close second. These two industries, together with hemp and cordage, tobacco and a few minor others, responded mightily to the golden temptation of the American market and became almost the total substance of Philippine economy.

During normal years the Philippines sells about 80 percent of its exports to America. On the other hand, the islands absorb only less than 3 percent of the total U.S. exports. Up to the war, however, we were the best American foreign market for cotton cloth, galvanized steel sheets, dairy products and cigarettes, and the best or next best American Oriental market for steel and meat products, automobiles and automobile tires, and electrical machinery.

The resulting situation is incisively described by President Grayson Kirk of Columbia University as follows:

> To an almost appalling extent, the Filipinos perforce shaped their economy in such a way that the livelihood of the inhabitants as well as the financial stability of the government is now dependent upon an ability to sell a large volume of a limited number of commodities in the American market.

The possible fatal consequence of the free trade came with shocking clearness to the Filipinos during the early postwar years. With the sugar and other export industries completely wrecked by the war, the flood of imported American goods soared to staggering levels never before reached—no less than a billion pesos annually since 1947. The result was to unbalance the country's foreign trade to an alarming tilt, draining out most of the dollars with which America was trying to prime the pump of the all but dried-up economy.

Almost too late, this was cured by controls—on imports, on dollar allocations, and a special 17 percent tax on dollar purchases. This levy as well as the controls violated the Bell Trade Act and the Agreement implementing it, but the Truman Administration, realizing that they meant economic life or death to the infant Republic, approved them. This near-economic collapse more than ever convinced the Filipinos of the dangers of the free trade and the need for new markets abroad and for some measure of industrialization at home.

In opposing the establishment of free trade, leading Filipinos and the Philippine Assembly had feared two things: the loss of revenue in the form of duty on American goods and the forging of economic chains which would fasten the islands to the United States and render political separation difficult. Free trade, would, the Assembly's resolution declared, "be highly prejudicial to the economic interests of the Filipino people and create a situation which might delay the obtaining of their independence."

The first fear was true enough—in the books. If duties had been collected on American goods, the public treasury would have been richer by at least $150,000,000 annually during good years. But it should be quite obvious that without free access to the American market, it is very doubtful if the Philippines would have had the dollars to buy so much American or other foreign goods on which to collect customs duties.

The political fear took an ironic turn. The swelling volume of Philippine export to America, instead of delaying independence, finally hastened it. Largely on the plea of certain U.S. farm interests and the strength of the farm blocs in both houses, the newly-constituted Democratic 73rd Congress quickly enacted the Hare-Hawes-Cutting independence law. Behind the law was the belief that the elimination of Philippine competition from the domestic market would somehow ease up the situation of the sugar, dairy and other U.S. industries, then panic-stricken by the Great Depression. After the Philippine Legislature rejected the law, the U.S. Congress quickly re-enacted it as the Tydings-McDuffie Act, President Roosevelt readily signed it, and the Philippines got its independence anyway. Independence implied, of course, the termination of all special Philippine privileges under the American flag.

As far as the American Congress was concerned, the primary aim of the Independence Act was the liquidation of the free trade. The law imposed immediate quotas on Philippine sugar, coconut oil and cordage. Philippine exports in excess of these quotas paid the full American duty. After July 4, 1946, the full American duty was to apply on all Philippine exports to America. The Philippine Government was also to collect an export tax on all exports to America starting on the sixth year of the Commonwealth Government at 5 percent of the full American tariff and increasing yearly until it would be 25 percent in the ninth year. Collection from this source was to be earmarked for the redemption of the country's bonds most of which had been sold in America.

The orderly carrying out of this plan was prevented by the war. Fortunately, the Act itself provided that at least a year before July 4, 1946, the future trade relations between America and the Philippines would be considered in a conference of representatives of both nations. This directive and the great war destruction the islands had suffered led the U.S. Congress to enact two companion measures, the Bell Trade Act and the War Damage Act, on April 30, 1946.

The first was intended to liquidate the free trade in an orderly manner and encourage American investment so as to stimulate Philippine economic rehabilitation. To assist the second purpose, the law provided that American citizens would have equal rights with Filipino citizens in the exploitation of natural resources and in the operation of public utilities. And to make sure that this right would be beyond the reach of ordinary politics, it was to be incorporated in the Philippine Constitution. The law also contained provisions on immigration, currency and other matters.

The War Damage Act appropriated $620,000,000 as payment for war damage to the Government, Filipino and American citizens, and religious, educational and charitable institutions that suffered destruction due to the war. It also provided that payment of this money would be limited to claims not over $500 each, unless the Bell Trade Act was accepted and the so-called parity right for Americans, inserted in the Constitution as an amendment.

Under the Bell Trade Act and the Executive Agreement based on it, tariff duties were to be levied on the exports of both countries beginning July 4, 1954. It was to start at 5 percent of the full tariff that year and increase every year by 5 percent to become 100 percent in 20 years. With the imminence of the tariff provision's effectivity, the law came into closer scrutiny.

Easily the most searching critic of American policies in recent years is Recto. A former justice of the Supreme Court, President of the Philippine Constitutional Convention, and called the "foreign policy expert" of the Nacionalista Party until he broke up with President Magsaysay, Senator Recto concluded an address before the University of the East in Manila, devoted to Philippine-American economic relations, as follows:

I shall not end my exposition and analysis of the Agreement without making allusion to the diabolical scheme resorted to by the string-pullers in the United States Congress to force the Agreement upon us. It will be recalled that the Bell Trade Act specifically provided for parity rights in favor of Americans with regards to public utilities and utilization of natural resources, and called for an appropriate amendment of our Constitution in order to guarantee as firmly as possible for the Americans such rights as can be inherent only in Philippine citizenship. A rejection of the Parity Amendment meant, according to the Bell Trade Act, a termination of the Trade Agreement. On the other hand, a provision was inserted in a sister Act of the United States Congress, better known as the War Damage Act, prohibiting payment of any war damage claim above 1,000 pesos if the Trade Agreement did not go into effect. The result was that if Parity were not approved, the Trade Agreement did not become effective, the Filipinos who suffered damages during the last war would not receive reparations over the sum of 1,000 pesos   We had to take it or leave it in its entirety. We took it. We had no way out. Our country was in ruins, the national economy was completely dislocated, there was no food, nor shelter, nor clothing, for our people as a result of the war

Some of the provisions of the acts, taken out of their historical and statutory context, could indeed appear sinister. The trade and immigration arrangements were not reciprocal. While Philippine duty-free exports to America were on a quota basis, American exports to the Philippines were not similarly limited. The Law permitted the entry into the Philippines of at least 1,000 American citizens a year to reside for a period of six years as against the Philippine immigration quota of only 50 persons.

Other parts of the law seemed to curtail Philippine sovereignty. The provision on currency pegged the peso to the dollar at the rate of two to one and provided that legislation affecting its value or free convertibility would be subject to agreement by the President of the United States. Another provision gave American citizens the so-called "parity rights." Filipinos have, of course, no such rights in America: in fact, they may not even engage in gainful occupation while there on a visitor's visa.

Gen. Emilio Aguinaldo, with the second Mrs. Aguinaldo, a niece of his dean of Ambassadors, Felipe Agoncillo, shown together in a recent photograph taken in their home in Kawit, Cavite. Refused official recognition, Agoncillo was nevertheless received unofficially by President William McKinley and thus won the distinction of being the only member of Aguinaldo's Government who ever made contact with the War President.

Gen. Aguinaldo is here shown starting to troop the line of his honor

The co-authors, Gen. Aguinaldo and Vicente Albano Pacis photo-
graphed February 18, 1957.

The currency provision of the Act was however evidently intended for mutal protection. The Philippines owes considerable sums to the U.S. Government in budgetary loans and to American investors in bonded loans. By plunging itself into the abyss of inflation, Germany had repudiated billions of dollars in foreign debt after World War I. It would therefore seem reasonable for a creditor in America's position to have some means of preventing devaluation by the debtor.

But there is still another side of the coin. Hitler rode to power and raped German democracy on the crest of the runaway inflation. For when a nation's money becomes worthless at home and abroad, its future teeters between anarchy and dictatorship. American support of the peso was as much for the protection of American loans as of Philippine democracy, economy, and credit against the shocks of political and economic adjustments at home and of shrinking markets and the cold war abroad.

On the surface, too, the immigration arrangement was discriminatory. But it had a good explanation. If Americans were to assist in the economic development of the Philippines, American financiers, businessmen and technicians must be able to enter the country. The American Government's vast program of dollar and technical assistance through FOA, now ICA, could not be effectively administered unless American scholars, educators, technicans, experts and others were able to come to the islands.

Behind the so-called parity was a similar story. Since the Treaty of Paris at the turn of the century up to now Americans have enjoyed equal rights with Filipinos to Philippine natural resources and the public utility business. The concession in the Bell Trade Act was merely an extension beyond the withdrawal of American sovereignty of a right which, under ordinary circumstances should, like the free trade, have simultaneously ended. Again, the reason was the expected mutual benefit to be derived: by the Americans from investing part of their surplus capital, and by the Filipinos from the aid of much-needed capital in their post-war economic rehabilitation and development. We have no capital to export to the United States.

The plain fact is that, without Philippine prompting, the American Government itself had originated the rigid laws which for over half a century protected Philippine natural resources and the public utility business. The Spooner Amendment of 1901 prohibited the sale or lease of public lands, forests or mines and the grant of public utility franchises until a civil government was established. Where an exception was to be allowed because of its extreme urgency, the approval of the President of the United States was required and, in any case, it was to expire within one year of the establishment of the civil government. The Bill of 1902, the first Philippine Organic Act enacted by the U.S. Congress, followed this up with conservative provisions on franchises and natural resources. Homesteads and individual land purchases were limited to 16 hectares to any one person and sale or conveyance to any corporation or association, to 1,024 hectares. The disposition of forests and mineral properties were similarly regulated.

Once we Filipinos observed that there was no undue American attempt at exploitation, and once we understood that natural riches are wasted unless they are rendered usable, we began to welcome American capital. But it came only in trickles. Up to the war, U.S. investment in the Philippines did not exceed $300 million, most of it profit made in the islands. This, out of a total U.S. foreign investment of over $10 billion of which only about $1 billion was placed in Asia, most of it in the Middle East oil industry.

When the Bell Act was drafted in 1946, however, it was hoped that American venture capital would come in greater volume. This hope was premised on the grant of independence and the common Filamerican sacrifices in Corregidor and Bataan, both of which newly cemented Filamerican friendship. The fall of militarist Japan, Nazi Germany and Fascist Italy was also believed to have made the world safe for democracy and honest commerce. But creeping world Communism, with its Philippine version in the Huk rebellion, altered the picture entirely. Very limited American capital—$10,682,248 as of October 1954—found its way to the Philippines. The trickle virtually dried up when the Government controlled imports, taxed dollar exchange, and regulated dollar remittances.

It would seem therefore that what is bothersome and burdensome to us Filipinos in the Bell Trade Act was more the theory than the substance.

The late President Roxas, arguing in 1946 for the acceptance of the so-called parity provision of the Bell Trade Act, asked:

> Should we fear a nation that, after liberating our country in compliance with the promise of President Roosevelt, is helping us to rehabilitate this country; a nation that has voted out of its substance $400,000,000 to pay for the damage wrought by war; a nation that has voted $120,000,000 to pay for the damage suffered by the Government and Government institutions; a nation that has given us $100,000,000 worth of surplus property without asking a cent in payment? Should we fear a nation that is going to transfer to us not only all the arms and equipment for our army but even the arms and equipment that you will use for the training of our citizen army . . . a nation that is going to transfer eighty-three ships, fighting ships, for our off-shore patrol (navy); a nation that is going to send beginning next month, 500 students to study in the universities of the United States at her expense . . . ?"

Like an indulgent parent, America allowed the Philippines more or less to have its way. On top of permitting Manila to set aside provisions of the Bell Act to try and conserve its dollar reserves by imposing restrictions on the importation of goods, mainly American, and the exportation of money, mostly to America, Washington extended further concessions. The effectivity of the application of tariff duties under the Bell Act was postponed for six months as the Philippines requested. The period of grace was to be utilized for a revision of the Act.

Such a revision was agreed upon in 1955 and embodied in the so-called Laurel-Langley Agreement which both governments have since adopted as law. Under its terms, America relinquished control of the Philippine currency and relaxed the immigration provisions. Effective January 1, 1956, tariff duties have been applied on the export of both countries, with the Philippines getting a head start. While it now collects 25 percent of the full tariff and will raise it by 25 percent more every five years for 20 years until the full tariff applies, the United States started on the same date with only 5 percent of the full tariff and will increase it by 5 percent each year for 20 years to apply the full rate.

The duties are still on the first year of their application, yet the economic situation in the Philippines has apparently worsened. Imported goods are rising in cost, and domestic goods are following suit. The cost of production is also increasing, but labor is demanding higher wages and increased benefits with resulting strikes and other labor disturbances. Some industries are closing, and unemployment is increasing. As the Government is vigorously implementing a social justice program, it has to increase taxes. Yet production is almost stationary, except in the area of "new and necessary industries," which are however completely tax-exempt. Criticism of the Laurel-Langley agreement has begun.

The often patronizing manner in which American economic and military policies have been implemented has been aggravated by the unwitting snobbishness of American cultural policy, arousing Filipino nationalism and hurting racial sensitiveness. This snobbishness was particularly apparent in the early postwar treatment of Filipino visitors to America, together with the very limited Philippine immigration quota, the strict restrictions on Filipino students, and what can only be characterized as the "supreme indifference" of American publications and publishers to aspiring Filipino writers.

As American nationals between 1899 and 1946, Filipinos entered or resided in Ameirca at will, worked in her farms and factories, or studied avidly in her colleges and universities. Today, they find it strange that they are on a U.S. immigration quota of only 50 persons a year. They are vexed that they are allowed to travel to America only on a six-month visa at a time. Students must first secure formal admission to American institutions before they are permitted to enter the United States.

Whether tourists or students, they must have sufficient funds; they may not accept jobs while in America, although, under a recent relaxation of the law, foreign sudents including Filipinos may now secure work upon the recommendation of the schools in which they are enrolled. As a result, the only young Filipinos able to enter American universities today are the children of the rich or the fortunate ones who can secure scholarships. And in spite of the substantial number of scholarships available the number of Filipino students in America is fast dwindling to an insignificant handful. This is most unfortunate, since the best Filipino friends of America are those who have drunk deep of U.S. democracy on the spot—on college campuses especially.

The increasing economic and academic exclusion is aggravated by American literary snobbishness. Since the turn of the century Filipinos have accepted English as their adopted tongue. Starting as the language of the schools, it has become as well the language of the government, business and finance, the professions and society. Until very recently, the Filipinos have been well on the way to making it their home language also. But thoughtless criticism and lack of encouragement are altering the situation.

Filipinos have often been inconsiderately ridiculed by thoughtless Americans for the necessarily differently-accented English that they are developing. It is true that, just as Americans, Australians, South Africans, Indians and others speak varieties of English different from that of the British, the Filipinos talk an English combining the characteristic phrasing, enunciation and intonation of Spanish and the native vernaculars.

What perhaps hurts even more is the apparent American policy of literary exclusion. Very few Filipinos, and only as the rarest of exceptions, have had works accepted by American publications and publishers. Lack of merit is undoubtedly the main reason, but the superior assumption that no Filipino could possibly produce good work in English is certainly much of it too.

To the aspiring Filipino, this is particularly tragic. For in the Philippines there is yet no literary market to speak of. In the book field, only school textbooks sell enough copies to pay for the cost of publishing and give their authors and publishers a modest return. General works are completely labors of love. Only libraries, collectors and a few people of culture buy them. The few newspapers and magazines do use limited quantities of short stories and articles, but the average pay for such works is about $15.00. No Filipino freelance writer or author completely dependent on the Philippine literary market could possibly live on his earnings. No wonder his mouth waters every time he contemplates the wealth of the American literary market. But, as of now, that is about all he can do.

"It is . . . a good guess," says Stanford University's Wallace Stegner, explaining the situation from a neutral angle, "that the Filipino literature of the future will have to be considered a branch of English, or more properly American. This should mean that American media of publication are freely open to Filipino writers. They are—but the competition is brutal. With his little bolo in hand, a Filipino story writer is asked to step out against the massed firepower of all the English-writers of the world.   "

But the fact is that the Filipino is not even asked to step out. He does not get a hearing.

It has been said that much of the motivation of the so-called National Language movement, in addition to its inherently nationalistic origin, stems from humiliations and disappointments suffered in the use of English. To speak and write in Tagalog has become a way by which some Filipinos with literary aspirations have achieved unchallenged supremacy. A sort of an escape, it is at the same time in conformity with the old and respectable philosophy, "I would rather be the first man in a village than the second in Rome."

Some measure of American cultural hospitality to Filipinos should however not be amiss. Founded by Americans, the Philippine school system is in effect an extension of the American educational system. And English as the educational, intellectual and literary language of the Filipinos is a consequence of the long American trusteeship of the Islands. Political separation and the growing economic alienation will eventually leave culture as the only available bond between Americans and Filipinos. It should be strengthened towards permanence rather than weakened and thus also inevitably liquidated.

A Philippine Republic linked with America by the strong ties of language, culture and friendship is, after all, a necessary appurtenance of American world leadership.

CHAPTER XVI

THE SUPREME COMMANDER'S SUPER-IRRITANT

THE SUPER-IRRITANT in Philippine-American relations was the making of the Supreme Commander himself.

A series of inter-related gripes, mainly spawned by the American armed forces during and after the war, has left an acute sense of disappointment and injustice among the generality of Filipino soldiers, guerrillas and veterans. All this was only a backdrop. On stage, in his wonted histrionics, General MacArthur administered the unkindest cut of all. And the wound has left a permanent scar of the deepest humiliation in the very souls of some of our most respected political leaders, jurists, professionals, editors, financiers and businessmen.

First for the backdrop. Tens of thousands of claims for guerrilla pay and guerrilla currency redemption were turned down by the U.S. armed forces. Each unsuccessful claimant, whether guerrilla or civilian, became disgruntled. All are potential fomentors of discontent against the United States. Even with the best of intentions some of this result would have been inevitable. But the truth is that there was considerable confusion in the processing of guerrillas and guerrilla claims.

I am not one to minimize the services that guerrilla fighters can render an ally through the torment and harassment they can inflict upon the enemy. It can be said that even after the Japanese had established complete control over the Philippines, they enjoyed no peace of mind nor security of life mainly because of the activities of guerrillas. Some of the feats credited to the latter were brave, intrepid and patriotic to the extreme. But it was also true that, for the purpose of collecing backpay, guerrilla groups sprouted like mushrooms at liberation time. Even the rolls of some genuine guerrilla units were padded with new names. It has been estimated that the various guerrilla lists submitted for processing contained no less than a million.

As a result, the screening officers were themselves almost as badly harrassed as the Japanese had been. They made mistakes. Thousands of truly deserving guerrillas were left out in the division of the much-coveted backpay melon, while many strictly liberation and postwar outfits with glib leaders and convincing promoters were favored and honored. The screening was finally so slowed down by conflicting claims and tales that much of the money the U.S. Congress had appropriated for guerrilla compensation was reverted to the U.S. Treasury or spent for other purposes. Resentment among those who failed to collect, whether deserving or not, was the result.

But even of greater potential danger to Philippine-American friendship is the apparent injustice committed against Filipino soldiers and veterans. It is estimated by finance officers of the Philippine Army, partly relying on the computations of the U.S. Administration of Veterans' Affairs, that Filipino soldiers and veterans have been deprived of at least $3,457,274,000 which they should have received from the U.S. Government under the provisions of various American laws and Philippine Government executive orders approved by General Douglas MacArthur as Allied Supreme Commander in the Pacific. In addition, they believe that $35,000,000 of unexpended USAFFE funds earmarked for payment to Filipino soldiers and veterans and which the Philippine Government loaned to itself and used for other purposes, should not be paid back to the United States as is being done but should be utilized, when made available, for the original purposes for which it was appropriated. The men affected actually went to court to claim the money but lost the case. The Philippine Government itself claims having expended $41,500,000 in meeting obligations to army personnel and equipping the USAFFE which the U.S. Government should have made good.

Some of the other claims are interesting for they reveal the apparently careless and arbitrary handling of the interests of Filipino veterans and soldiers by American authorities.

The claim of the Philippine Government is made up of the following items: $5,000,000 for expenses incurred for the operation and maintenance of the Recovered Personnel Division, AFWESPAC, Allied Forces West Pacific, an agency charged with the processing and adjudicating of claims for arrears-in-pay of members of the USAFFE and recognized guerrillas; $10,000,000 for advances in the payment of bonus to enlisted men, an expediency resorted to due to the payment of only prewar salary rates to army men after the liberation when the cost of living had soared to about 500 percent more than prewar; and $26,500,000 for furnishing initial equipment and supplies to the USAFFE in 1941.

The claims for the soldiers and veterans are more formidable. Upon landing in Leyte, President Osmeña issued, with the approval of General MacArthur, Executive Order No. 22 raising the pay of members of the USAFFE and recognized guerrillas to the level of the U.S. Army pay. Ignoring this order, AFWESPAC continued to give Filipino soldiers the lower rates prescribed in an Executive Order which President Quezon had issued in Corregidor. The arrears-in-pay arising out of this discrepancy is $345,000,000.

Other claims are for refund to individual veterans of the following: for erroneous deductions of National Life Service Insurance premiums, $200,000; for erroneous deductions made from their arrears-in-pay equivalent to 3-month advanced pay which was not received, $500,000; for deductions made from their arrears-in-pay for guerrilla notes received by them during the Japanese occupation, $6,500,000; for erroneous deductions made from their arrears-in-pay for clothing issued upon their return to military control, $324,000. Set against the fact that even civilians were issued Army clothing, the last deduction seems especially unkind.

There are still other items. But by far the two most important are the following: Over 30,000 officers and enlisted men of the USAFFE and of the Philippine Scouts did not receive full arrears-in-pay by virtue of AFWESPAC Staff Memorandum No. 14 declaring members of the Philippine Army as civilians upon release as prisoners of war from concentration camps. This Memorandum is believed illegal and these men should receive full arrears-in-pay amounting to $100,000,000. The biggest single claim is $3,000,000,000 arising from the cancellation of benefits due Filipino veterans under the GI Bill of Rights. It is alleged that benefits which had accrued to them under the Bill were abolished retroactively and illegally by a rider to the Surplus Appropriation Recision Act, Public Law 301, 79th Congress.

So large do these combined claims amounting to $3,533,744.000 loom in army and veteran circles that the Philippine Congress, under date of May 19, 1954, adopted a Senate Concurrent Resolution urging the President of the Philippines to negotiate with the American Government on the highest level at the earliest possible time for the final settlement of the claims. President Magsaysay partly took heed of the Resolution when he subsequently submitted a claim of $860,000,000 to Secretary Dulles.

Not all the various claims may be justified or, if justified, they may not be in the amount indicated. Blundering subordinates may also have been largely responsible for the discrepancies. They at least painted a backdrop not unworthy of the Supreme Commander.

On stage General MacArthur committed a grave error of judgment and foresight in dealing with the relatively small number of key Filipinos who had supposedly given help and comfort to the Japanese invaders. The ill-will he thus incurred for the United States has become one of the greatest perils to Philippine-American friendship.

When the American forces approached the Philippines, most of the high Filipino officials of the puppet republic who had not been flown to Japan had fled to Baguio in Northern Luzon. This in the belief that the mountain city would be spared from military action, being of no great strategic value. They were mistaken.

The Japanese had made full use of Camp John Hay, the nearby American military reservation. Furthermore, when the spearhead of the American forces pouring through the Gulf of Lingayen cut across the Central Plain and severed the enemy forces in Luzon, the northern segment retreated up to the Baguio area, perhaps hoping to make the place its own Bataan. Perched some 5,000 feet high upon pine-clad mountains, Baguio is accessible only by two roads, the Zigzag and the Naguilian, both running through easily-defensible mountain passes. Before air power—during our own war—it would have been a natural and impregnable fortress.

But the Americans denied the Japanese the pleasure of feeling safe very long. Now pouring in from the Gulf like a great on-rushing tide, the Americans split into two columns. One rolled down to Manila while the other column clambered up the mountains northward to Baguio and other points. Simultaneously the artillery which brought up their rear and U.S. carrier and land-based planes which gave them a protective umbrella blasted far ahead of the columns. Before long American bombs and shells were exploding almost everywhere like gigantic popcorns on the roast, and nowhere more intensely than Baguio. Filipino guerrillas, sensing that it was now or never, rushed out from hiding to support the Americans.

There was now the greatest danger where the Japanese were and the Americans weren't. For reacting to the American assaults by land and air and the stepped-up guerrilla strikes in their rear like maddened beasts trapped in a conflagration, the Japanese went completely berserk. They burned, blasted or looted properties and slaughtered unarmed civilians including women and children.

The extremely dangerous situation to which Baguio was reduced soon set off a great exodus to the lowlands. As the roads continued to receive daily aerial blastings and poundings, the refugees avoided them. On foot, most of them with only the clothes on their backs but others loaded down with children and bundles of every description, they rushed down pell-mell in all directions over mountains and ravines like scared ants fleeing their smashed nest. Among the refugees were the top Filipino puppet officials. They and thousands of other Filipinos who had sought refuge in Baguio now raced down headlong towards the American lines.

But a strange thing happened. A group of puppet cabinet men, rushing in panic down to safety, like all the rest of the refugees, reached the American forward lines well below Baguio. They thought that they were now among friends and their ordeal was over. They were mistaken.

The next day, the official American Government newspaper, *Free Philippines,* announced that Manuel Roxas had been *rescued* while his companions had been *captured.* Roxas was soon back in his USAFFE uniform of brigadier general and was assigned by General MacArthur as assistant to his chief of military intelligence, Major General Charles A. Willoughby. His former cabinet colleagues were in jail.

This was the start of what I believe was General MacArthur's greatest error from the standpoint of Philippine-American friendship.

His CIC, Counter Intelligence Corps, now rounded up everyone who had had any dealings with the Japanese. These included businessmen like Vincente Madrigal, perhaps the richest Filipino; former puppet ministers, including Claro M. Recto; former cabinet members under President Quezon and the American Governors General; former Senators and Congressmen; ex-members of the puppet legislature and former judges; at least three former prewar Speakers of the House of Representatives, one retired Chief Justice and several Justices of the Supreme Court; newspaper and magazine editors, myself and many others.

We were confined in the Bilibib Prison like ordinary criminals and, later, the more "dangerous" among us were shipped to the Iwahig Penal Colony on Palawan Island. Bilibid is the Sing Sing and Iwahig, the Alcatraz, of the Philippines. The economic, political and legal elite of the country confined in the very prisons to which, as lawmakers, prosecutors or judges, they had themselves sent ordinary criminals! It was the ultimate in humiliation.

Jose P. Laurel, Jorge B. Vargas, Camilo Osias and the other

high puppet officials caught in Japan were also thrown into Tokyo's notorious Sugamo Prison by order of General MacArthur.

Although it turned out later to be a farce, wounded pride and dignity have never become completely healed. The resentment was aggravated by the special treatment accorded Roxas, yet it was this special treatment which finally turned what had promised to be a great tragedy into an amusing comedy. As the victims, we could, of course, never see the joke.

In due time MacArthur turned over his prisoners to the Commonwealth Government to be prosecuted for treason against America and the Philippines or, in the euphemism of the day, collaboration with the Japanese. The Osmeña Government set up a special tribunal, the People's Court, to try the cases. Meanwhile, however, Roxas became a candidate for President against Osmeña with MacArthur's tacit backing. When he won the election and took over the Government, winning at least partly on his assertion that collaboration had been a myth, the task of prosecuting the accused became impossible.

Witnesses who had signed affidavits prepared by CIC lawyers often suffered amnesia—they could not remember. Since an act of treason, according to law, must be testified to by at least two witnesses to justify conviction, Government prosecutors suddenly found themselves with insufficient witnesses and evidence. Like the Government, public opinion became apathetic. The only recorded outburst of popular temper was in Cebu where a crowd tried to mob an accused on his way to trial. When President Roxas, with the Congress concurring, proclaimed amnesty, only one alleged top-rank collaborator, a former puppet cabinet minister, had been convicted and he, of course, also went scot free.

It all came to so much ado about nothing. But the deep humiliation suffered by those who had been herded to prison and haled before the Court like ordinary criminals remained seared in their souls. And since almost all of them shortly returned to their former prominence in the political, professional, financial, economic and journalistic life of the country, they could exert tremendous influence on public opinion.

It is perhaps correct to say that the anti-American outbursts which now and then sour Philippine-American friendship can be traced at least partly to the deep-seated resentment over General MacArthur's arbitrary and discriminatory policy.

General MacArthur should never have started anything which he could not or did not wish to finish. My own wish is that he should have finished it. Because he failed to do so, we Filipinos continue to have no clearcut concept of treason and loyalty.

My colleagues in Malolos who deserted the rest of us, crossed the battle lines and offered their services to the Americans were rewarded with high honors and offices in the subsequent American regime. We who remained loyal to our Republic and defended it as long as we had strength suffered a different fate. Many of us died. In the struggle, we risked our lives; in defeat and capture, we still risked punishment.

There is no doubt whatsoever that many of MacArthur's prisoners were loyal. But there may have been some of them who were truly traitors. Among the men and women of lower categories who were also arrested, imprisoned and indicted, there were undoubtedly quite a number who could not pass the loyalty test. Because of the election of Roxas to the presidency and his amnesty proclamation, it was never established who the patriots and who the traitors were. What is probably even more lamentable, we repeated our failure at the turn of the century: we failed to clarify through the pronouncements of courts of competent jurisdiction the norms of conduct which distinguish loyalty from treason.

The intense disappointment among thoughtful Filipinos was voiced by Rafael Roces of the newspaper publishing family of Manila when he said: "Next time an enemy invades us, the people will meet him at the beaches with a brass band."

Roces had lost a guerrilla son, Rafael, Jr., to the Japanese.

A postscript to the messy affair has been furnished by General MacArthur himself. Late in 1954, the president of the Japanese puppet republic of the Phillippines, now Senator Jose P. Laurel, went to the United States at the head of an official mission to seek the revision of the Bell Trade Act. He and MacArthur met at the Waldorf-Astoria for the first time since the war. The *United Press* reported the meeting in a dispatch to Manila datelined New York, Oct. 12.

"It was MacArthur who did the explaining," the U.P. stated. "One might almost say that he made a long overdue apology."

The press service went on to quote MacArthur as saying to Laurel: "There was never any doubt in my mind but what you and the others who worked with you during the Japanese occupation acted in what you believed to be the best interest of your country. President Quezon completely approved of your actions. But I was against a very tough proposition. I carried instructions in my pocket to have you tried as a war criminal."

This, I think, is making a confused situation worse confounded.

CHAPTER XVII

NEW, IMAGINATIVE U.S. POLICY URGENT

SOME FILIPINOS have brought down the old toy of imperialistic exploitation from the attic and dusted it off and painted it new and bright with patches of nationalism and vestiges of Japanese propaganda, cultural humiliations and anti-military and anti-MacArthur resentments.

It is claimed that Japan invaded the Philippines solely to attack America, that the Philippines was really a mere bystander who was caught in the crossfire. This echoes the occupying Japanese forces' propaganda greetings to the sullen Filipinos: "Japan and America enemies, *Hiripino* and Nippon *tomadachi!*" America, it is also asserted, has wanted to make sure that its postwar assistance to the Philippines would be made good many times over by embarking at last upon a systematic economic exploitation of the country.

Fortunately Philippine-American friendship is not, in the main, of the fair-weather variety. This was amply demonstrated during the war and enemy occupation. Later, when some of the bitter war aftermaths brought forth new tensions, it became strained but remained unbroken and steadfast. Even as Filipino politicians today denounce American policies and manners, they often protest their personal admiration of America and admit the value of American friendship to the Philippines.

The seed of good will is surely there, and there are gratifying evidences that, even while there has been a political drought, it has not been entirely unwatered. But in this precarious existence, it can undergo unpredictable mutations. It can even perish.

Although the visible manifestations of continuing mutual respect and friendship are apparently superficial, they are in truth significant. In recent years, the treatment of Filipinos who

235

travel to the United States has improved, at least socially and in some ways even legally. Those Filipinos who had long endured the status of displaced persons in America, if able to meet the requirements, have been admitted to American citizenship. Before the war, of the thousands of Filipinos who resided and made their living in the United States, only those who had served honorably in the American armed forces could avail themselves of this boon.

On the part of the Filipinos, there is a durable feeling of admiration and gratitude—and a pervasive respect for America. The mark "Made in USA," whether on an article of commerce or a way of life, is readily accepted by them as the best. How Filipino public opinion, in spite of articulate protests to the contrary, accepts the verdict of American public opinion is perhaps one of the most profound signs of Filipino respect and liking for America.

Ramon Magsaysay, then relatively unknown, had first been elected President in the American press and in American minds before he ever became a candidate for President of the Philippines. He was a young and obscure congressman doing his best to serve the people. Appointed by President Quirino as Secretary of National Defense, he went after the Huks simply yet effectively, unconventionally yet dramatically.

American writers began to take notice of him. In the on-the-spot news dispatches to American dailies and in magazine articles and books of renowned observers, like Mr. Justice William O. Douglas, his victories over the Huks became battles won on behalf of world democracy against communism. It was then, and only then, that the Philippine press and people took serious notice of Magsaysay. And, lo, they beheld an exceptional public servant—a man of great industry and honesty, of courage and action. From that moment no other Filipino had a chance to be elected President in 1953.

But these remaining threads of good will cannot by themselves last long. Something must be done to strengthen them. I feel that the kind of original massive thinking and ingenuity, boldness and daring, imagination and vision which conceived the McKinley Instructions—an idea completely new under the sun of European imperialism in 1900—must once more be applied to post-war and post-independence Philippine-American relations. All Asia is watching to find out if American friendship and leadership has staying and lasting power.

The crux of Philippine-American relations today is commerce —commerce as shaped by the free trade. While this commerce is perhaps of little moment to America, it is of paramount importance to the Philippines. The nation's entire economy has been shaped in the image of the free trade. Yet America's post-independence economic policy in the Philippines has so far followed the old American taunt when the Filipinos demanded their freedom: "You cannot have your cake and eat it too!"

This policy has consisted simply of predicating Philippine political independence on the liquidation of the free trade and, consequently, the destruction of Philippine-American commerce. This was the formula of the Philippine Independence Act. It was the formula embodied in the Bell Trade Act. It is still the formula on which the Laurel-Langley Agreement is based. I am strongly of the belief that the assumption on both sides of the Pacific that Philippine-American free trade be abolished and its consequences endured is backward and anarchronistic. It is at best an over-simplification of a complex and dynamic situation which involves the life and death of an infant Republic, a new votary of democracy.

The free trade was adopted on the basis of unilateral American decisions and against Philippine opposition at a time when American economic policy was firmly based on tariff protectionism. Since then, America has been slowly coming around to the view that free trade is the only tenable basis of the well-distributed world prosperity that she seeks to promote with billions of dollars of annual foreign aid. "Trade not aid" is becoming the new world assistance policy of the United States and the new hope of her beneficiaries.

Leading American chambers of commerce and outstanding

generally conservative Report of the Randall Commission on American industrialists now advocate free trade. Even the "United States Foreign Economic Policy" submitted to President Eisenhower declares the following:

> The strength of our domestic economy requires adherance to three fundamental principles: 1. The freest possible opportunity for the development of individual talents and initiative in the utilization of private resources and through the free association of workers. 2. The maintenance of vigorous, but fair, competition. 3. The maintenance of a broad free market for goods and services. Our primary reliance should therefore be upon the incentive of the free enterprise system, the stimulating effects of competition, and the stabilizing influence of free markets.

Clearly, the soundest goal of American foreign economic policy is free trade. Philippine-American free trade has been, as it were, the spearhead, Why then sacrifice it?

Yet, obviously, the free trade must be modified to permit the natural and desirable growth of the economies of both countries. The modification must be based not only on the facts of history but also on the actualities of economic life. The fact of history is that, the free trade as the basis of America's economic policy, shaped Philippine economy into its lopsidedness and precariousness. The actualities of economic life in both countries are a little more complicated.

Having expanded its foreign markets to parallel its industrial and technological developments, the United States no longer needs the Philippine market as much as in the 1910's when the European powers were still the dominant trading nations. Less than 3 percent of American export finds its way to the Philippines. On the other hand, the Philippines depends mainly on the American market. The American market absorbs about 80 percent of the total Philippine export. Furthermore, the Philippine export to America is made up of only a few items, the products of several industries expressly and artificially developed to cater to the United States market.

While the American export to the Philippines is a flood in the limited Philippine market, Philippine export to America is a mere drop in the ocean that is the American market.

The facts should also be taken into consideration that America is a country with a highly developed economy, not only well able to supply the domestic demand for raw materials and manufactured goods but also dominant in most open markets abroad. On the other hand, the Philippines, by the operation of the free trade, has been imprisoned in an agricultural straitjacket. Inspired however by the example of America and realizing that a certain amount of industrialization would greatly improve our economy, we Filipinos also aspire to have our own manufacturing industries.

We must be assisted to undo the consequences of the free trade; we must become less dependent on American goods and the American market—with positive American help.

On the basis of these historical and contemporary facts, it is possible to propose a mutually fair and beneficial formula of Philippine-American trade relations. Roughly, such a formula should have the following bases:

1. The Philippines will continue to buy capital goods from the United States.

2. The United States will continue to develop the Philippines as a capital goods market.

3. The Philippines should be encouraged to establish industries which manufacture consumer goods.

4. The United States must gradually forego the supplying of the more common consumer goods to the Philippines.

Some of the ways and means of carrying out these objectives include tariff preferences and quotas. Of necessity, the plan involves a measure of mutual sacrifice.

On the part of certain American industries such as the tobacco, toilet and pharmaceutical interests, there must be a deeper sense of understanding and justice than heretofore. But considering that the Philippine market is relatively small and unimportant compared to the vast American domestic and other foreign markets, the sacrifice is not too great.

The Philippines should also undertake a corresponding measure of sacrifice. Its principal exports like sugar, coconut oil and hemp will continue to be restricted by quotas. The purpose is partially to relieve corresponding American interests of their competition as well as to force the Philippine export industries to seek new markets, reduce their cost of production or retrench and diversify to new industries. In the meantime the Philippines also limits its industrial dream to the production of consumer goods mainly for the domestic market. Such a balancing of the Philippine economy will however result in a more balanced trade and a more stable dollar reserve.

In the field of loans and investments, it is plain to see that while Nehru is being plied with hundreds of millions, Garcia is being half-heartedly offered only a few millions. Very little of the ordinary consideration of profit enters in each situation. The main basis is the cold war and how each of the leaders and countries concerned can be lined up. The situation is indeed extraordinary and warrants urgent and extraordinary arrangements.

But it is an error to appraise each country mainly by the number of its population or its location on the map. To be sure, India is the second largest nation in the Orient and the leader of the neutralists. These surely are formidable considerations. Yet, in its proper position in the structure of American world leadership, the Philippines is no less important. If America loses the Philippines, she loses all Asia and Africa as well. Wherefore it also deserves extraordinary and special American attention and treatment.

The scheme already in use in a limited measure of insuring or guaranteeing loans and investments channelled to underdeveloped countries should be expanded. At least in the Philippines American interests will never risk confiscation as they once did in Mexico and as they constantly risk in other Central American countries and the Middle East. But parity rights and other inducements have failed to attract the expected American capital to the Philippines.

Of the greatest urgency is some change in the workings of ICA. The requirement of peso counterfund for every project has slowed down dollar and technical aid, since the Philippines is also short of pesos. The requirement has a good motivation; it is to habituate the assisted country to help itself. But in many cases, it often has the effect of paralyzing assistance.

The proportion of local counterfund in relation to the dollar aid should therefore be reduced. This will make the assisted countries more able and happy to help themselves. What is probably equally important, it will dissipate the suspicion that America sees to it that all dollar aid eventually goes back home to roost. For then some of the dollars would be expended where it is most needed—in the country assisted.

Something must also be done to correct the impression that American experts and technicians are overpaid, overproud and over here. They should be as well selected as the pioneer American teachers who lovingly built the Philippine school system from the ground up. They must love to help other peoples, they must be social and science missionaries imbued with the spirit of Switzer and Taft.

Except for the private consulting firms which are supposed to bring about efficiency and economy in the various agencies of the Government, Americans in the Philippines are not really overpaid. The consultants' contracts do call for as much as a million dollars in some cases. This is too much money, considering the fact that the consultants and experts depend mainly on low-paid regular Government personnel and the possibility that their reports and recommendations may only gather dust in some Government pigeonhole. This definitely has happened before. The personnel of ICA and the university professors under contract by the University of the Philippines however receive very reasonable sums in terms of American salary scales.

"The average salary and allowance for ICA employees," ICA's Manila headquarters has revealed, "is $13,600 of which the United States government pays $10,203 in dollars and the Philippine government $3,392 in pesos. For the employees of the contract groups, the average salary and allowance is $15,330, of which $11,330 is paid in dollars by the United States and $4,000 in pesos by the Philippines." The average age of ICA technicians is 45.7 and of contract employees, 42.2 years.

Some such improvements in the American assistance to the Philippines are urgent. No longer can America rely on routine measures. She must once more search her soul and bring forth a bold and original basis of post-independence relations with the Philippines. With Philippine statesmanship, now more articulate and more experienced than before, assisting American statesmanship, such a basis can be discovered. But it must be discovered now—not after it is too late.

It is axiomatic that if America fails in the Philippines it fails everywhere else in Asia. For in the Philippines she found her mission of world leadership. It is here that she dealt the first fatal blow to European colonialism in Asia. This she did not only by defeating a leading European colonial power in war but also by assisting a country long oppressed by European imperialism to attain social and political progress and, finally, nationhood and independence.

The new American policy in the Philippines reverberated all over the East. The impact of her new international philanthropy shook the entire system of European colonialism to its very foundation. It was on the strength of America's Philippine record that the late President Roosevelt could urge Britain and Holland and France to liberate their colonies. It was partly her Philippine feat that gave America moral stature as a leader nation, and it is her Philippine policy which she has expanded into a world policy of assistance. America's Philippine record was also definitely the germ of the mission of human liberation and peace which has become that of the United Nations' Trusteeship Council.

Exulting over Dewey's Manila Bay victory, American statesmen at the turn of the century, led by Senator Beveridge and Secretary Vanderlip, envisioned the Philippines as America's gateway to the commerce of the limitless Orient. But most of that commerce has gone glimmering behind the Bamboo Curtain, and America has severed political relations with the Philippines. Yet the Philippines can still become the natural gateway to the East for American friendship and leadership. With the Filipinos wholeheartedly accepting them—accepting them as the first beneficiaries of enlightened American influence in the East —they will sooner be welcomed by the rest of Asia.

CHAPTER XVIII

CONCLUSION

ONE OF the basic virtues of Democracy is its power of self
correction—although sometimes the process takes a terribly long
time. Dictatorship, on the other hand, cannot correct itself—
except by total explosion and disintegration. The freedom of
discussion and the control by public opinion enable Democracy
to purge itself eventually, emerging stronger from the experience. But the evils of Dictatorship can end only if the regime is
completely destroyed as were the reigns of Mussolini and Hitler.
And some dictatorships—Russia for instance—are frightfully
durable.

"In this country," says President Eisenhower, "public opinion
is the most powerful of all forces, and it will straighten this
matter (McCarthy-Army controversy) out wherever and whenever there is real violence done to our people." This can be said
of any true Democracy and about other matters of public
interest. But Democracy's slow and lumbering pace on the one
hand and susceptibility to propaganda on the other are nevertheless an inherent weakness.

A classic case unearthed after the war pinpoints this short-
coming. It took no less than a thorough inquiry by a Royal
Dutch Commission to vindicate Felix Kersten and expose the
hoax perpetrated by Count Folke Bernadotte for his benefit at
Kersten's expense.

Kersten enjoyed some mesmeric influence over Himmler,
Hitler's ruthless Gestapo chief. Taking advantage of this, Kersten
was able, through Himmler, to frustrate Hitler's decision to exile
up to 3,000,000 "irreconcilable" Dutchmen to Polish Galicia
and to liquidate thousands of Dutchmen, Germans and Jews.
He was allowed to evacuate the condemned hordes out of
Germany, thus saving them from torture and death. But Berna-

dotte, having been the Swedish Red Cross official who had directed the convoys, rushed three books to print in fast succession, the first one within six weeks of Hitler's death, to recount the task of rescue. In them, he said not a word about Kersten but assigned himself the role of hero.

"Later," Oxford University Historian H. R. Trevor-Roper, author of the authoritative *The Last Days of Hitler,* adds, "Bernadotte circularized prominent Englishmen to draw attention to his (supposed) achievements, and then had those English letters translated and published in Sweden."

Bernadotte thus neatly succeeded in publicly claiming the credit for the splendid war-time humanitarian feat. He had been covered with medals, loaded down with honorary degrees and hailed as "The Prince of Peace," "Savior" and, after his assassination in Israel as a United Nations peace commissioner, "Martyr of Humanity," before the facts finally prevailed over his propaganda of self-glorification. With the truth enthroned at last, members of the Dutch government nominated Kersten for the Nobel Prize for Peace.

A similarly interesting footnote to Philippine-American history, one more directly pertinent to my narration, is an *Associated Press* dispatch datelined "Buffalo, New York, April 17, 1954" and printed in the Manila newspapers on April 18, as follows:

Veteran Edward M. (Ted) Rogers, 73, of Suburban Kenmore, had a purple heart citation Friday, awarded 55 years after he was wounded in naval action at Manila Bay. Rogers was wounded slightly Feb. 15, 1899, while serving on the gun crew of the cruiser *Buffalo*. He said the ship had been bombarding the insurrectionists at Malate.   The award was signed by Vice Admiral J. L. Holloway, Jr.

The bumptious and the braggart, especially if they know their public relations, seem to be able to hoodwink most of their contemporaries. Their lies prevail until some crusading spirit takes the trouble of disinterring the truth. Likely as not, the liars have died by then. If still alive, they have deceived so many respecta-

ble people and medal-awarding associations and diploma-confer-
ring institutions that their victims, rather than confess gullibility,
strangely become their staunch defenders. That is why, to oppor-
tunists, the policy of self-inflation is often not unprofitable.

To people who don't blow their horns, however, it seems the
day of vindication is later than sooner—if at all. My own case is
an example. Not only do the old scurrilous slanders and libels
against me still have currency in many quarters. The deliberate
attempt to blacken me also continues with brand-new smear
concoctions.

In a book I have previously mentioned, advertised as the
latest official biography of Admiral Dewey and prepared with
the collaboration of his only son, the following statement appears with the finality of an oracle:

> Aguinaldo, after 40 years of exile in Japan, returned to the
> Philippines with the Japanese conquerors in 1942.

The authors make this charge in the same breath with the give-
away statement which I have quoted earlier: "Dewey was especially careful never to put anything in writing, a step which permitted Aguinaldo later to allege that he had received from the
admiral numerous promises of sovereignty." To prove to their
readers that my claims were false, they now present me as a man
who had turned his back to his Motherland and later returned
as the invading enemy's bellwether. The fact is that the only
Filipino who came from Japan with the Japanese was General
Artemio Ricarte about whom I have previously spoken.

But no matter. The prevarication serves as an excellent example of the method employed in the insistent and persistent
attack upon my person which has been going on since the Philippine-American War. In sensational books, magazine articles and
newspaper stories, features and editorials—in millions upon
millions of words—I have been subjected to the treatment
known as *argumentum ad hominem*. Stuart Chase describes this
method as a process of switching "the argument from the issue
to the man, and might be freely translated, 'Get personal'." It is

usually resorted to when the arguer has run out of arguments, yet is more afraid than ever that he has not dented those of his opponent.

Failing to damage Thomas Henry Huxley's case for evolution, Bishop Wilberforce resorted to this trick and asked Huxley, "Are you descended from a monkey on your grandmother's or your grandfather's side?" In contemporary politics an equally classic example has been furnished by Senator Joseph McCarthy. Answering the charge of Vermont Senator Ralph Edward Flanders that he was practicing Hitler's brand of anti-Communism and in effect really helping the Communists more effectively than a paid agent, McCarthy sneered, "I wonder whether this has been a result of senility or viciousness."

I, however, have taken all my misfortunes as the toll of the inevitable accidents of history. My conscience is clear. In all my acts, I have done what I have believed the best for my country and people. General Anderson, among others, left undisputed testimony that my first question when I met him for the first time was whether America was going to recognize our Government. It stands to reason that if I asked this of Anderson, I had asked it of Dewey and Pratt and others. And if Pratt and Dewey had made me no promises of independence, it is equally logical that I would have refused their request for my cooperation in fighting the Spaniards.

While I regret the Philippine-American War, it was not our own making. If we persisted in fighting after it had been started it was because our peace efforts had been spurned. But I feel now that our natural and justified resistance accomplished a two-fold historic purpose. Defeated in war, we won by our last-ditch defense of our homes and our freedom the respect of mankind. What is perhaps more important, especially in the light of the present world situation, we helped cure America of the sickness of imperialism.

Personally I have not harbored any rancor nor resentment against America or the Americans. Those with whom I had dealings acted, as I have shown, in good faith. With American officials assigned to the Philippines as well as with American residents, I have been sincerely friendly, and I believe they have reciprocated. Evidencing my desire that they may know America better than I have managed to know her, I sent two of my children to study in American schools. My son and namesake went to Phillips Academy in Andover, Massachusetts, and to the U.S. Military Academy in West Point, New York. My daughter Carmen studied in the University of Illinois in Champaign-Urbana and Wellesley College in Wellesley, Massachusetts. On our side of the Pacific, they are among the greatest admirers of America.

It can perhaps be said that America received her summons to world leadership via the Philippines. Heretofore, she had not shown consistent humanitarianism in dealing with other peoples. She had all but exterminated the American Indians. The Monroe Doctrine was in the main a negative rather than a positive international policy. Neither was the American Cuban policy of liberation a deliberate and long-range plan of international leadership. It was mainly a necessary justification for intervention in Cuba. It was in fact later vitiated by the Platt amendment which forced the Cubans to incorporate into their Constitution an acknowledgment of the right of the United States to intervene and to purchase naval and coaling stations in Cuba. South of the border, Americans had not been held ideal neighbors.

But between 1900 and 1946, with the Philippines as a sort of a pilot plant, the United States developed a new international policy of altruism. This policy is applicable to all the rest of the world, especially to the colored peoples who constitute over three-fifths of the earth's population and most of whom have groaned under the heels of European imperialism. They have been the victims of what Churchill calls "designs which belonged to those dark ages when men felt themselves entitled to conquer yellow, brown, black or red men, and subjugate them by their superior strength and weapons." The outlawing of race segregation in schools and public carriers by the U.S. Supreme Court, if accepted in time and in good faith by the South, will vastly improve what Editor Fleur Cowles calls America's eye-dropper-effect public relations among these races.

According to Elliott Roosevelt, his father, President Franklin D. Roosevelt, having gained the leadership among the Western leaders of World War II, directly demanded of the latter the liberation of their respective colonial empires. It was some such demand which is said to have sent Churchill bridling with the declaration. "I shall not preside over the liquidation of the British Empire!" What gave the greatest validity to Roosevelt's moral posture was America's definite plan to liberate the Filipinos in 1946 under the Independence Act enacted by the U.S. Congress in 1934.

The independence of the Philippines, taking place soon after the war—together with the war-time "Asia-for-the-Asiatics" agitation of the invading Japanese—helped to precipitate Britain's decision to give independence to India, Pakistan, Burma and Ceylon, and Holland's to free Indonesia. Because France hesitated she was caught in a whirlwind. Yet, the movement has gone full circle at last. On April 4, 1956 the Spanish Government declared the end of Spain's protectorate over Spanish Morocco and recognized its independence.

The intense nationalistic ferment in all the East and Africa today is part of the chain reaction which began in Manila. The contemporary liquidation of European imperialism, the work of the United Nations Trusteeship Council of assisting backward countries to political and economic competence and independence, and Point Three of the 1954 Eisenhower-Churchill Washington Declaration promising peaceful assistance to all peoples desiring and capable of independence—all these are definitely an outgrowth of the labors of America in the Philippines.

It was especially apropos that the *Pacific Charter,* signed by both Britain and France together with the United States and five other nations, was sponsored by the Philippines and adopted by the Manila Conference of 1954. For its declared first objective is "to promote self-government and to secure the independence of all countries whose people desire it and are able to undertake its responsibilities." All this sequence of facts should be made clear—credit should be given where credit is due—before a rampaging Russia or a resurgent Japan still under the urgent compulsion of expanding or exploding claims the credit with some plausibility.

More than a symbol, the Philippines is a living witness to American philanthropy in international relations. More than a "show window of Democracy in the East," a phrase by which it is often described, the Philippines is the first beneficiary of and witness to the fact that America, far from being the heir to European imperialism, really started this ancient evil's complete and orderly liquidation.

But in the East, America has nevertheless to overcome certain handicaps which in Europe are her advantages. Europeans accept Americans as kin for they are in fact descended from European forebears. But this very closeness of America to Europe makes her suspect in the East. For the leading countries of Europe either have once been or continue to be the oppressors and exploiters of the Eastern races. A white country like their tormentors, America, with her great power and wealth, is easily believed by the colored races the logical heir to Europe's imperialism. And, indeed, by defeating Spain and subjugating the Filipinos, America, to all appearances, succeeded Spain as a colonial power in the Orient. Yet, this impression need not have been lasting.

The independence of the Philippines, it is true, took place at the wrong time. The war having but recently ended, the Philippines' ascension to nationhood occurred when victors and vanquished were painfully and busily licking their wounds. The event failed to register clearly among the peoples of Asia, confused as they were by the recent Japanese propaganda which fuelled the flame of Asian nationalism with hate of the white West. And with the Filipinos still bewildered by years of cruel enemy occupation and with the Americans at the start of their colossal task of helping to occupy and administer the defeated aggressor nations, both failed to dramatize the deep meaning of Philippine independence before the eyes of the world. A great landmark in human emancipation, the event should have been

no less than an international pageant, a memorable and unfor-
gettable historic spectacle.

But it is not too late. To my mind, American world leadership will be considerably strengthened by the following steps:

1.

By the fullest use of all the media of mass information, the
true Philippine story should be broadcast and rebroadcast
throughout the world. And to give the story ultimate authen-
ticity, the Filipinos should be given ample opportunities to tell
it as eye-witnesses and initial beneficiaries.

It is a paradox that while American salesmanship is believed
to be the world's best, America has so far failed to sell to the
peoples of the world her truly great achievement in human
welfare. It is true, as John Foster Dulles points out, that most
free Asians fear imperialism more than Communism because
they have suffered under the former but know the latter only
as a theory. Hence, it is the clear imperative of the situation that
America should clearly appear not as the agent of imperialism
but as the leader of a new international altruism.

The Philippine story is the key to the final disabusing of
Asia's confounded mind.

2.

The American influence in the liberation of European colonies should be established, documented and propagated. The
impact of that influence has derived from the example of the
Filipinos, which inspired the other subject peoples, and the direct
American pressure on the colonizing powers. Just as the Filipinos should tell the story from their viewpoint, so the European
colonial powers should acknowledge conspicuously America's
part in the liberation of their own colonies.

3.

America should study Asian nationalism more closely and
understandingly.

It will not suffice to simply say, as an American publicist

has said, "Nationalism is triumphing in Asia in an age when nationalism as such is bankrupt." Nor should the Communist claim that Russia and China are the sole champions of Asian nationalism be allowed to stand unchallenged. Asia's nationalism is becoming the Trojan horse of Communism.

Fortunately America has in her Philippine experience the weapon with which to destroy the Communist pretense. As Yale's Professor Ralph E. Turner points out, a Filipino, Jose Rizal (1861-1896), was the first to raise the cry of nationalism in Asia. It was taken up and given specific and peculiar meanings by others—China, India, Indonesia and the Arab world. America felt the full explosive impact of Philippine nationalism, veered it away from agitation to accomplishment, transformed it from emotion to tangible progress.

But even the Filipinos have refused to be made into the image of America; hence, their post-independence nationalistic confusion evident in their national language movement and their belated flirting with the slogan "Asia for the Asians." America can learn much of the nature of Asian nationalism from a meaningful statement of Senator Claro M. Recto, one of the leading lawyers of the Philippines: "A Filipino must of necessity, if he is not a bastard, be a nationalist."

President McKinley's directive for the Philippines should be adapted and made the general directive for American world leadership: ". . . the Commission (Taft's) should bear in mind that the government which they are establishing is designed not for our satisfaction or for the expression of our theoretical views, but for the happiness, peace and prosperity of the people of the Philippines, and the measures adopted should be made to conform to their customs, their habits, and even their prejudices. . . ."

As Professor Turner points out, the Asians do not want to be "Westernized"; they only want to be "modernized." They merely hunger for scientific knowledge. "Whereas nationalism is the driving force of the Asian revolution," he points out, "science is the recognized means to its realization."

4.

America must stop retreating.

The Asian hesitation to follow American leadership is due in a large measure to the massive Russian victories in the cold war. Eastern Europe, China, North Korea and North Indo-China have been lost to Communism. It is nibbling at other democratic salients. Communism today holds sway over 40 percent of the population and one-fourth of the area of the world. Meanwhile, Russia seems to have overhauled the United States in the arms race. She has tremendous armies in being, more planes and more submarines. Assisted by stolen American and British secrets, she has learned to make the atomic and hydrogen bombs. The Russians claim greater advance in guided missiles with hydrogen warheads. But since, as with the poison gas once every power learned to make and use it, thermonuclear weapons may never be actually used in warfare,* the arms balance is very much in favor of the Communists. The new American threat of "instant massive retaliation" in the form of atomic and hydrogen bombs may have become obsolete.

Safety for the West lies only in the demonstrated unwillingness of Russia to risk open warfare for herself. This is evidently due in part to her ability to use satellite cannon fodder, as in Korea and Indo-China, and more to the uncertain loyalties of the Russian and satellite masses. The defection from Communism at Panmunjom of 14,000 Chinese prisoners of war as

---

* Especially after the frightful warning made in a 1954 scientific conference in London by Dr. E. O. Adrian, Nobel Prize winner and president of the British Association for the Advancement of Science, and others that any extensive atomic warfare would eventually subject the entire world to fatal radioactive dusting such as befell the 22 Japanese crewmen of the tuna ship *Lucky Dragon* in Bikini in mid-Pacific. The first of the victims to die and thus becoming the first martyr to the bomb, Aukichi Kuboyama, when autopsied, was found to have suffered from a general serious jaundice condition with a liver shrunken to two-thirds of normal, kidneys and heart enlarged, and virtually all other organs yellow and seriously affected. Dr. A. H. Sturtevant of the California Institute of Technology points to a biological danger from atomic radiation: damage to the genes in the individual's germ cells which may result in the production of defective offsprings or monsters.

against only 220 who chose to return home was a vivid glimpse caught by the free world of widespread mass resistance behind the bamboo and iron curtains. It is evident that the more the Russian bear snarls and bares its fangs the more it is really scared.

America should henceforth assume a posture of quiet but unyielding strength. As Teddy Roosevelt advised, America must speak softly but carry a big stick.

5.

America should understand Asian fears.

Asians respect America's strength, actual and potential, yet they fear being involved in another war. Realizing their enormous backwardness and their tremendous problems of poverty and ignorance, sanitation and disease, population and production, they want peace in which to solve them. With her threats of "instant massive retaliation," America, they fear, is often ready to stride to the brink of war.

It will be well to heed former Ambassador Chester Bowles, even if what he says is only partially true. According to him, Asians cannot understand and, therefore, fear "our concentration on military answers to complex problems which Asians believe are basically political and economic."

Asians fear that if they gravitate to the West they will become conspicuous Communist targets. They fear even more that in the event of war, America, as in the last war, will first rush to the aid of Europe and abandon Asia to its own fate, at least temporarily.

They fear Communism less, not only because, as John Foster Dulles says, it is merely a theory to most of them, but because of its more subtle ways. This is especially so today when Bulganin and Khrushchev go from capital to capital with smiles and handshakes and offers of gold and coexistence to cover the grim and gruesome developments at home.

6.

America should try to understand Asian needs.

Asia needs butter more than bullets. It needs education and sanitation, food and clothing, capital and technical knowhow. It needs irrigation systems and electricity, tractors and fertilizer, a new system of land tenure, an altogether new concept of society and politics.

It needs to extricate itself from the traditions of centuries that have kept its peoples away from the blessings of modern civilization.

7.

Asia needs a more original and more imaginative plan of practical assistance.

America should use the Philippines as a pilot plant for its program of assistance in Asia. Just as the Philippines has been the ideological model, so it can become the material model.

But to help all Asia, America must have help. The rest of the West, especially those colonial powers which once sucked much of the substance of Asia, must now pool their resources with America in a vast program of assistance.

And if the Russians mean their talks of disarmanent, a great part of the many billions of dollars heretofore annually spent in the arms race by East and West, both, should be channelled to the Asian program of assistance.

Such an eventuality will be a great historic justice. Instead of being the bone of contention, Asia—perhaps Africa as well —will then be the object of the world's good will.

In the Philippines the United States has committed many errors. From Dewey to MacArthur, there have been American acts which, if taken out of their context and put together as the authentic American policies, could make Uncle Sam deservedly the most-hated and the most-despised in the world. These mistakes have spawned resentments, disappointments and even a war.

But all in all, taking these mistakes together with the impressive accomplishments, America's record stands out as an example of international magnanimity. While there are indeed varied grounds for criticizing American policies and methods, the broad soundness, the abiding honesty of purpose, and the ultimate worth of America's Philippine work cannot be questioned. It has shown that there is in the American people a depth of goodness and humanity which, to my mind, is the greatest hope of a world anxious to see the return of prosperity, peace and security.

We Filipinos have benefited from American guidance. We have learned the worth of disciplined work and acquired an outlook of life which values competence, material success, spiritual contentment, and cultural achievement. Above all, through America, we have finally earned our share of human freedom.

From America's work in my country the world at large has also profited. It has rendered colonialism obsolete and substituted international philanthropy as a basis of relationship between advanced and backward countries. Instead of the old evils of imperialism, America offers guidance and assistance. America's Philippine experience has demonstrated that peoples, being possessed of soul and reason, inherently desire freedom.

Americans seem to fear that the projection of the United States as the world's leader nation is not good public relations. "We are trying not to be the leader," says Harold Stassen, "but to participate in a leading role with other free peoples in what might be called a democracy of nations." Ambassador James Bryant Conant, former president of Harvard, agrees with this view, and would limit American claim to that of "leading partner." Many do feel that American leadership would be more effective if it were less aggressive. They are probably right, but America must nevertheless lead. A leaderless West will be a weaker antagonist of communism.

Out of friendship with America, of loyalty to Democracy and of sheer self-preservation, the Filipino people will, I am absolutely certain, fight a hundred Tirad Passes and Bataans, if need be, to help preserve human liberty and dignity.

INDEX

Little, Richard Henry, 111
Lodge, Sen. Henry Cabot, 19, 50, 58, 59, 87-89, 131, 163, 173
Long, John D., 41, 46, 55, 56, 59, 63, 64
Lopez, Sixto, 91
Lowenstein, Prince, 44
Luna, General Antonio, 100, 103-107
Luna, Joaquin, 106
Luzuriaga, Jose, 149

Mabini, Apolinario, 99, 102-104, 115
Macapagal, Major, 25
MacArthur, General Arthur, 100, 101, 103, 114, 126
MacArthur, General Douglas, 47, 48, 61, 69, 172, 174, 176, 181, 183, 184, 186, 188-191, 226-229, 231-234, 255
McCarthy, Sen. Joseph, 247
McCutcheon, John T., 73
McKinley, William, 18, 46, 50, 53, 55, 57, 58, 60, 61, 63-66, 82, 84-86, 90-94, 101, 102, 116, 131, 134, 138-141, 144, 149, 161, 164, 252
Madrigal, Vincente, 231
Magellan, Ferdinand, 19
Magsaysay, Ramon, 210, 212, 213, 217, 229, 236
Mahan, Capt. Alfred T., 50, 58
Marsh, Major, 109-112
Marshall, Thos., 166
Merritt, Maj. Gen. Wesley, 74
Michener, James A., 186
Millis, Walter, 58, 64, 66, 162
Montojo, Admiral, 42
Mountbatten, Lord Louis, 124
Murphy, Justice Frank, 15
Mussolini, Benito, 244

Nehru, Jawaharlal, 13
Nimitz, Admiral Chester, 186
Noriel, Gen. Mariano, 25, 26, 75, 76
Nye, Lt. General Archibald, 124

Osias, Camilo, 231
Osmeña, Sergio, 132, 152, 167, 171, 178, 179, 186, 189, 190, 228, 232
Otis, Gen. Elwell S., 82, 93, 94, 98, 99, 102, 114

Palma, Rafael, 152
Pardo de Tavera, Dr. Trinidad H., 27, 99, 149
Paterno, Pedro, 28, 103
Polavieja, Governor, 27
Pratt, E. Spencer, 18, 33-35, 37, 39, 46, 48, 50, 52-55, 62, 63, 83, 85, 109, 116, 247
Primo de Rivera, Capt. Gen. Fernando, 27, 28

Quezon, Manuel L., 15, 16, 18, 70, 153-157, 167-169, 172, 174, 177-180, 183, 184, 187, 189, 191, 214, 231, 234
Quirino, Elpidio, 160, 190, 213, 214, 236

Recto, Sen. Claro M., 211, 214, 217, 231, 252
Reid, Whitelaw, 19, 60
Ricarte, Gen. Artemio, 184, 185, 246

Rizal, Dr. Jose, 20, 21, 71, 132, 135, 136, 150, 252
Roces, Rafael, 233
Rodriguez, Eulogio, Sr., 190
Roosevelt, Elliott, 249
Roosevelt, Franklin D., 46, 47, 144, 160, 172, 173, 177, 183, 184, 216, 242, 249
Roosevelt, Theodore, 19, 41, 42, 50, 58, 59, 66, 144, 150, 155,, 254
Roosevelt, Theodore, Jr., 156
Root, Elihu, 139
Roque, Ramon, 119
Roxas, Manuel, 160, 171, 176, 179, 187-191, 221, 231, 232

St. Clair, W. G., 53
Schurman, Jacob Gould, 61, 64, 101, 102, 105, 107, 117, 141
Schurz, Carl, 87, 133
Segismundo, Cecilio, 117, 126, 127
Segovia, Lazaro, 117-122, 124, 127, 128
Smith, Maj. Gen. Wayne C., 212
Stalin, Marshal Josef, 46
Stassen, Harold, 256
Stegner, Wallace, 224
Stimson, Henry L., 156
Story, Moorefield, 133
Stowe, Harriet Beecher, 20
Sukarno, Achmed, 13
Switzer, Rear Adm. Wendell G., 211, 241
Taft, William Howard, 16, 131, 134, 139-142, 144, 151, 159, 241
Tal Placido, Lt. Col. Hilario, 118-122, 124, 125, 127, 128
Tañada, Sen. Lorenzo M., 211
Tirona, Candido, 22
Trevor-Roper, H. R., 245
Truman, Harry S., 17, 47, 144, 145, 160
Turner, Ralph E., 252

Vanderlip, Frank, 242
Van Fleet, Gen. James A., 67, 68, 81
Vargas, Jorge B., 187, 231
Villa, Col. Simon, 120-123, 127, 128
Villanueva, Prof. Honesto A., 84, 92
Von Bulow, Chancellor Bernhard, 44
Von Diederichs, Vice-Admiral, 43

Weyler, Gen. Valeriano, 131
Wheaton, Gen. Lloyd, 100, 101
Wheeler, Gen. Joseph, 90
White, Henry, 59
Wilberforce, Bishop, 247
Wildman, Rounseville, 35, 36, 38, 39, 46, 50, 52, 55, 62, 63, 78, 83, 85, 116
Wilhelm II, German Kaiser, 44, 45
Williams, Consul, 63
Willoughby, Maj. Gen. Charles A., 231
Wilson, Woodrow, 152, 165-167, 169, 173
Wood, Leonard, 15, 16, 18, 153, 154, 156, 168
Wood, Capt., 30

Young, Gen. Samuel M. B., 108-110

Zulueta, Clemente Jose, 27

CPSIA information can be obtained
at www.ICGtesting.com
Printed in the USA
LVOW13s2324230317

528320LV00022BA/535/P